UK Economic and Social Change 1700-2019 Supplementary Volume 1

*Being an investigation of the evidence that reveals the **best known facts** regarding the quantifiable economic and social history of the peoples of the United Kingdom of Great Britain and Northern Ireland (but particularly the English peoples) since the 18th century; including their population, economy, the role of the state, earnings, income inequality, living costs, household expenditure, housing, the retreat of real poverty, the air quality of their environment and their life expectancy.*

Collated, graphically presented with text written by:

J. R. Cooper

A data collation, analysis and presentation conducted from 2017 to 2023; but also founded upon five decades of the study of history, economics and the sociology of life and its political manifestations. Sources are derived from the most respected academic, authoritative and best researched origins. All underpinned by the thorough use of valid mathematical principles and the scientific methodology.

Text and Presentations ©2023 MM1 – J. R. Cooper.
Email: info@mm1.me.uk
Web: http://www.mm1.me.uk/

See references and bibliography for all source and data copyright acknowledgments

Title font Georgia
Text font Cambria
Chart font Arial

Self published with IngramSpark
Printed by Lightning Source UK Ltd.

Paperback (2023)	ISBN:	978-1-7395094-6-0
Hardback (2023)	ISBN:	978-1-7395094-0-8
Supplementary Volume 1 (2023)	ISBN:	978-1-7395094-1-5
Supplementary Volume 2 (2023)	ISBN:	978-1-7395094-2-2
Supplementary Volume 3 (2023)	ISBN:	978-1-7395094-3-9
Supplementary Volume 4 (2024)	ISBN:	978-1-7395094-4-6
Exploring Climate History (2024)	ISBN:	978-1-7395094-5-3

Dedication

Dedicated to my mother, father, sister and grandmothers.

Thank you for your unconditional love, care, support, guidance and tolerance (of which you needed a great deal).

To my maternal grandmother, who knew great hardship throughout her life, losing her father when she was aged three, losing her third baby in infancy, my grandfather in and out of work throughout the 1930's; with many debilitating consequences to her health and well-being.

To my paternal grandmother, losing her mother when she was six, forced to foster her first son (my father) for the first six years of his life due to extreme hardship in the 1930's; losing her second baby in infancy.

But also dedicated to my maternal great-grandmother, a lady I never met, but who was clearly a very resourceful and strong lady.

She was widowed in 1909, aged 32, with 3 young children (including her youngest, my maternal grandmother) and pregnant with her fourth child.

With only the Poor Law to turn to, instead she picked stones from local farmer's fields for coppers (old farthings, halfpennies and pennies) and took in washing.

She has described herself in the 1911 census as "Charwoman".

She had been forced to give her fourth child into the permanent care of her parents at her birth, yet still mistakenly listed her in her 1911 census return, before crossing her out from that return.

In 1926 her eldest daughter and son-in-law both died of tuberculosis within months of each other, leaving her to bring up her first new-born grandchild. Then in 1938 her eldest son also died of tuberculosis.

These ladies and the millions of other people of the time and all the millennia before, knew what **real poverty** was and struggled through.

Acknowledgements

I feel honoured to be able to thank several good friends for their reviews of aspects of the initial research, the presentations I have built of my findings, their notes and references and now this book.

In particular I thank Bill Young, a very good friend for many years now, for his careful and forensic checking of my blunders and his guidance regarding the understand-ability of the data, as I have tried to present it. Also MS for his checking of my presentations and then the pre-publication edition of this book, chapter by chapter, using his printer's and typesetter's eye to try to avoid blunders on the page, as well as the understanding of the narrative and spotting my many "apostrophic" errors.

I have also carefully checked the graphics and my explanations of these with my Mother in particular, as she has very strong views on politics and social organisation which I must confess are not at all in accord with my own in many respects. This has helped enormously to keep me scrupulously levelled in all facets of my interpretation of my findings.

Also I am very grateful further to Bill Young, my Mother, Rachel Turner and Alaine Mardle for their reading of the first printed draft and their notes and corrections of my errors and the oversights they have found therein and their suggestions for improvements throughout.

I have tried my very best to be even-handed and driven entirely by the "facts", the **best known facts** I could find from the evidence. All in the light of my natural and overpowering scepticism of all loud mantras of faith and ideologies (religious or secular).

If I have failed to be scrupulously honest, even-handed and factually correct then that is my error and no one else's.

Table of Contents

Commentary essay 1

UK Population and Life Expectancy 5

UK Economic and Social Change 25

An economy in transition 61

Growth of the state and world war 93

Quarter of a century of new changes 119

Stable income inequality 139

Bibliography, Selected Reading and Internet Data 171

    Bibliography and Selected Reading 171
    Internet Data 187

Population, Economy, State, Income and Inequality

"There can be no economy where there is no efficiency"

Benjamin Disraeli:
**Address to constituents,
(quoted in The Times)
1868**

A commentary on the current (2017/2019) media and campaigning discussion

As the UK and the world's population, life expectancy and wealth have increased over the last 200 years or so, and quite dramatically over the last few decades throughout the world, so the recent clamour by some campaigning and political causes has grown ever more shrill.

Whilst most of the campaigning to continuously improve people's lives throughout the world was and is justified, sadly, in common with the current instant judgement "sound bite" approach to discussion of important matters, many campaigns now *"make a drama out of a crisis"* and they clearly put their moral judgement, ladled with liberal doses of self-righteous indignation, ahead of balanced facts and consequent reasonable action.

One such is the widespread campaigning regarding UK economy and government policy in the 21st century.

Without any doubt, and by any measure, despite the 2008 international economic crisis, we in the UK are better off than any previous generation in history.

Before our age, the majority of people lived brief and hard lives in poverty, with life expectancy of only 30 to 40 years for most of the UK's and previously, England, Scotland, Wales and Ireland's history.

There was, is and never will be *a bucolic age or place as imagined by today's dreamers*. We have seen many attempts to impose self-appointed and self-righteously held images of the "*bucolic idyll*" throughout the UK's and world history. The result is always dire for the majority of people!!!!

Thanks to slack and lazy government thinking and behaviour, again "boom" turned to inevitable "bust" in 2008, after a sustained period of unrealistic and greedy speculation, allied to underlying unrealistic expectations of a wealthier populace. In the UK many joined the clamour to be a "millionaire by this time next year"!

Inevitably due to the desperate need to "reign in" government spending, and consequent plunging current account deficit, plus prevent further rise in the soaring national debt, the newly elected coalition of 2010 were duty bound to introduce many measures of painful austerity.

It remains an unavoidable reality that ultimately... "*Annual income twenty pounds, annual expenditure nineteen nineteen and six, result happiness. Annual income twenty pounds, annual expenditure twenty pounds ought and six, result misery.*"

Sadly, it is also inevitably true, that despite the earlier introduction of the new minimum wage (1998), the substantially increased lower tax thresholds (2010), and consequent improvements for the lowest paid wage earners, the least well off tend to disproportionately suffer from economic difficulties and austerity measures in real terms.

It is also true that all people tend to be naturally "relativistic" in their perception of their world. Thus tend to forget that despite some increase in economic challenges compared to a decade earlier (often many), they generally remain significantly better off than their parents at the same age and dramatically better off then their grand parents or any previous generation.

In addition, despite the tremendous gains in health and wealth throughout the world, the vast majority of people in the UK are amongst the richest people in the world.

When looking at the history of the UK economy for the last 120 years and looking back beyond at the reality of grinding, absolute poverty from before The Second World War and even more before The Great War, it is important to see our lives in the context of that "*foreign country*" and also the many, many *"foreign countries"* and their peoples now.

It is also true that every government, more and more since the Second World War is rapidly "damned if they do, and damned if they don't" in roughly equal measure.

As our freedom to express ourselves has grown, and in the 21st century ballooned, thanks to the near ubiquitous use of the facilities of the Internet, so the tendency to ill considered, ignorant snap judgements and knee jerk reactions has overwhelmed the world of thoughtful, consideration and fact based analysis; the latter is now showing every sign of being forced to take the Socratic path…when it's ideas are not already being burned on pyres of mass hysteria.

In contrast to all such campaigns conceived on the zealous moral high ground, the prosaic actual facts, be they economic, financial, mathematical, chemical or physical, by all measures, show that we are healthier, wealthier and longer lived than <u>ever</u> in human history.

No matter the naysayers and hand-ringers clamour that the sky is falling, that we are all dying (even *prematurely*), we still remain healthier, wealthier and longer lived than we poor everyday folk have EVER been in the whole of human history.

And yet the wealthier and healthier we have become the more miserable, niggardly, gloomy and doom laden many have become; it seems not also wiser!

Perhaps those same doom merchants would do as well to live the lives of the majority of the world's population, or the lives of their parents or grand parents, to put modern life in the UK for most in real perspective.

This is no call for complacency or rampant, unbridled economic free-for-all. There remain many, many issues to tackle, including slack, lazy government and rich individual and corporate greed, plus every day ignorance and complacency.

Rather it is a call for reason, balance and <u>fact based</u> argument, before dubious hysterical, zealous and knee jerk judgement.

And above all a call for firm, continuing governmental support for the REAL sustained improvements that have been wrought, so far, in people's lives in the last 100 years.

Rather than the modern penchant to ban or subsidise everything in a panicked sop to a minority of vitriolic dreamers, government, entirely paid for by the taxpayer (<u>"there is no such thing as public money – there is only taxpayers' money"</u>), should honestly and forthrightly live up to the broad social contract; to keep the nation safe, prevent excess of greed and set <u>and impose</u> the legal limits to balance economy and environment for everyone's benefit, **but with a light touch.**

UK Population & Life Expectancy

1700-2019 or fifteen generations

Continuous growth

Historical context

Population (UK, and nations),

Birth & Death rates and Age demographic,
Net migration rates and UK birth & ethnicity demographic

Death rates and life expectancy by age ranges

1700-2019

UK and England Long Term History of Population (Millions)

— BofE Pop England (Wrigley 1541-1841) — UK Population (Consistent) (Right Axis) — (including "southern" Ireland)

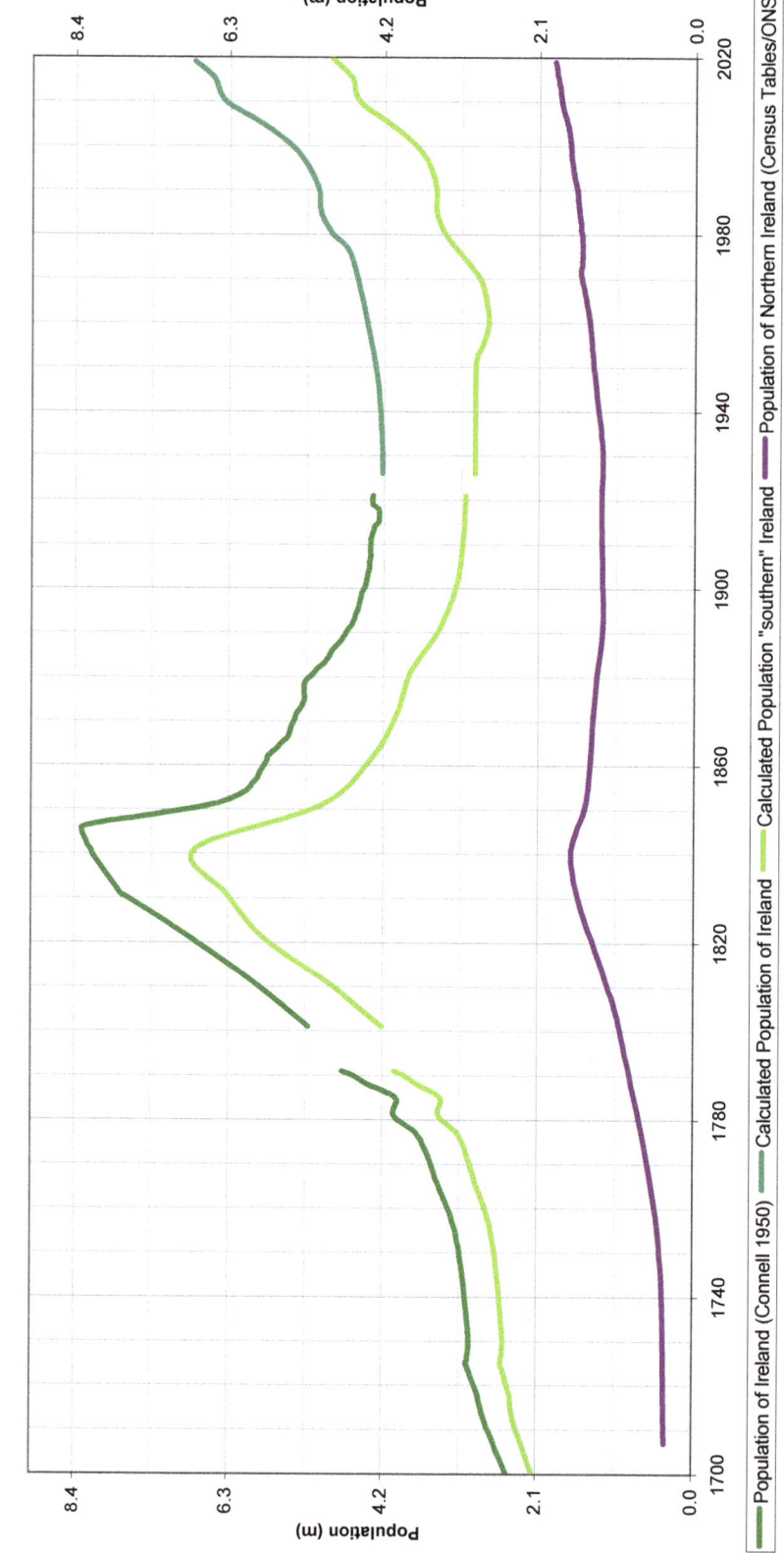

Webster's Census of the Population of Scotland, plus ONS mid-year estimates (m)

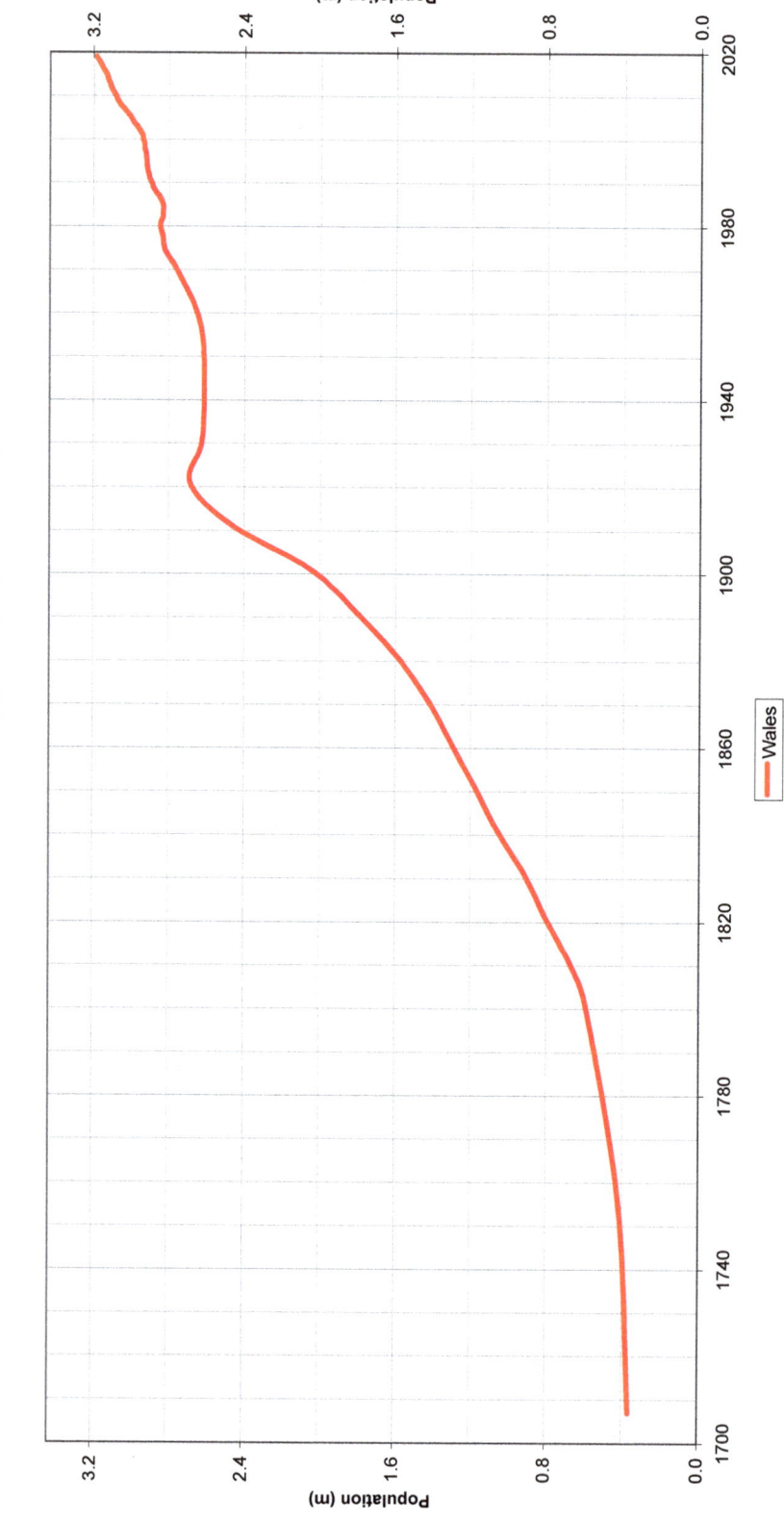

Population by age range

Birth and Death rates

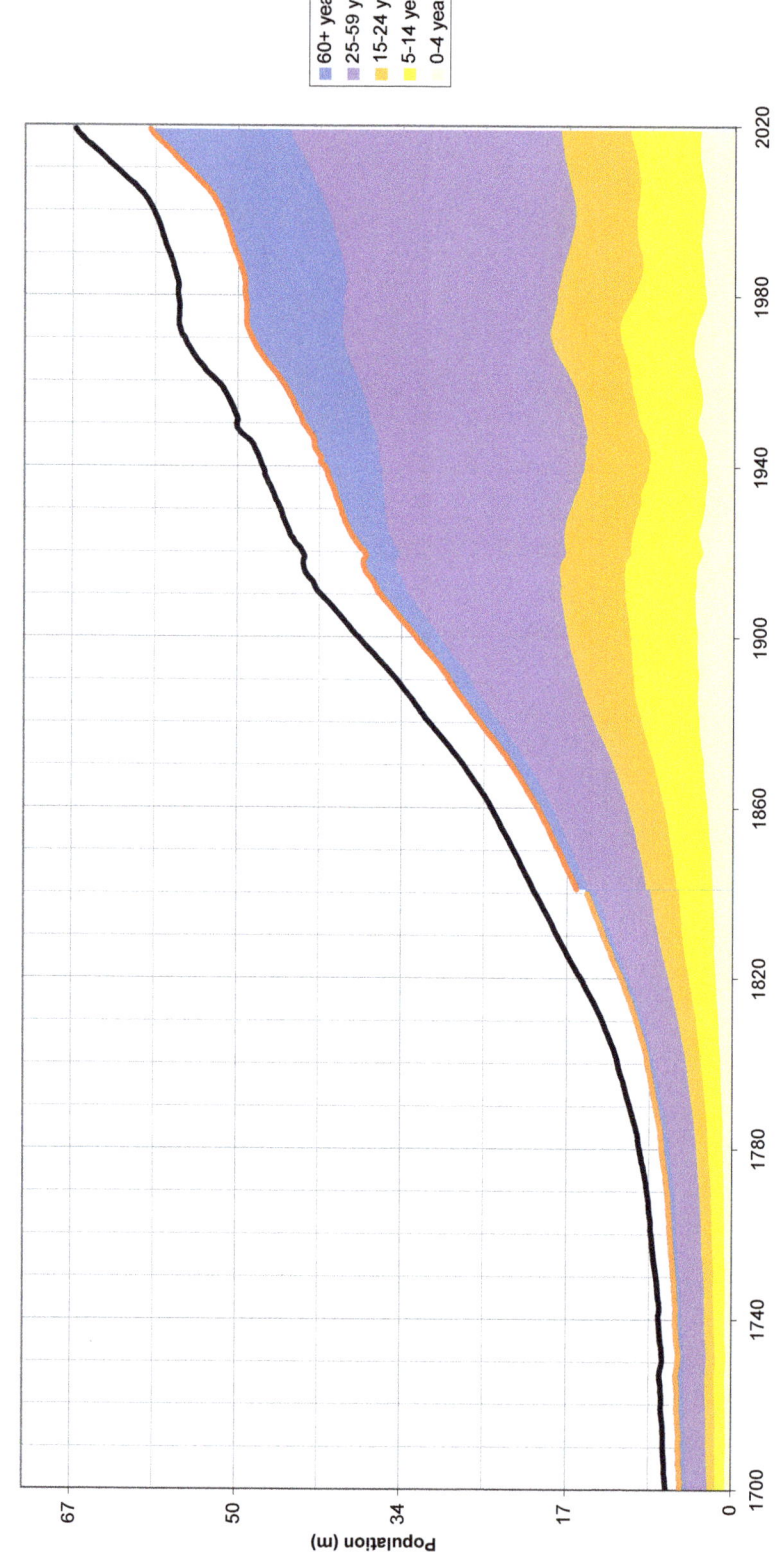

Population (m) England (Wrigley et al), England & Wales (ONS/Human Mortality Database) by age Range + UK (MW "consistent")

13

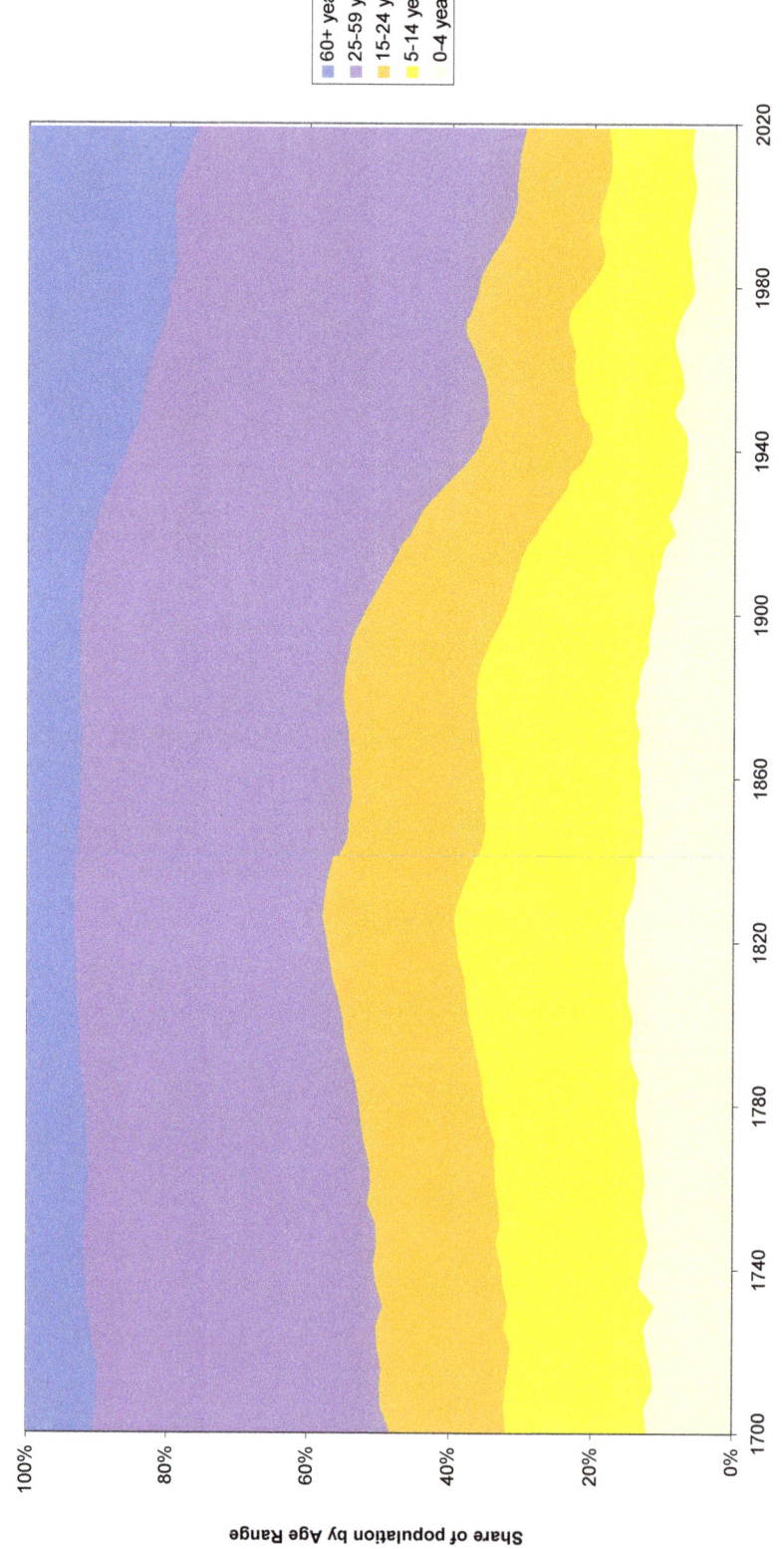

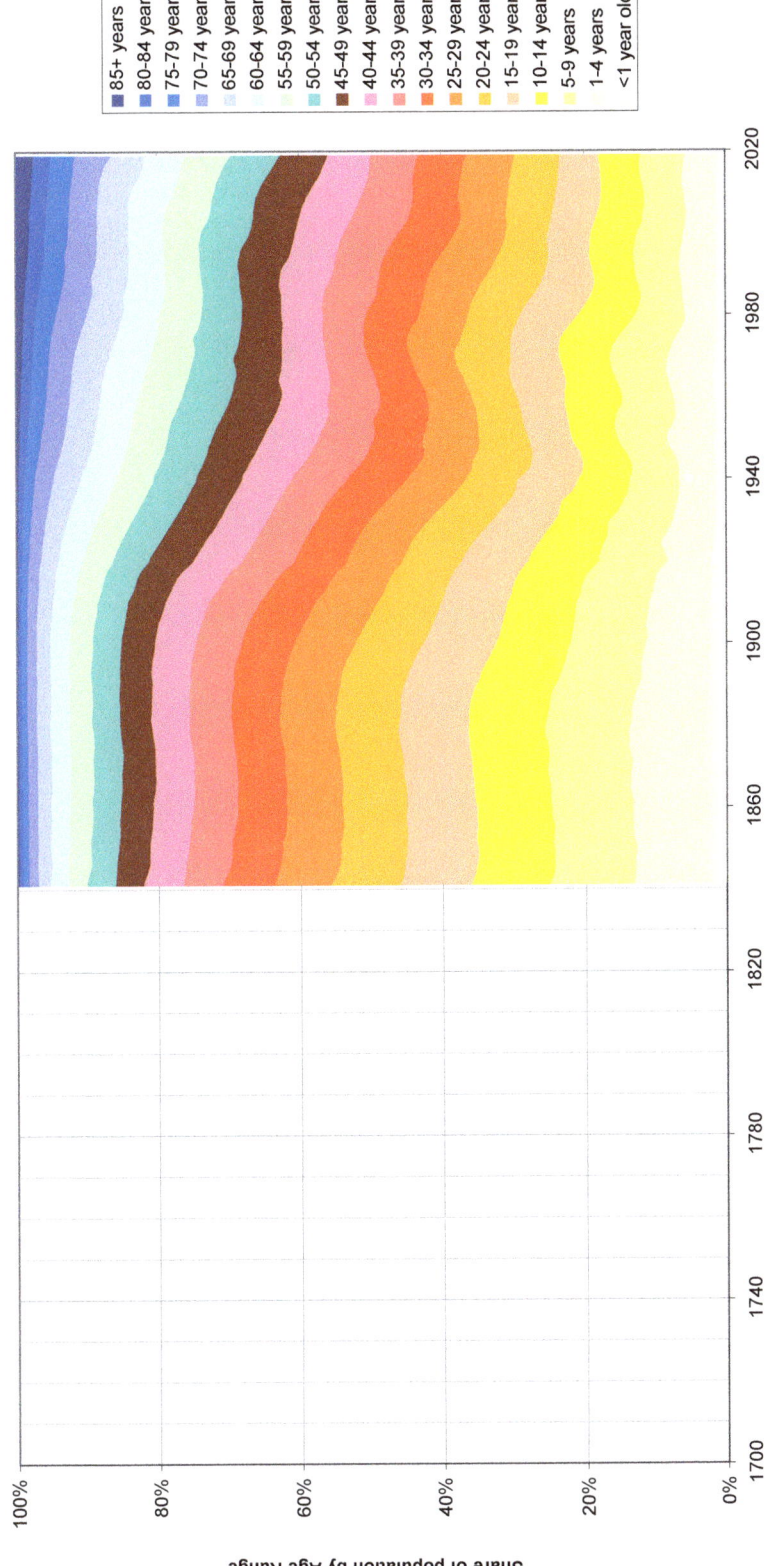

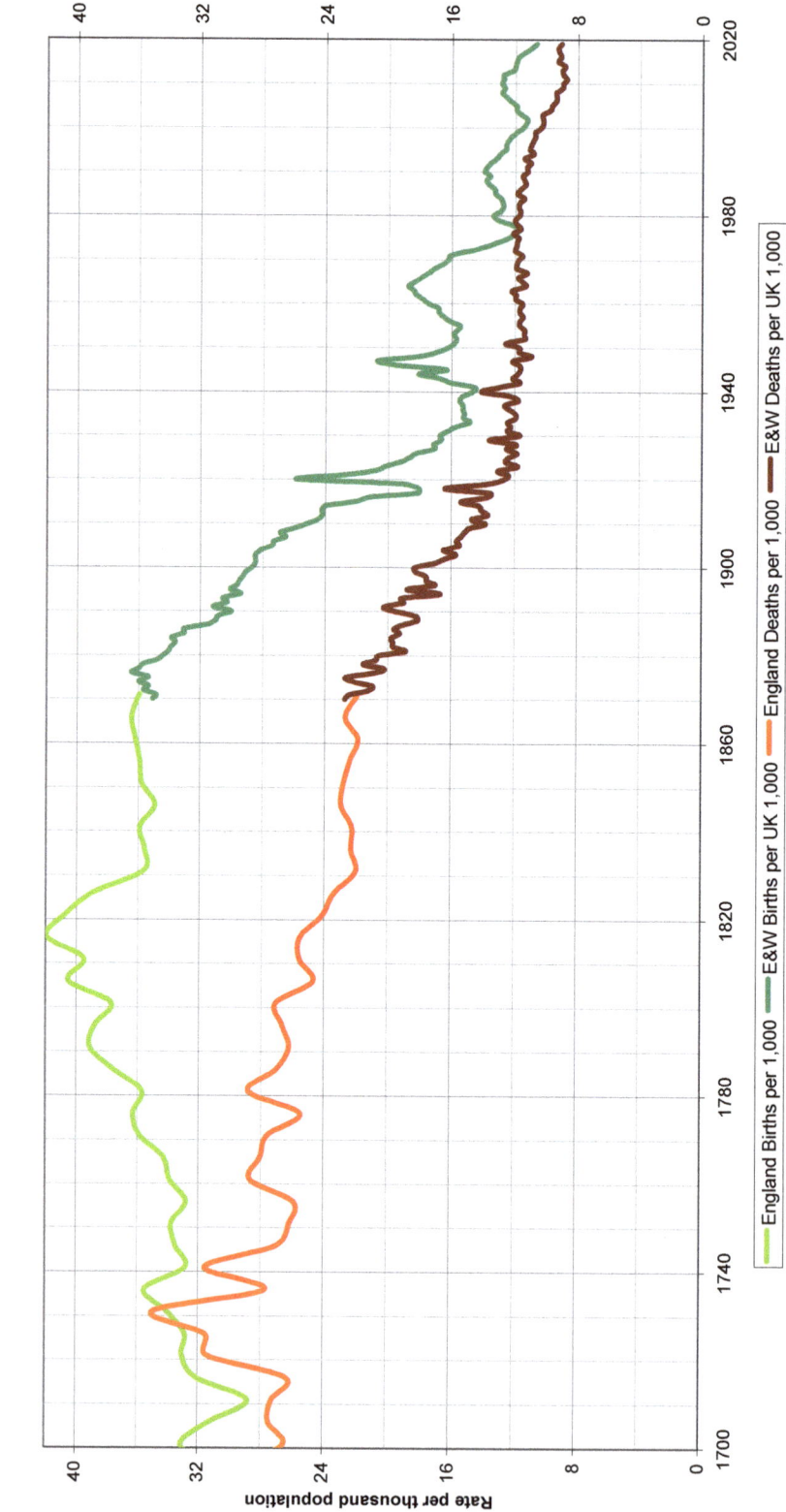

Population by "ethnicity"

Natural change rate (births minus deaths)

Net migration rate

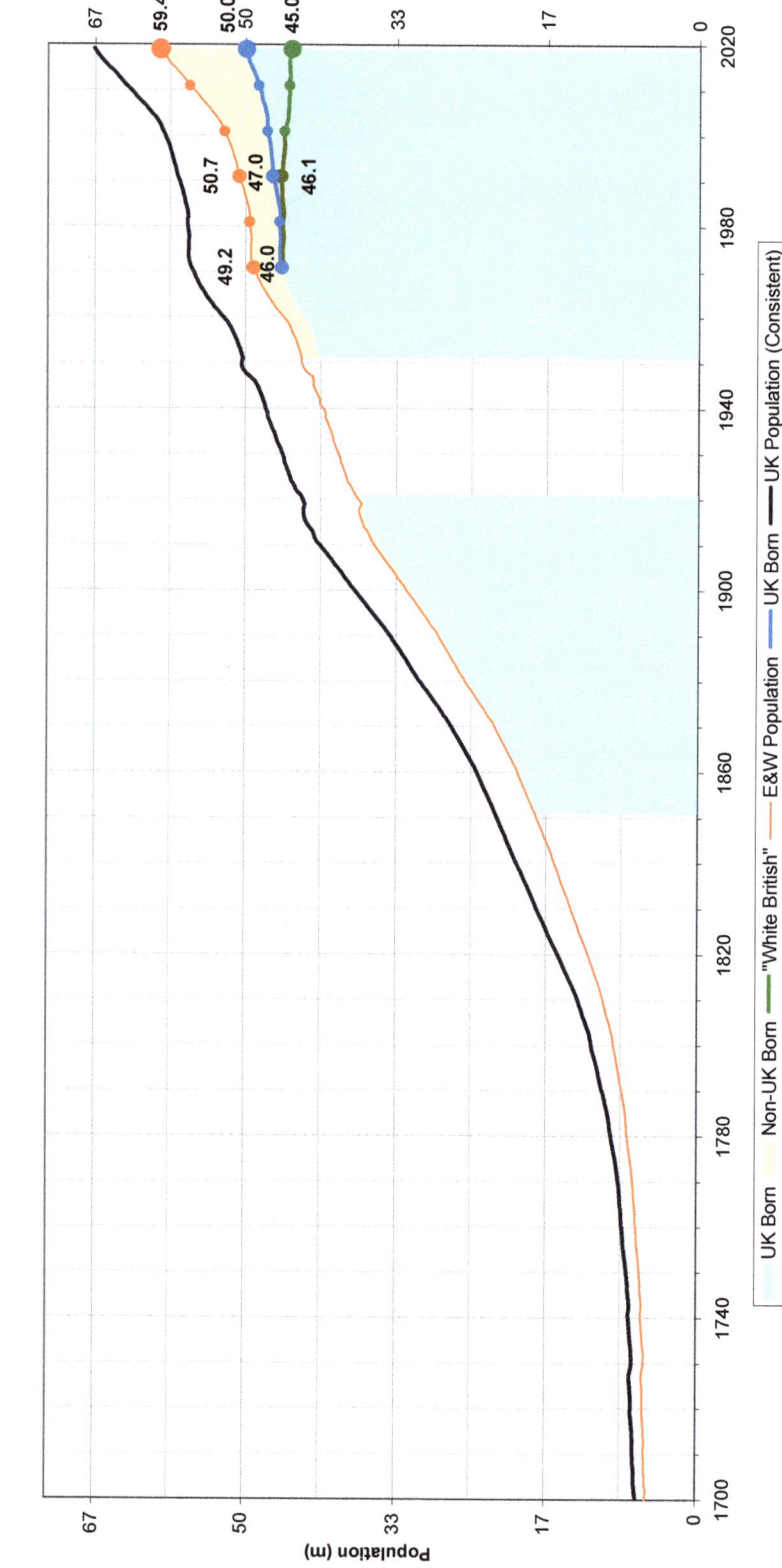

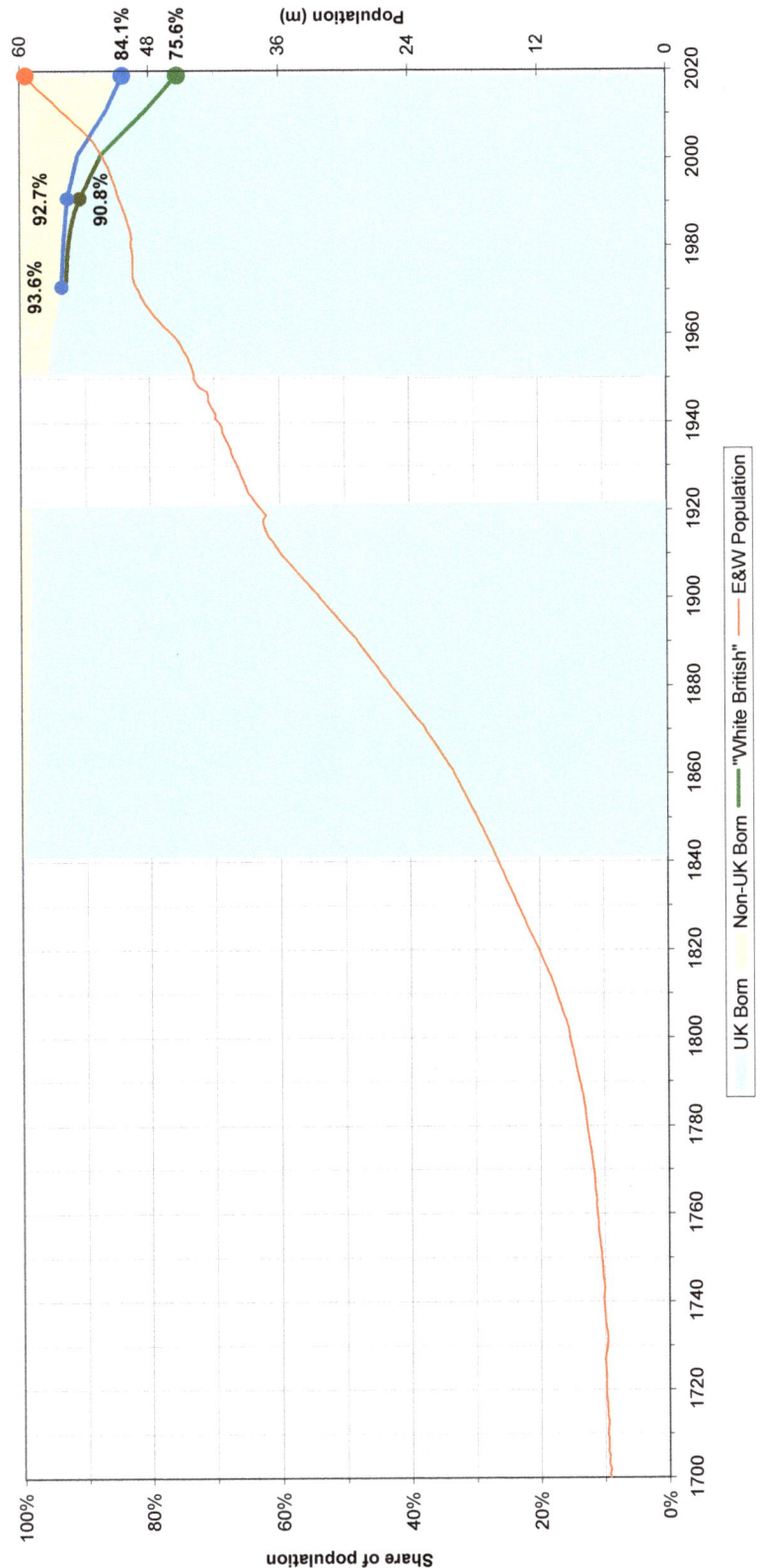

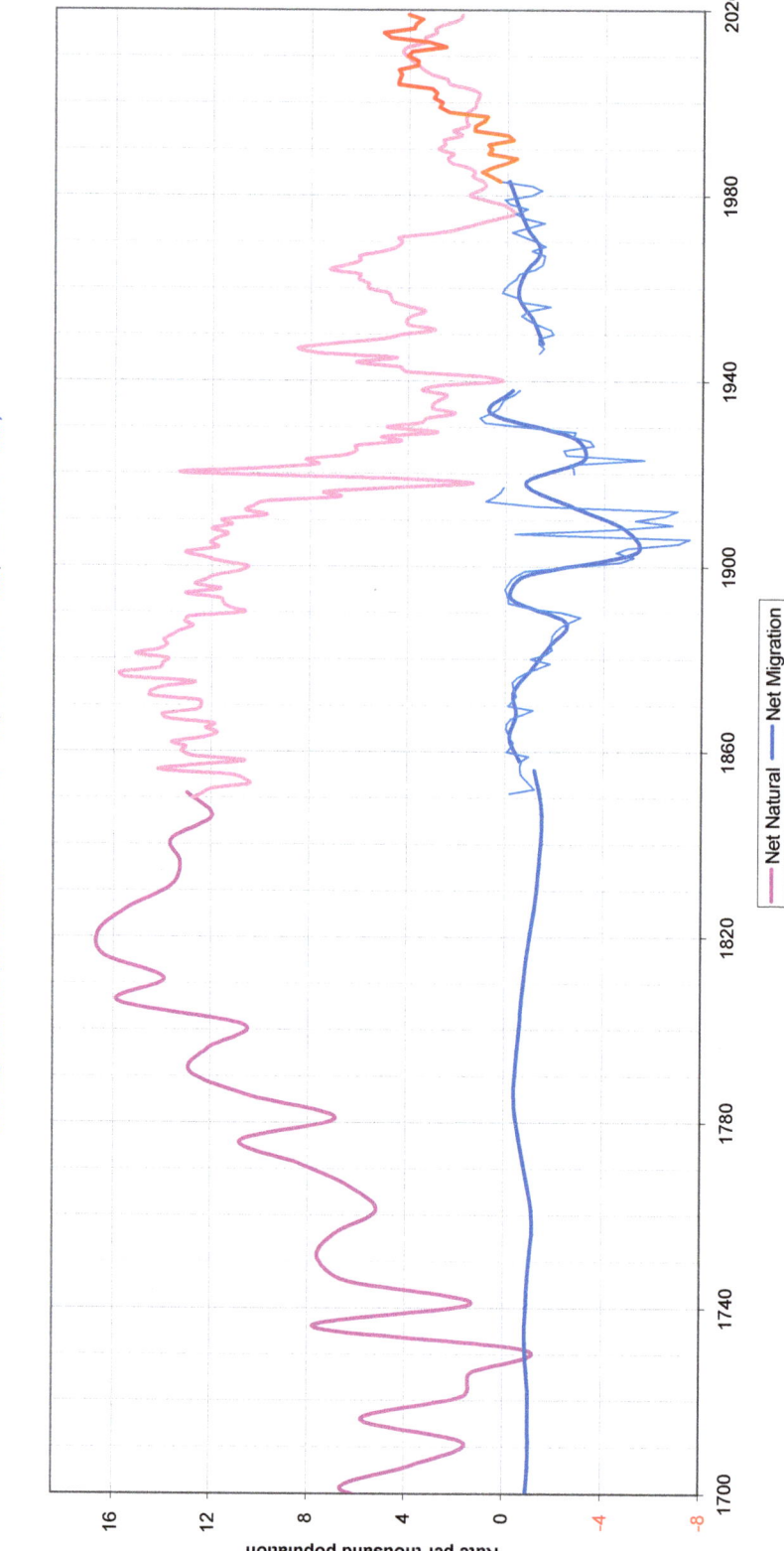

Death rates by age, Life expectancy by age

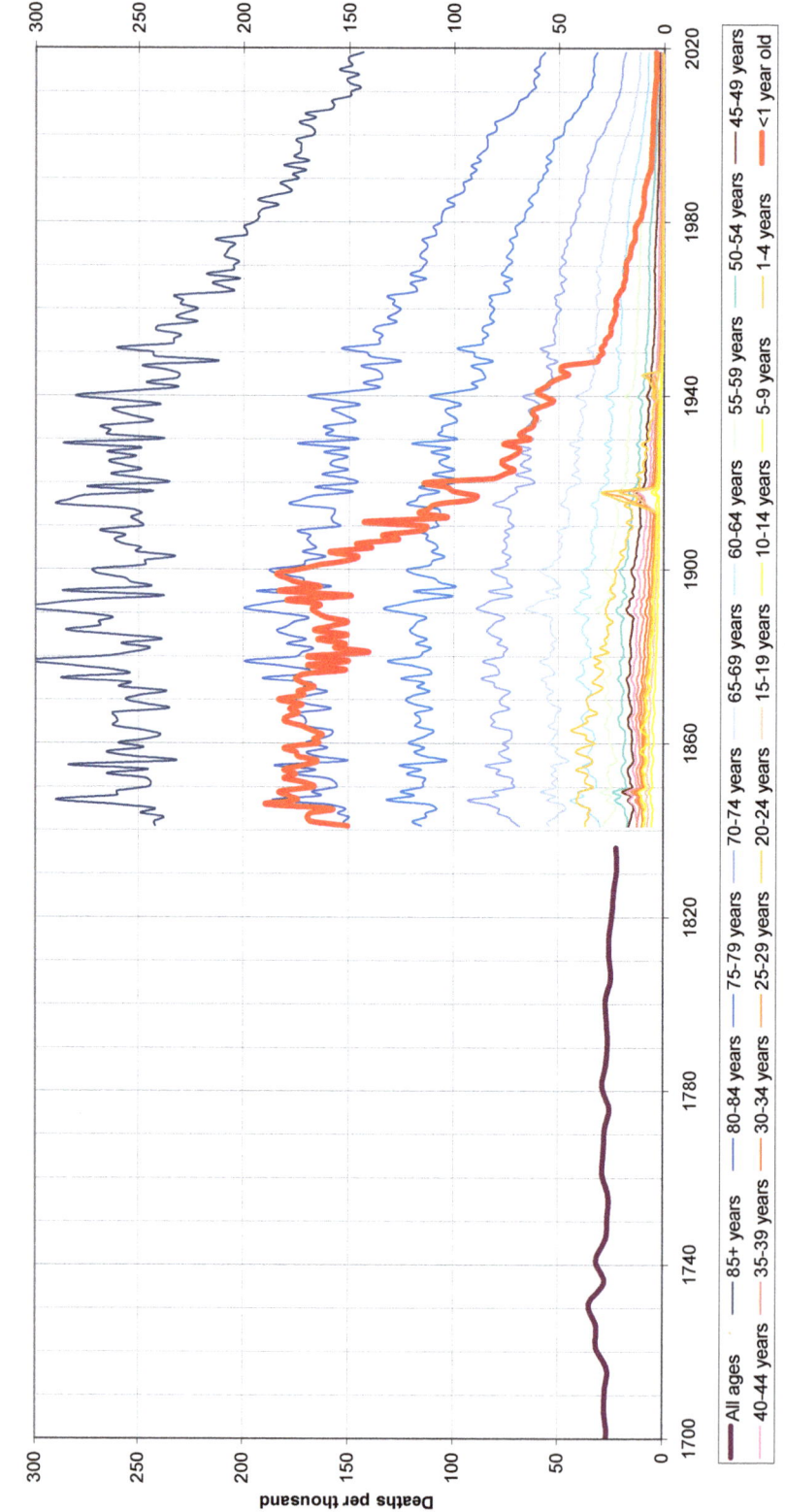

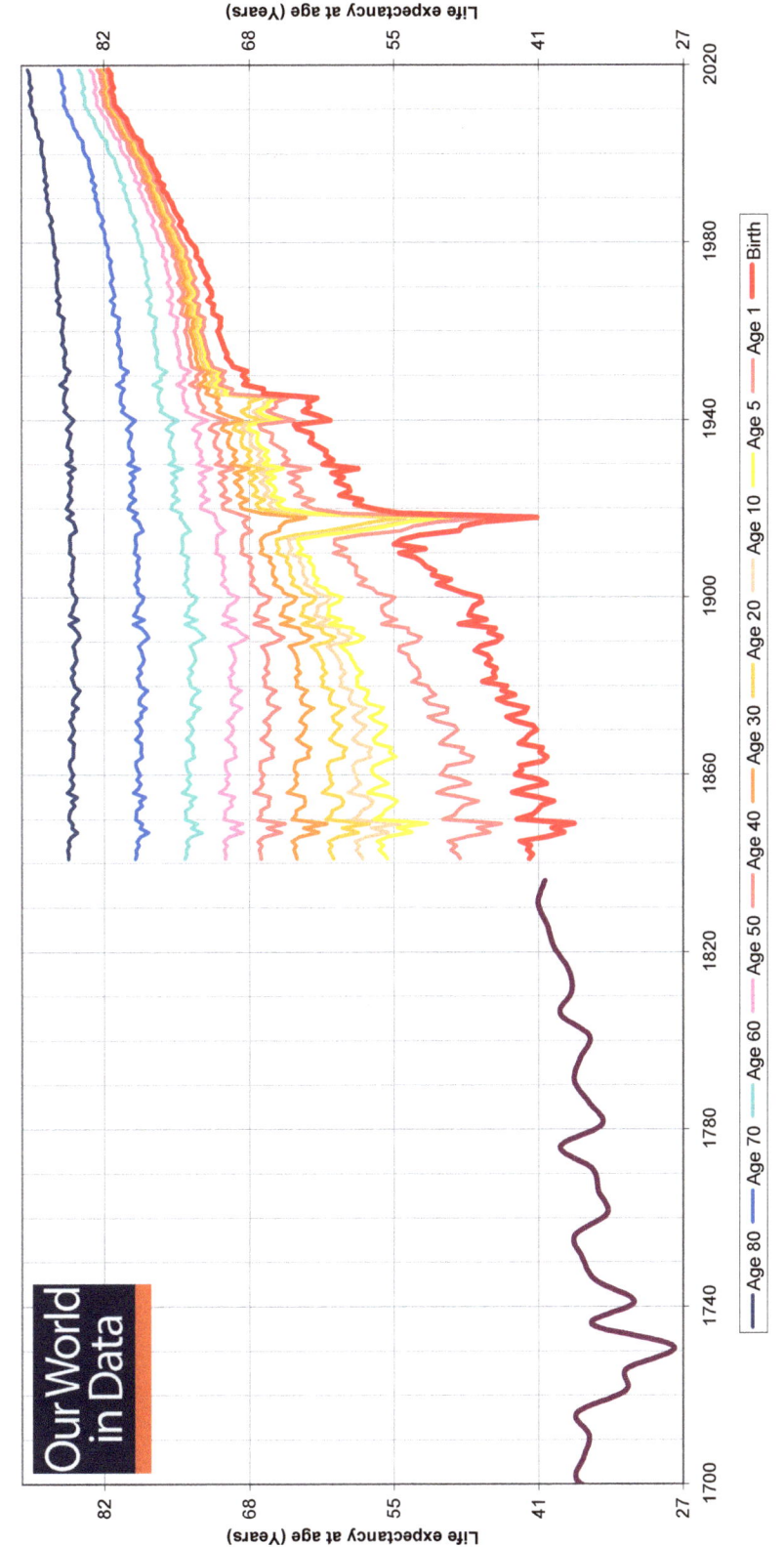

Part of a series - see also:

- UK Economic & Social Change – 1700-2019 – Three centuries of progress
- UK Economy – 1700-1913 – An economy in transition
- UK Economy – 1900-2019 – Growth of the state & world war
- UK Economy – 1990-2019 – Quarter of a century of new changes
- UK Economy – 1990-2019 – Stable income inequality
- UK Household Expenditure – 1700-2019 – Cost of Living
- UK Housing – 1700-2019 – Growth of home ownership
- UK Pauperism, Poverty and Hardship – 1700-2019 – The Retreat of Real Poverty
- UK Pollution (Air Quality), Cars – 1970-2019 – Continuous improvement
- UK Pollution (Air Quality), Energy – 1970-2019 – Continuous improvement
- UK Population & Life Expectancy – 1970-2019 – Continuous Improvement

UK Economic & Social Change

1700-2019 or fifteen generations

Three centuries of progress

Growth of population & Life expectancy

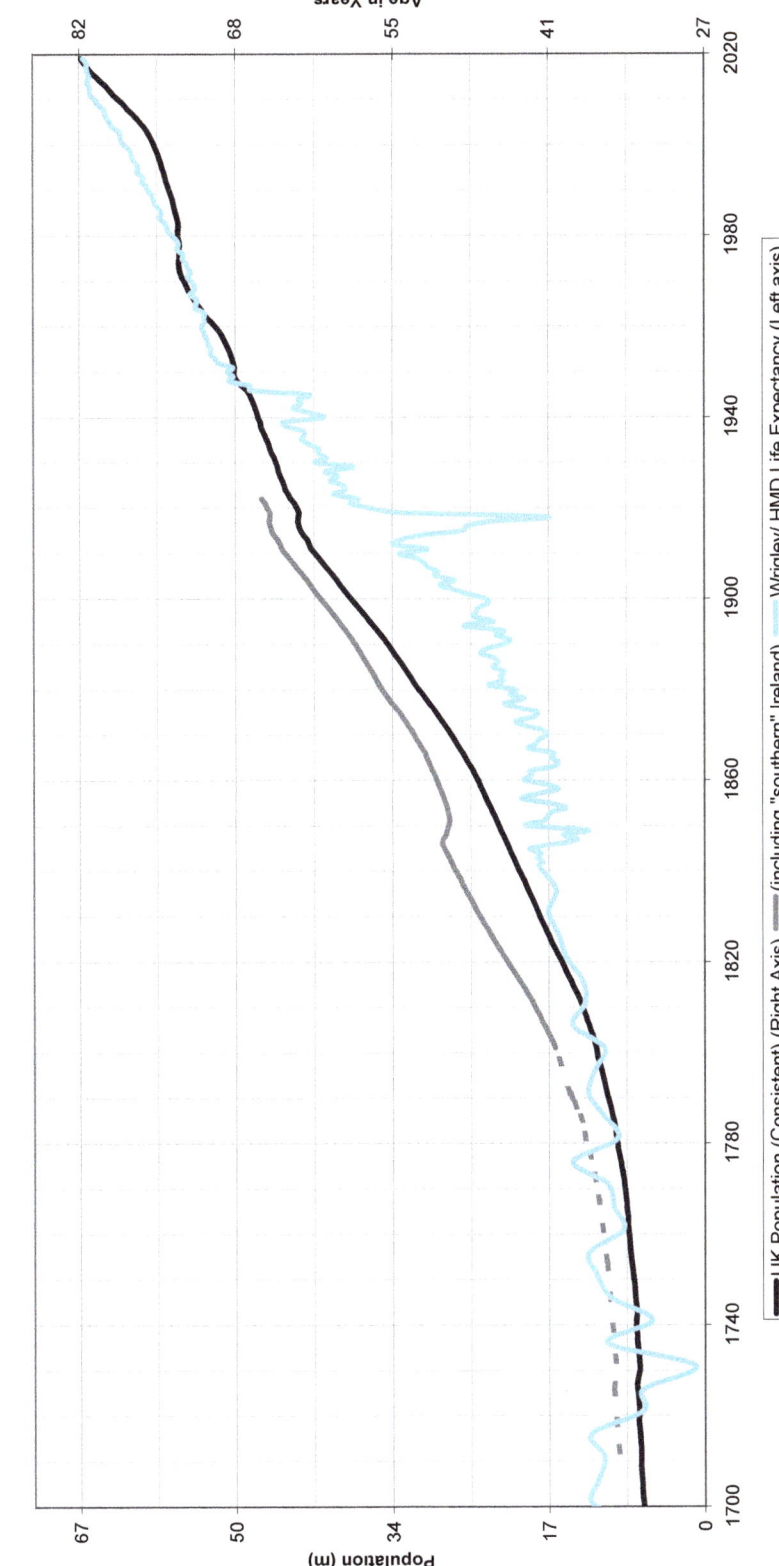

Growth of the economy
&
Effective (real) average earnings

Plus National Debt

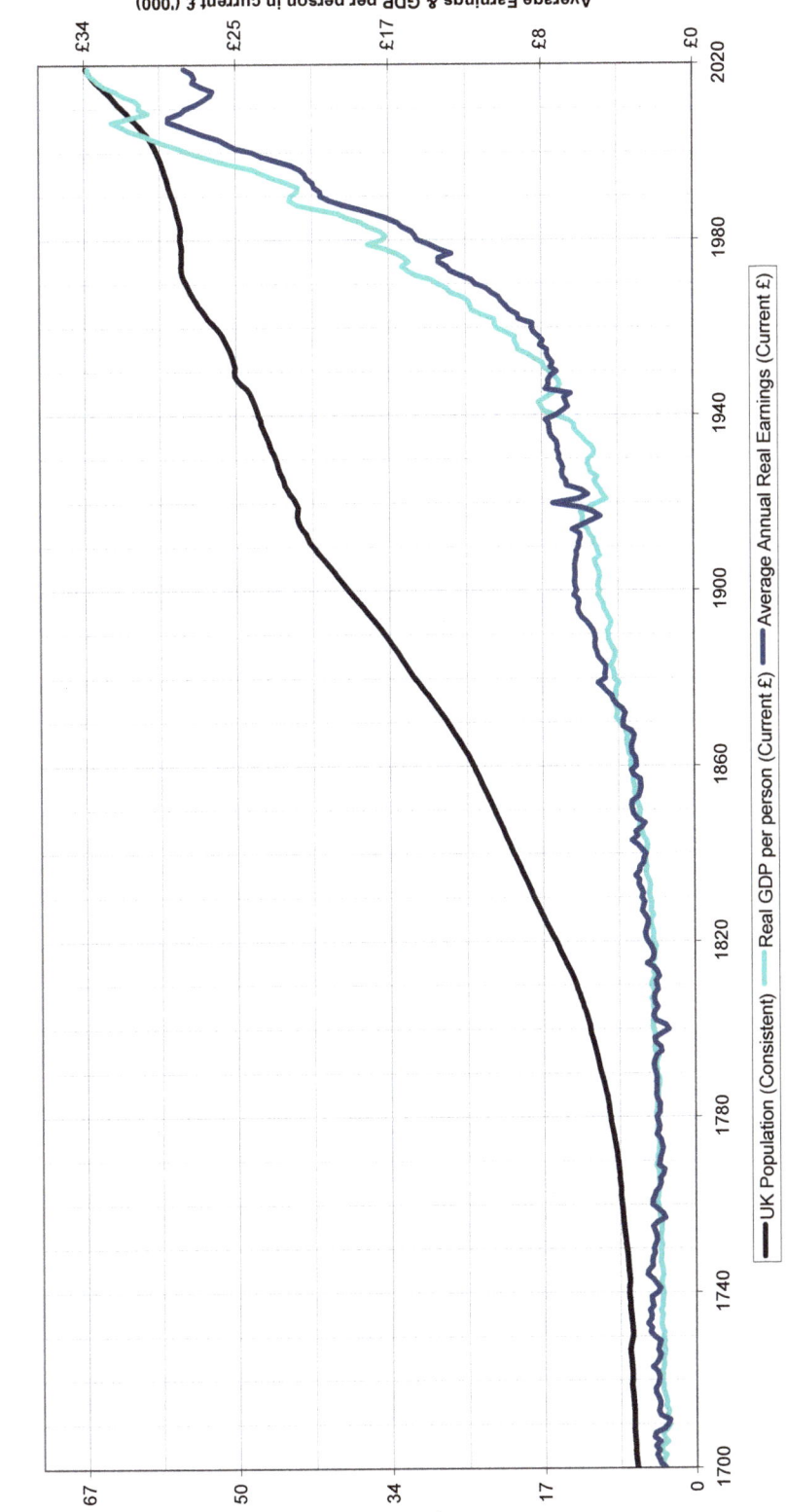

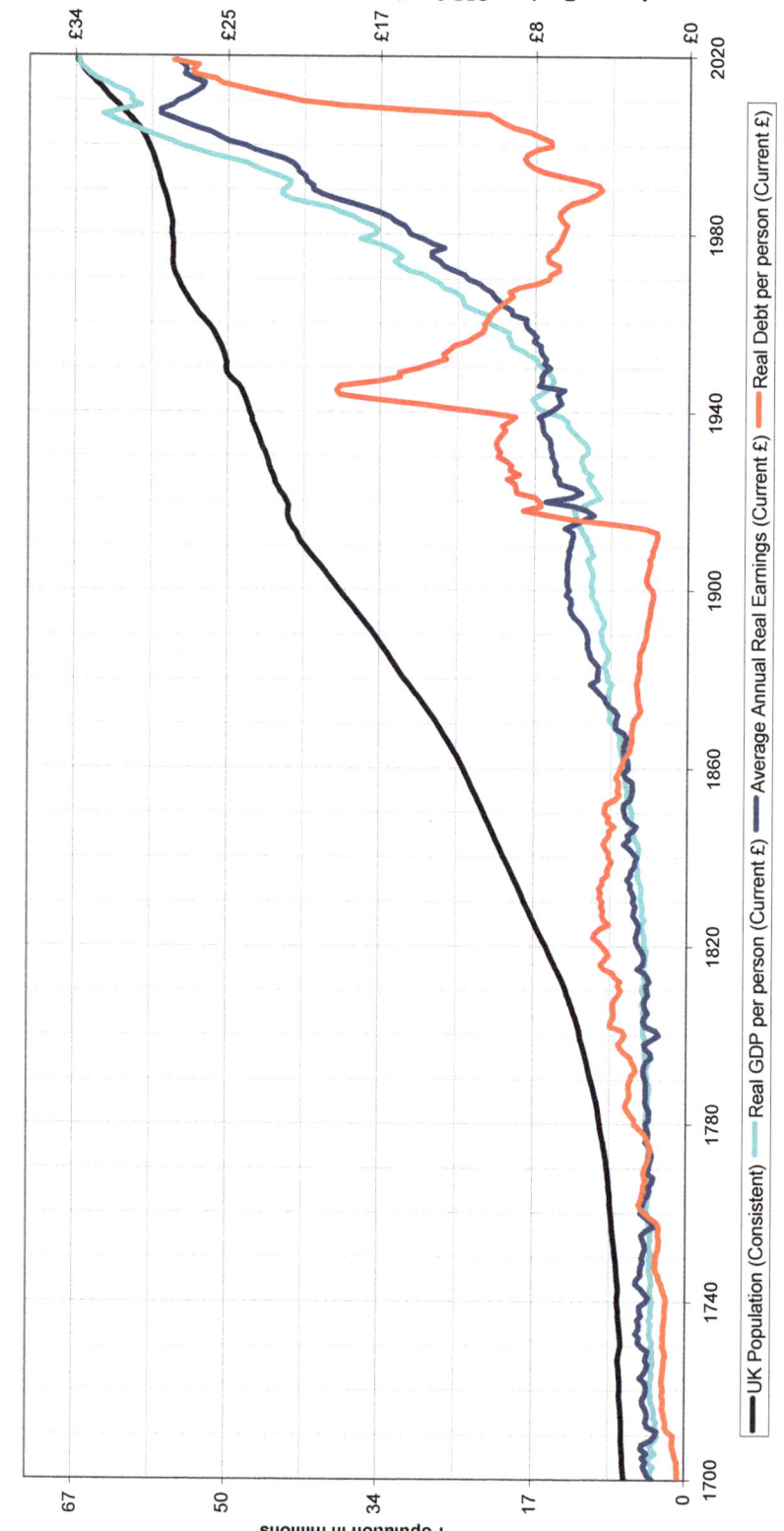

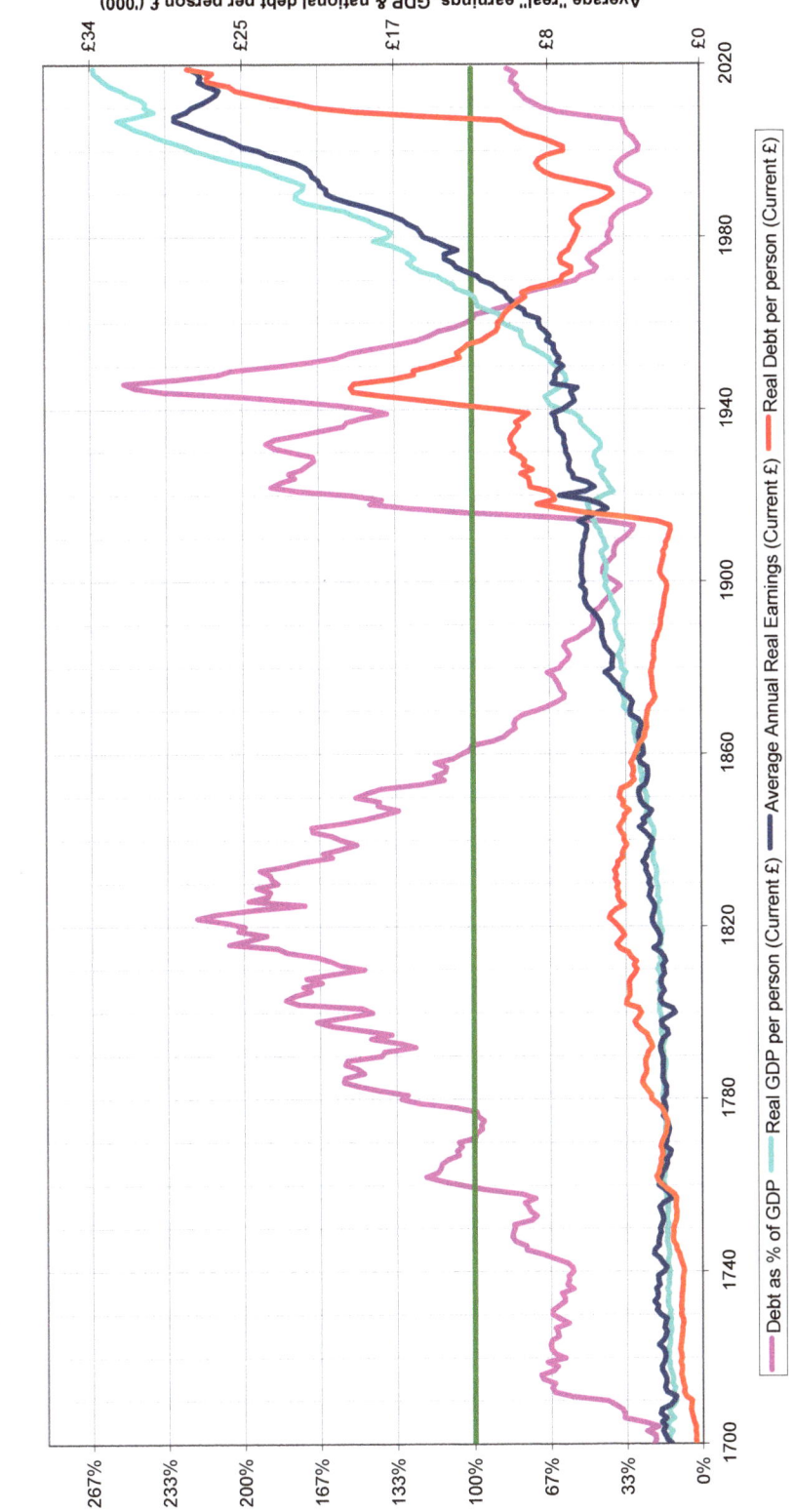

A State of War (with Debt) & Growth of the State

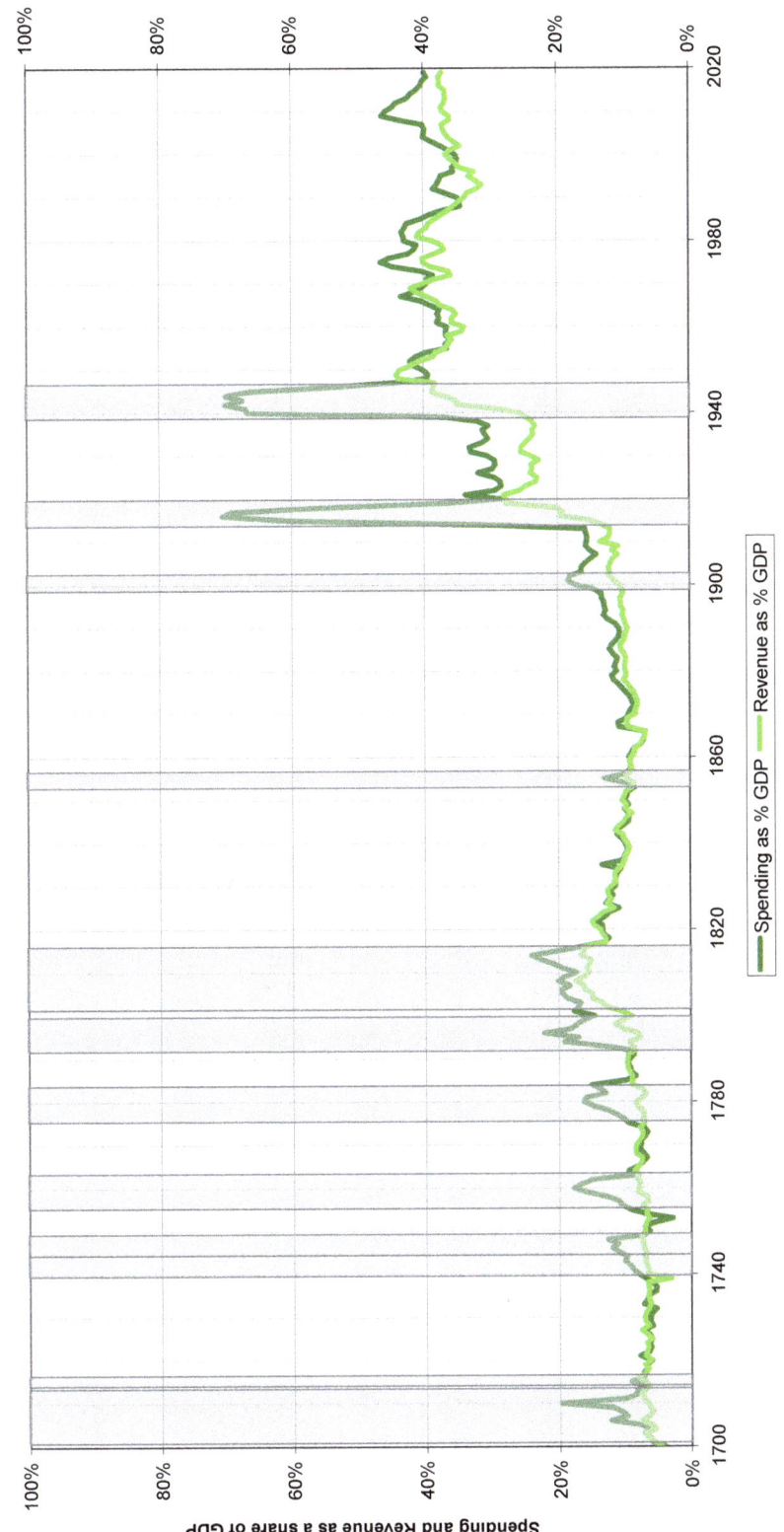

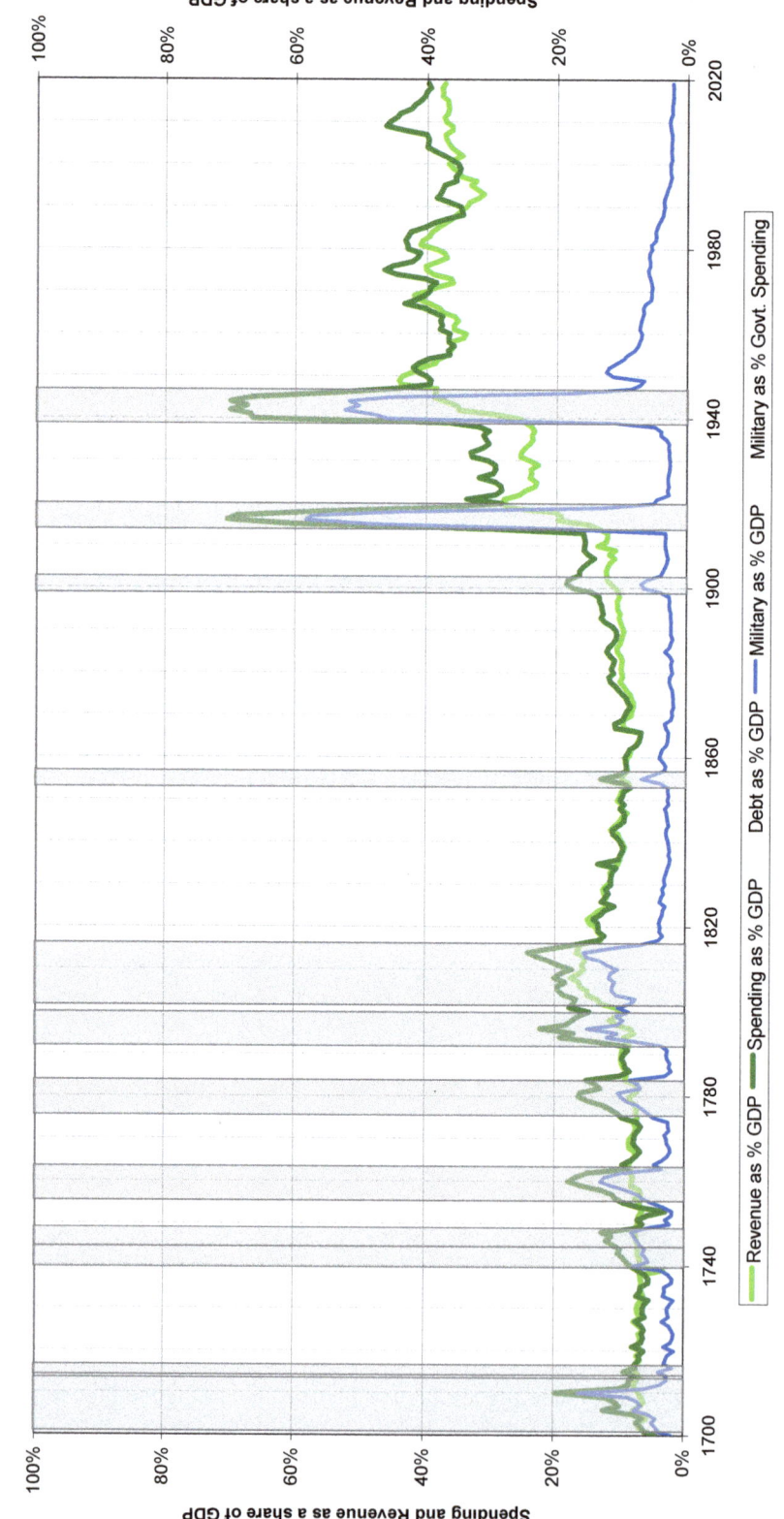

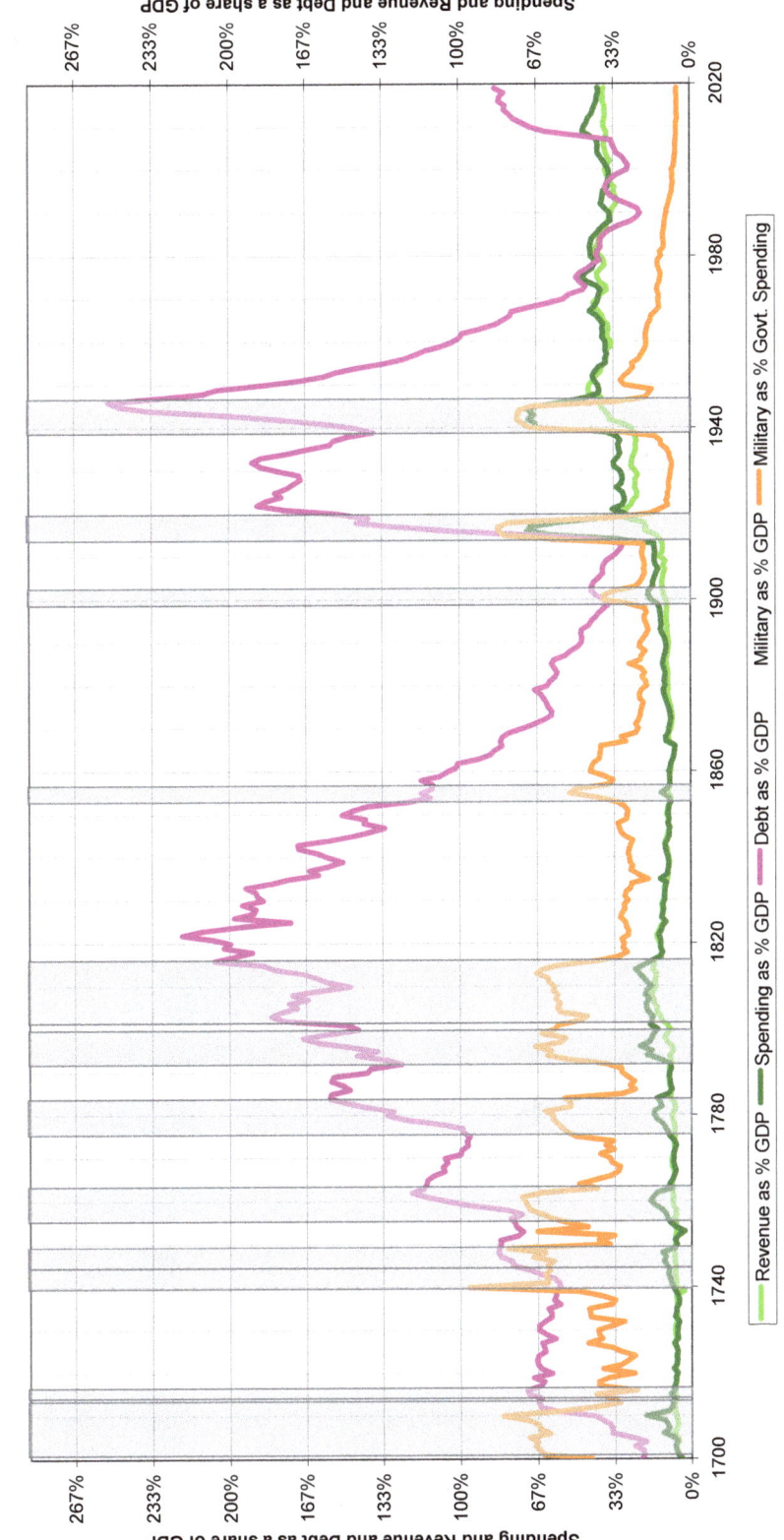

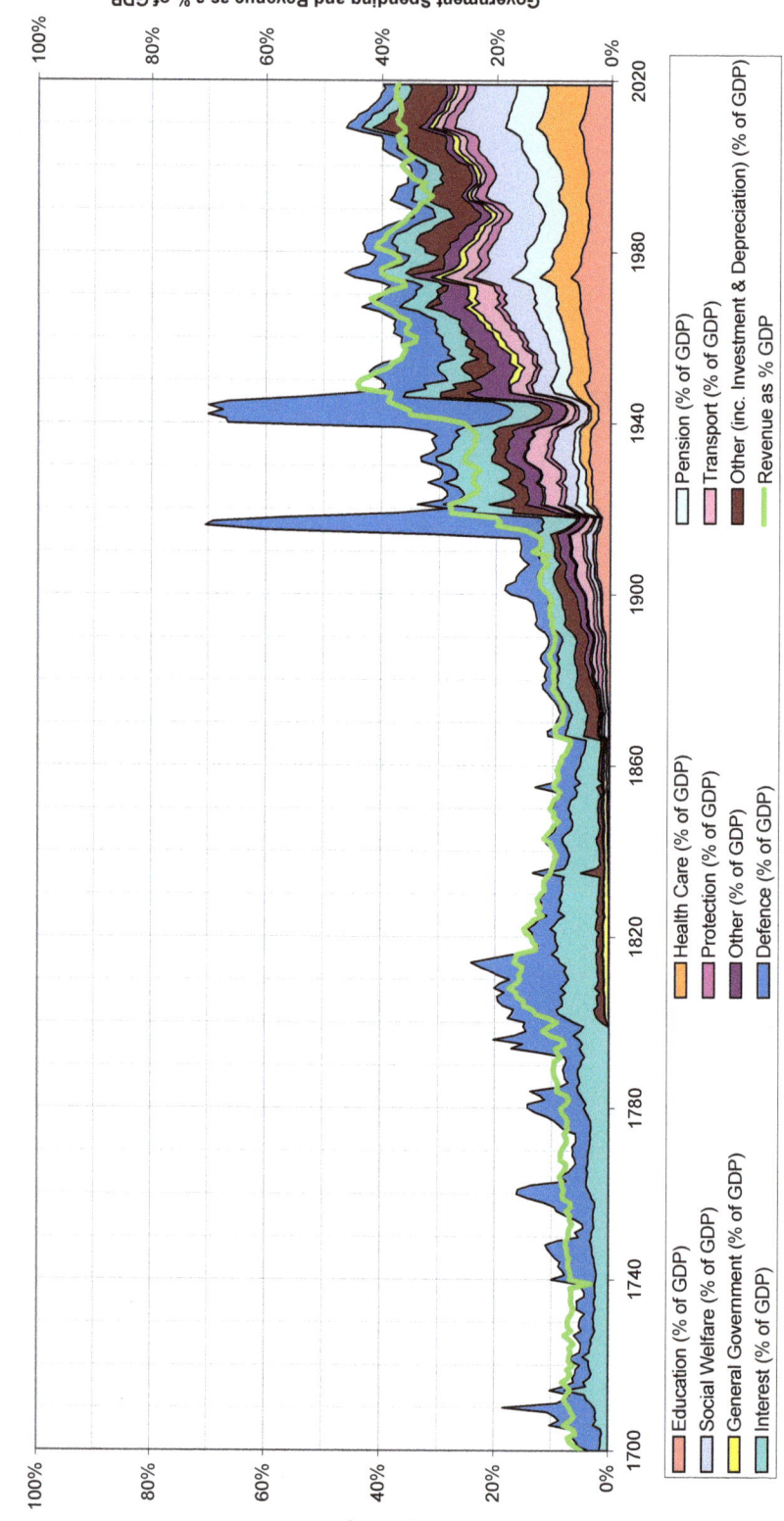

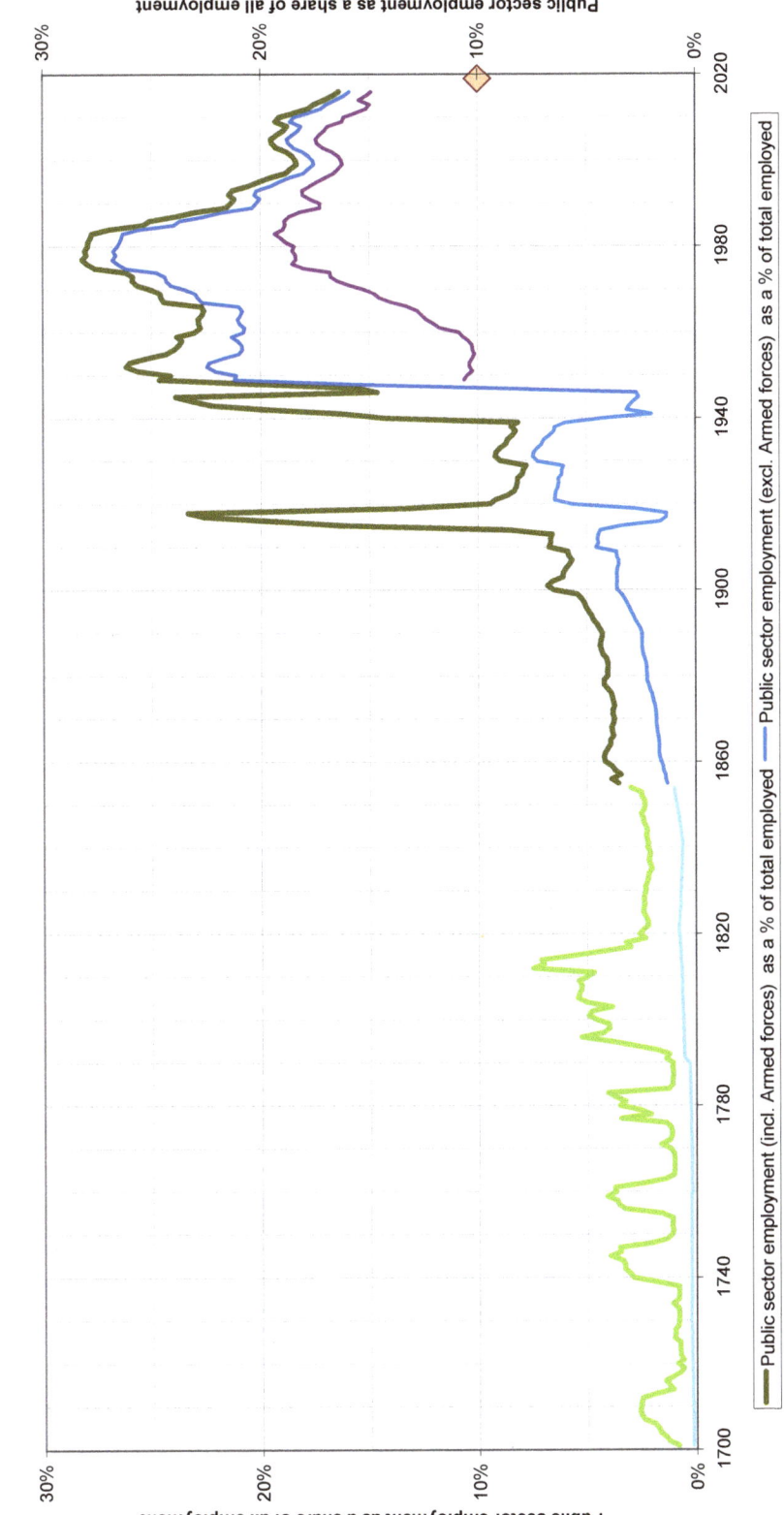

Various Annual Inflation Rates

&

Unemployment Estimates

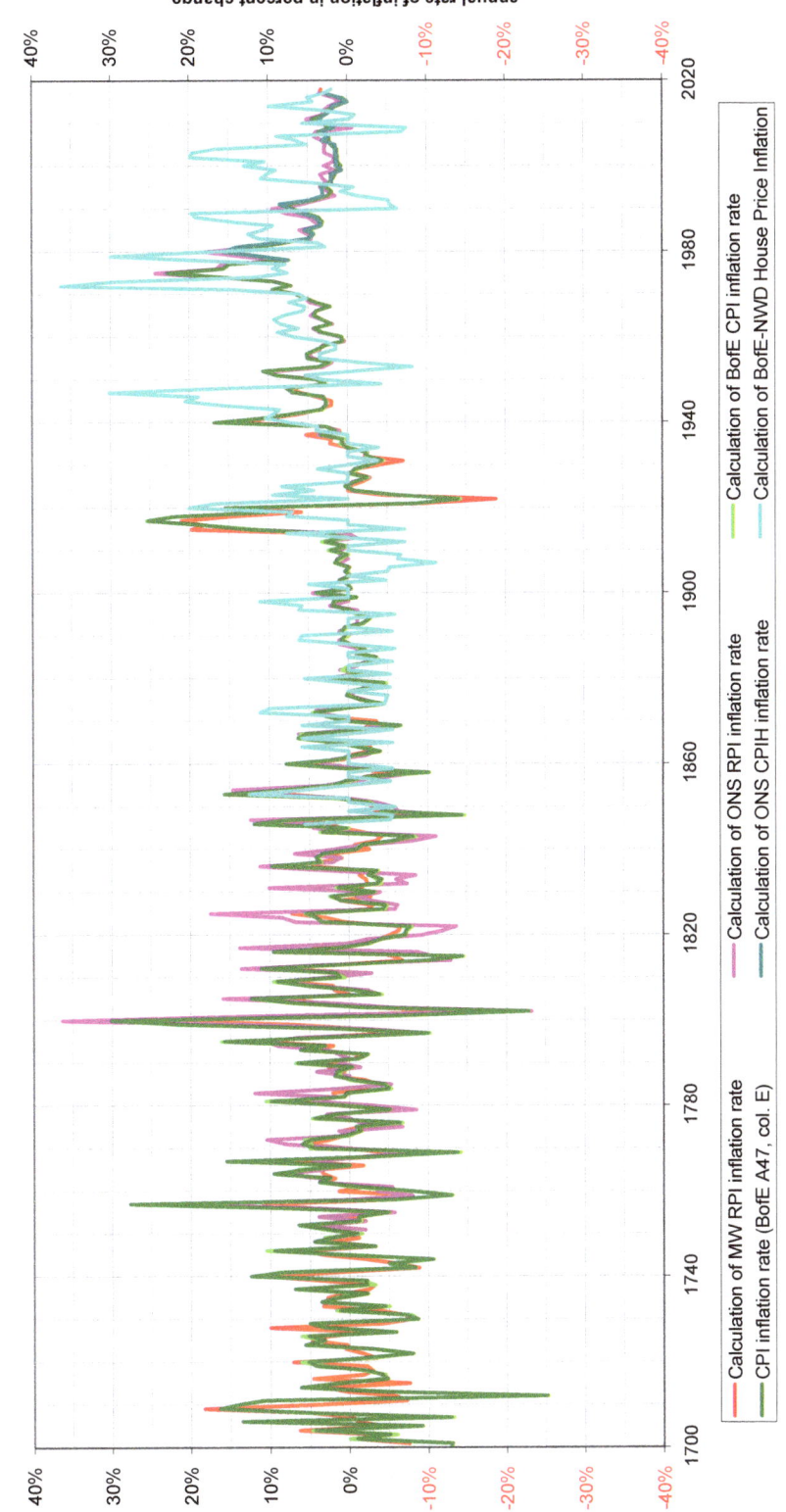

Unemployment as percent of workforce, BofE Millennium Okun's regression, from Feinstein, Solomou and Thomas 2019 plus Hatton and Boyer 2002

Legend:
- Unemployment rate – ratio applied to Feinstein 5yr averages
- Unemployment estimates calculated by Hatton & Boyer
- Unemployment rate based on 1855-1913 Okun's law regression equation
- Unemployment rate as a % of total UK workforce (incl. S.Ireland)

Inequality indicators

Gini, Top n% shares of income

Lorenz Curve & Income Distributions

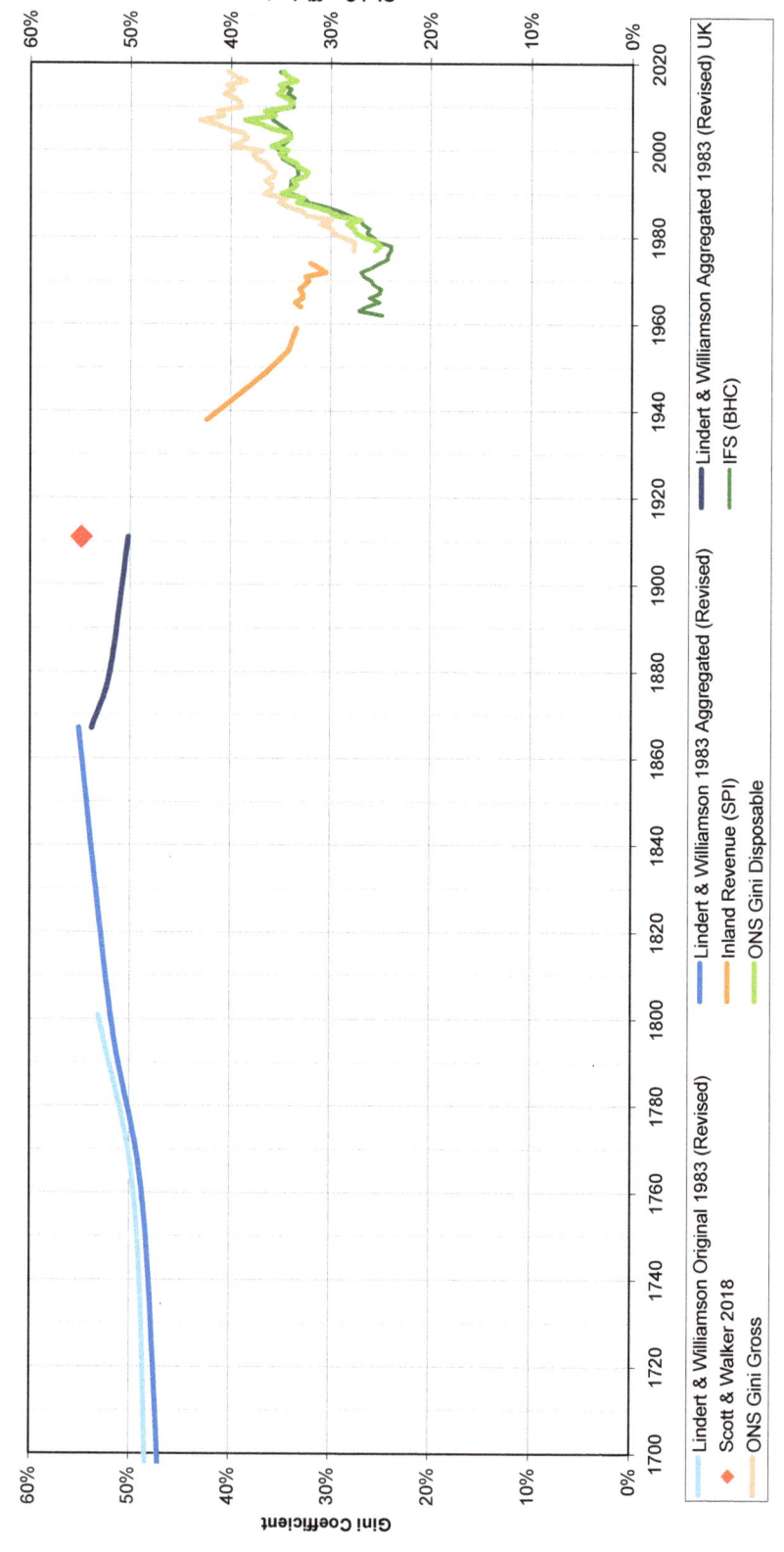

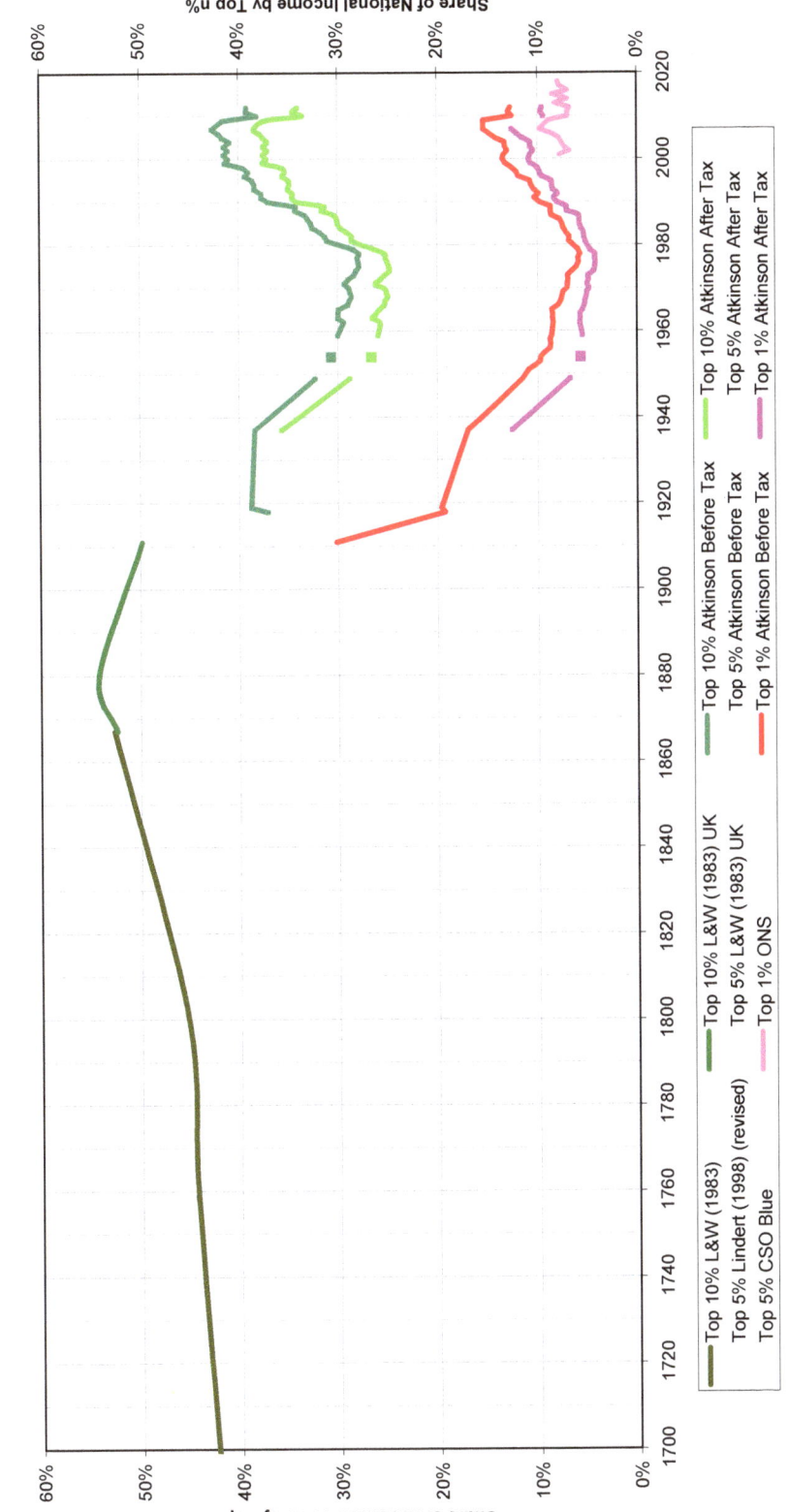

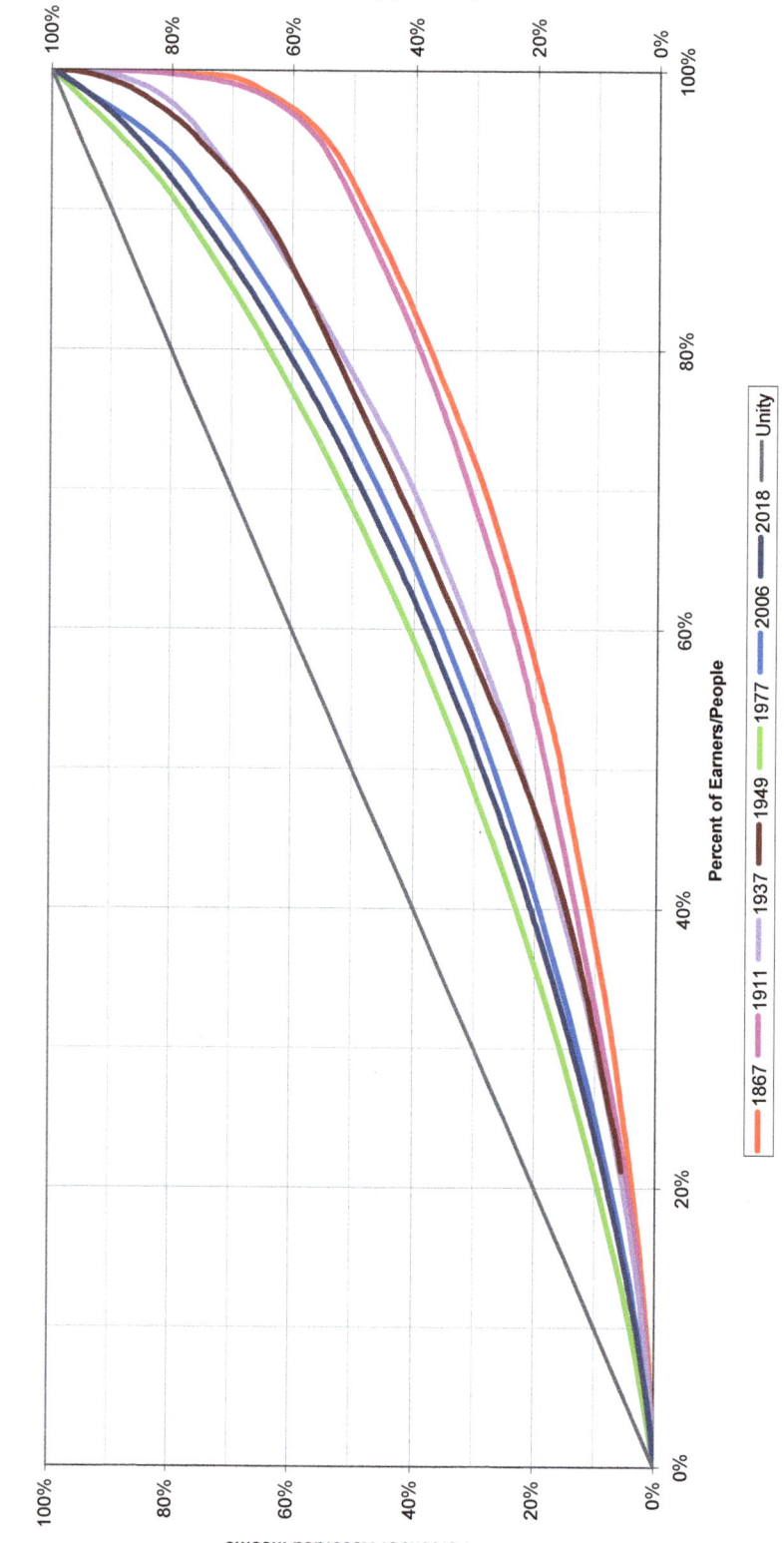

Lorenz Curves derived from Lindert/Williamson (1867/1911) and Scott/Walker Earners (1911/1937-38/1949) and ONS Equivalised Household Disposable (1977/2006-07/2018-19)

Compare real earnings/income distribution (CPI)

1867 (Baxter/Lindert '98 UK) - Gini **58.0**

2018/19 (SPI - factored for estimated non-taxpayers) - ONS Gross Gini **40.2**

Annual Income in Current £'s ('000)

— 1867 Baxter (ONS CPI) — 2018/19 ONS (ONS CPI)

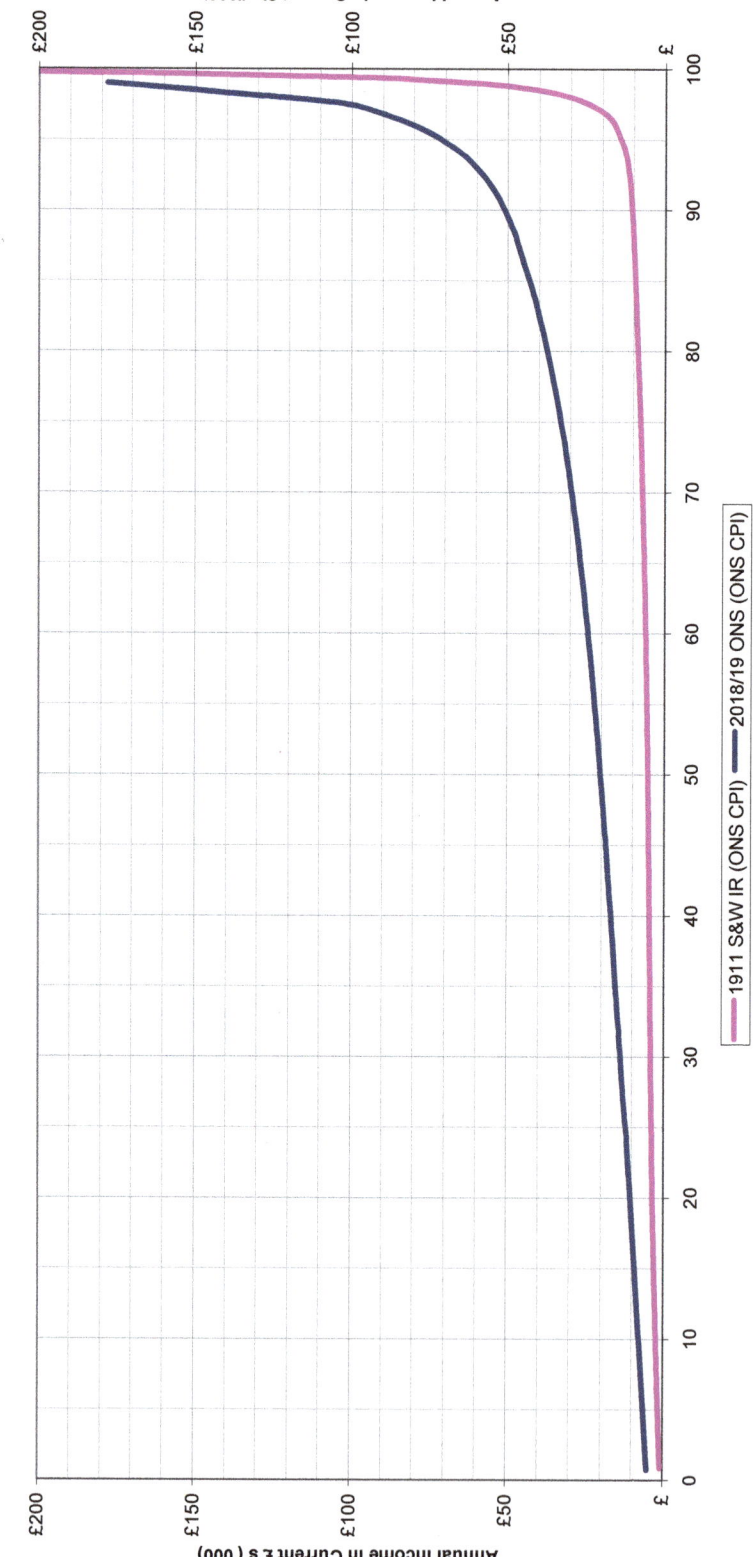

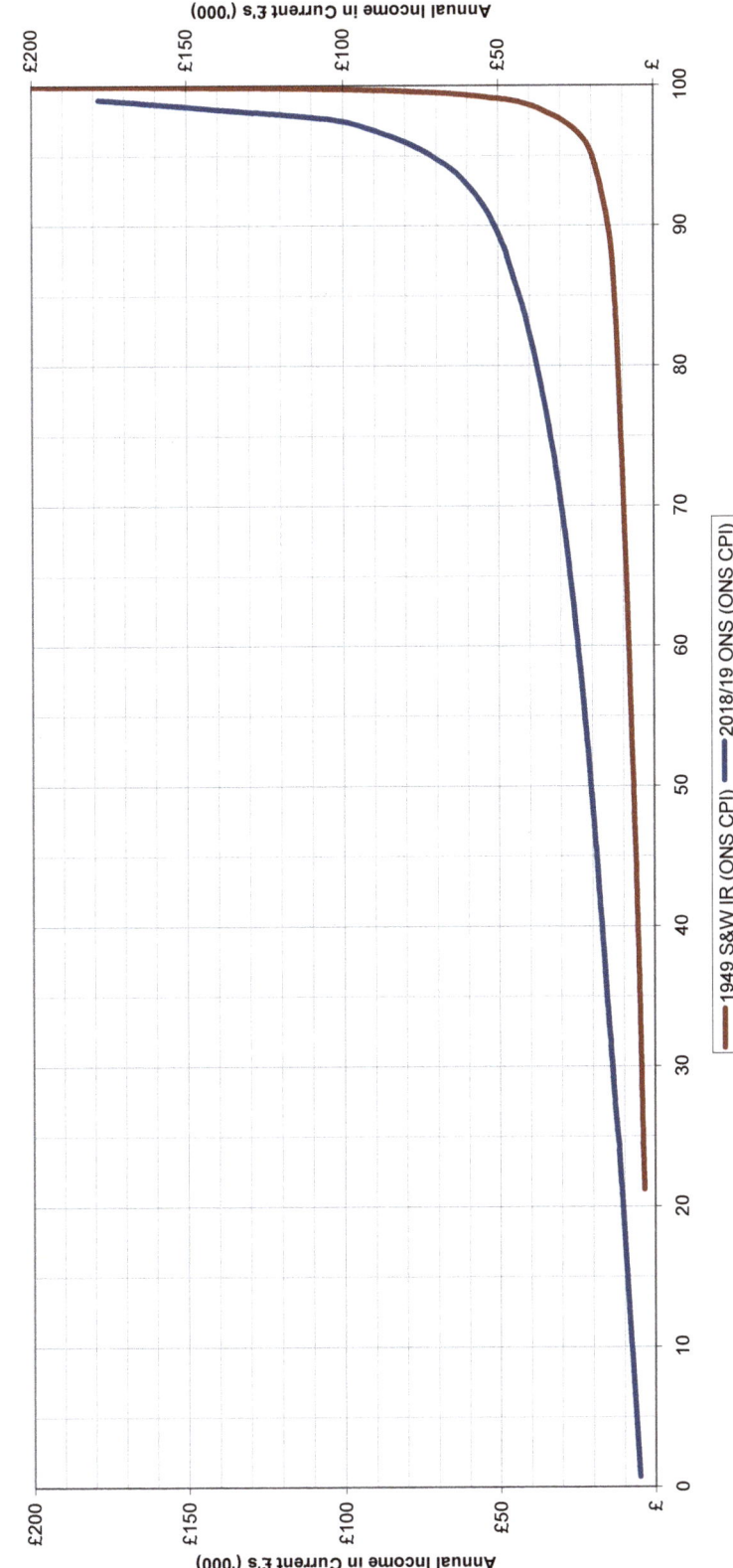

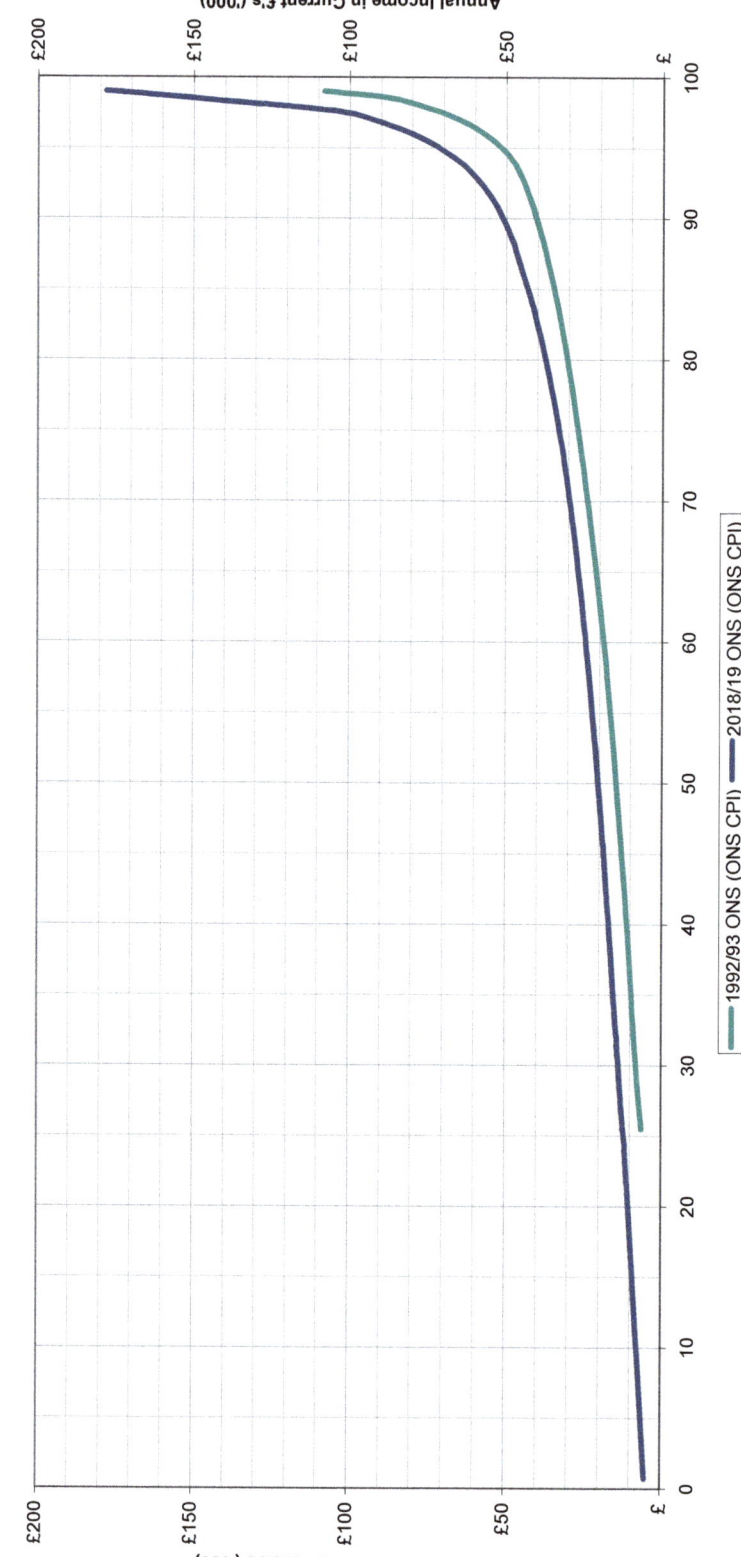

Effective (real) average earnings

&

The cost of living

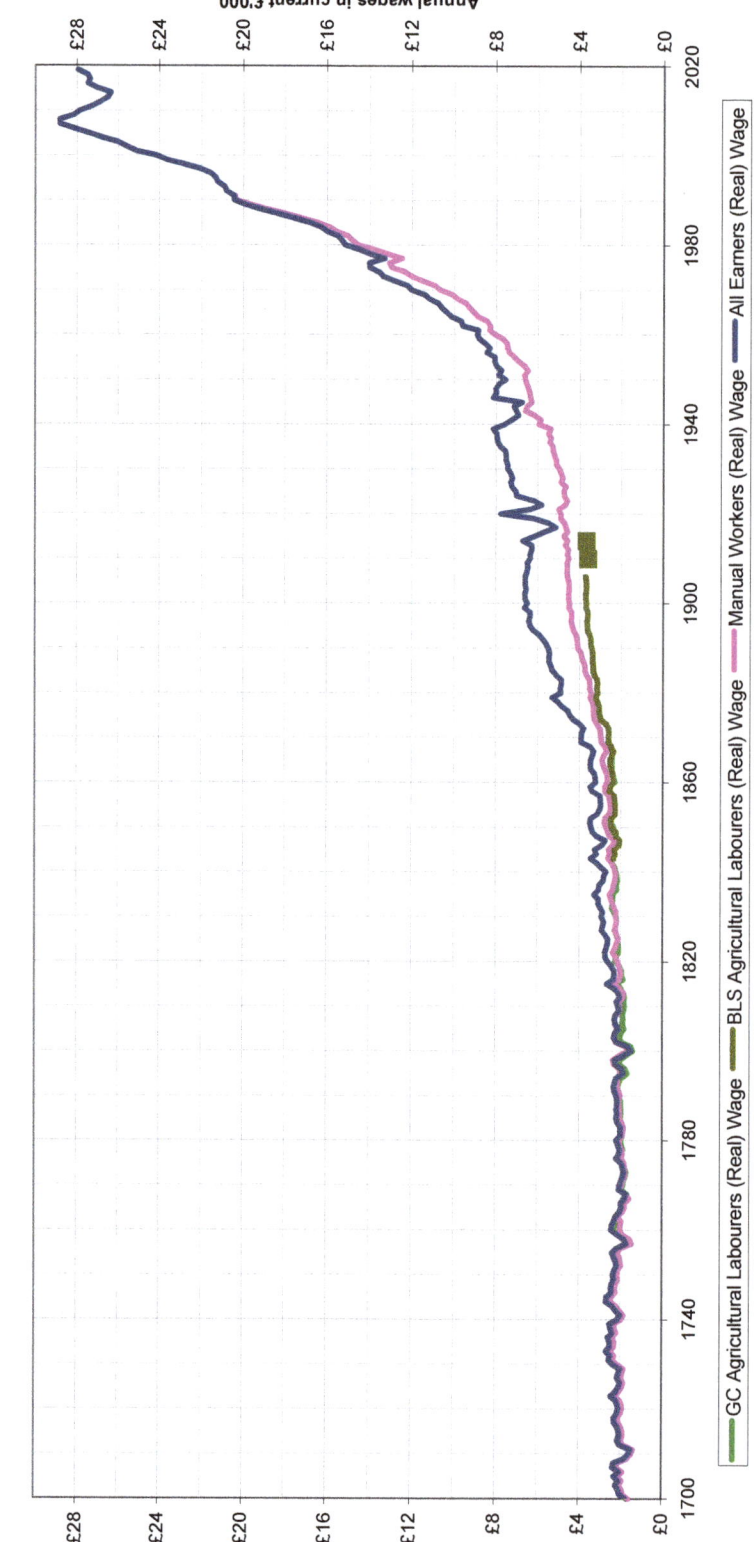

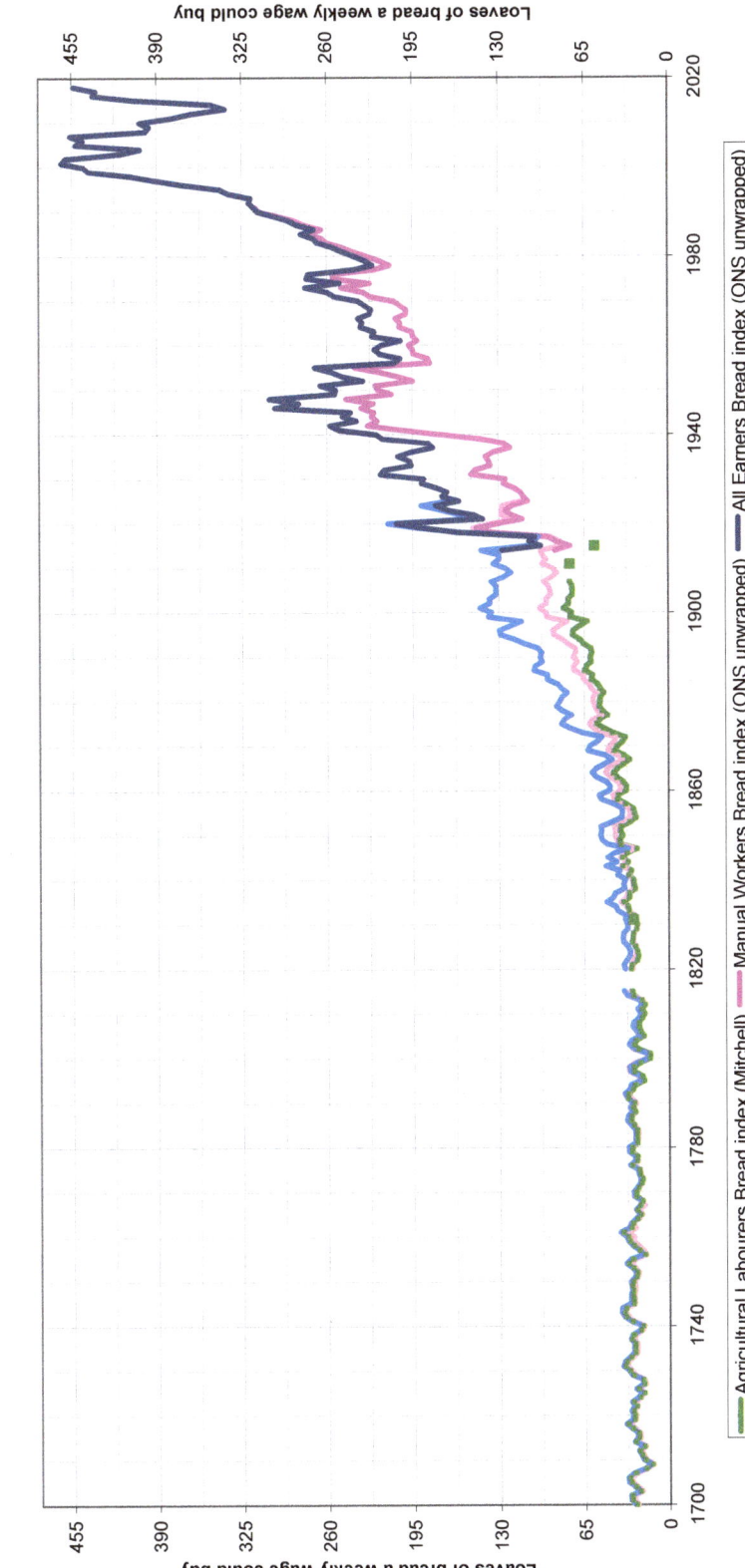

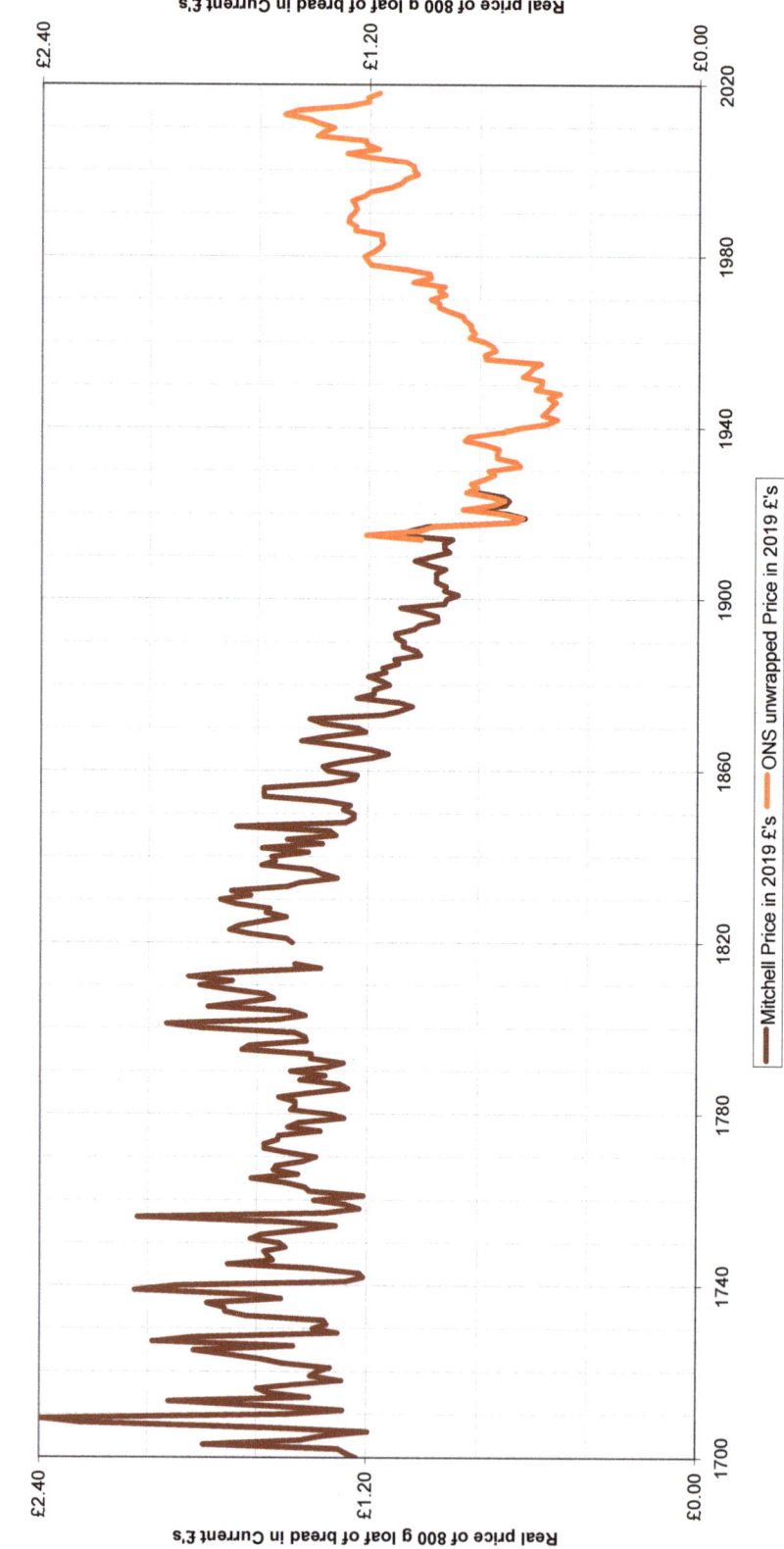

Social Spending

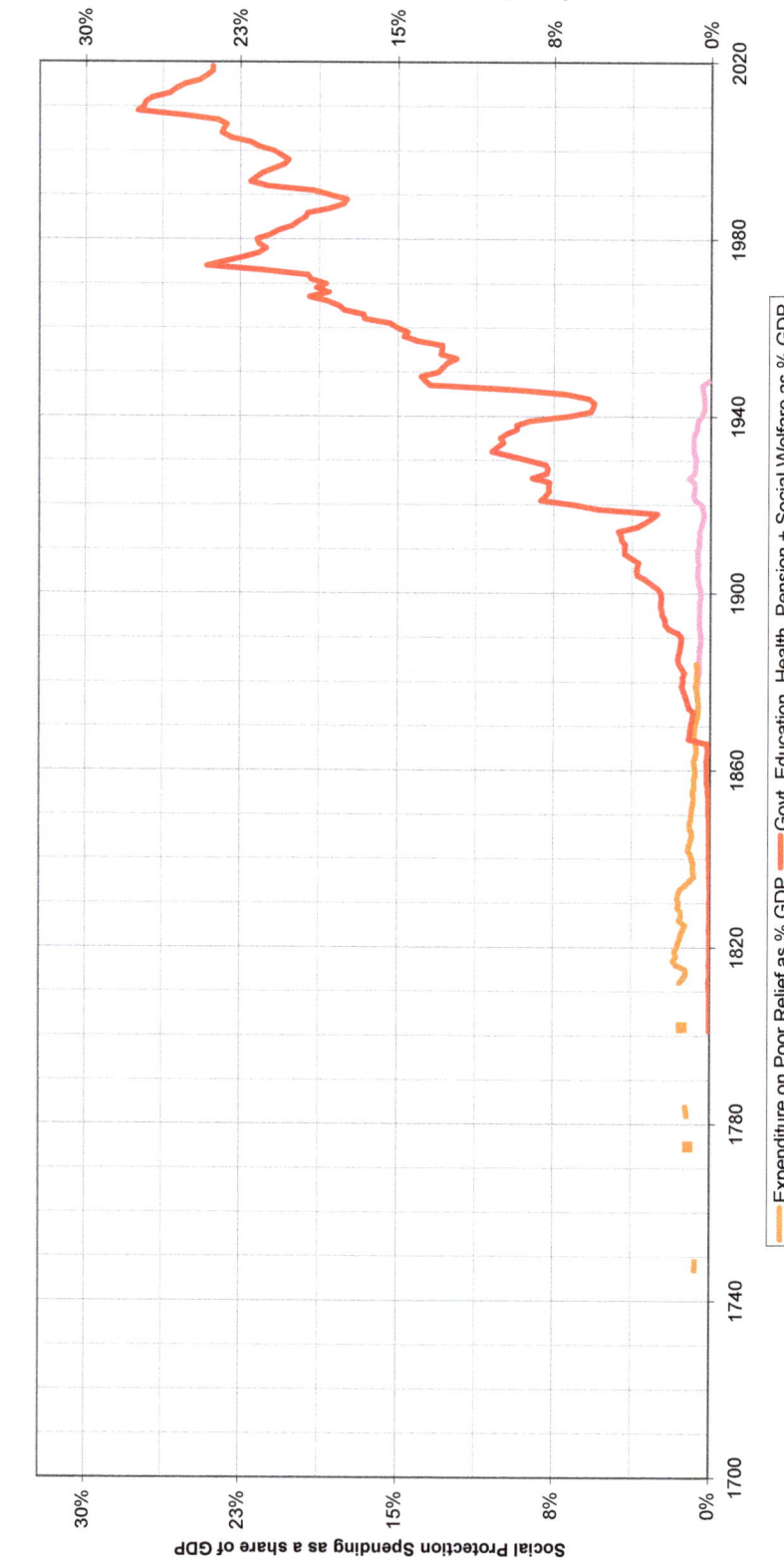

Historical Poor Law Relief and State Social Spending (Education, Health, Pension and Social Welfare) per capita % of MeasuringWorth/ONS Earnings

— Expenditure on Poor Relief % MW Annual Income — Govt. Education, Health, Pension + Social Welfare % MW Annual Income

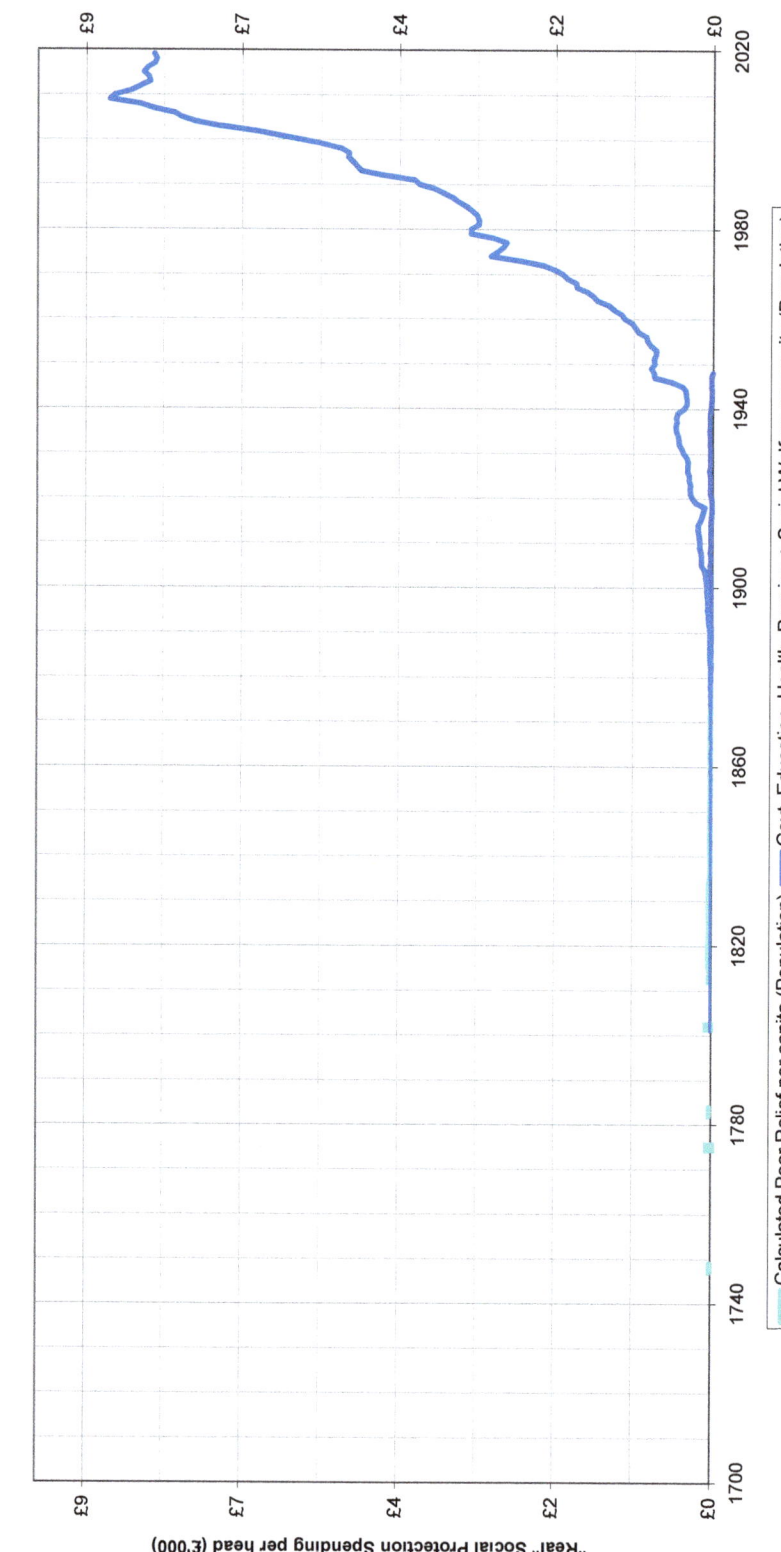

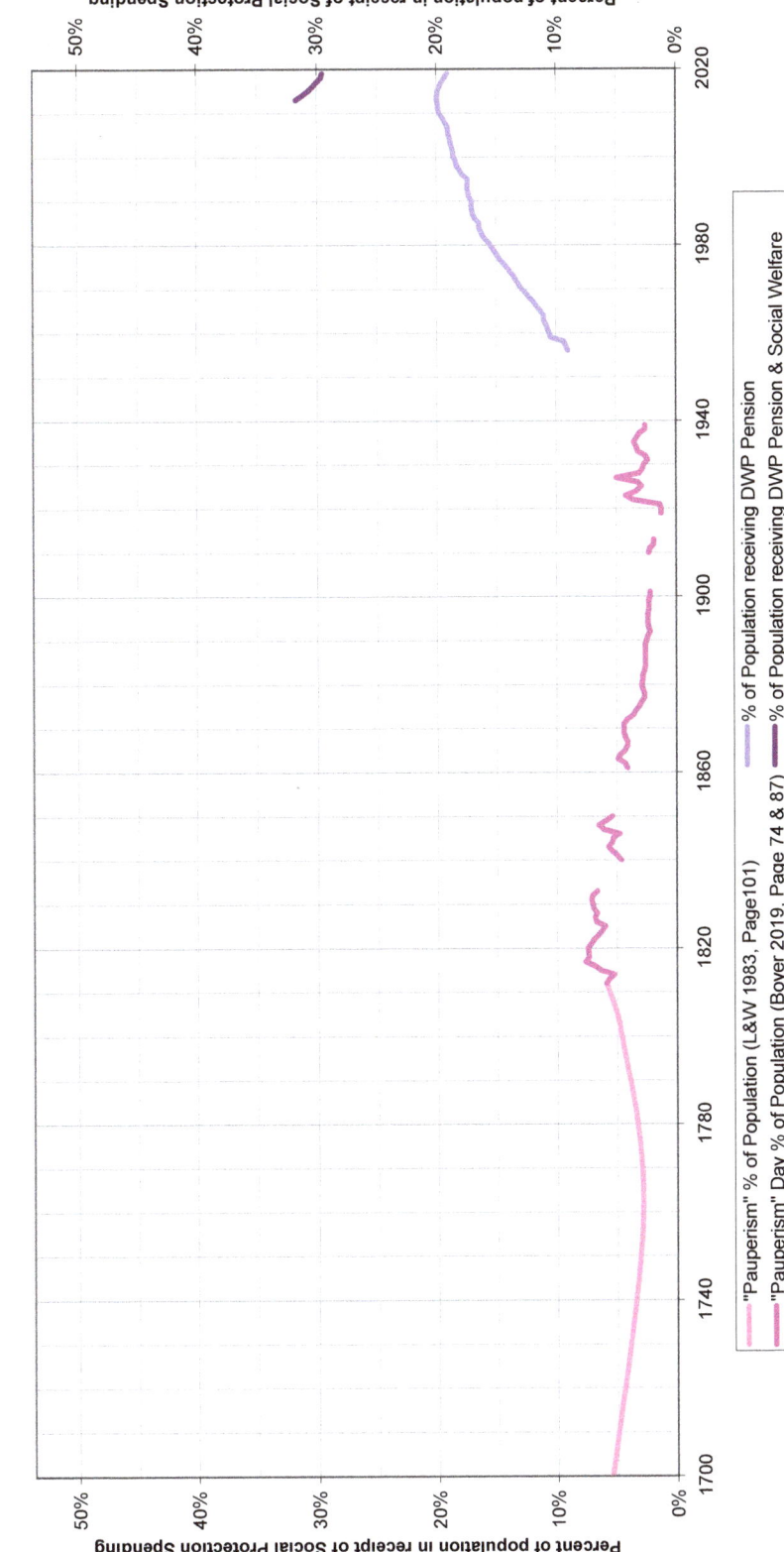

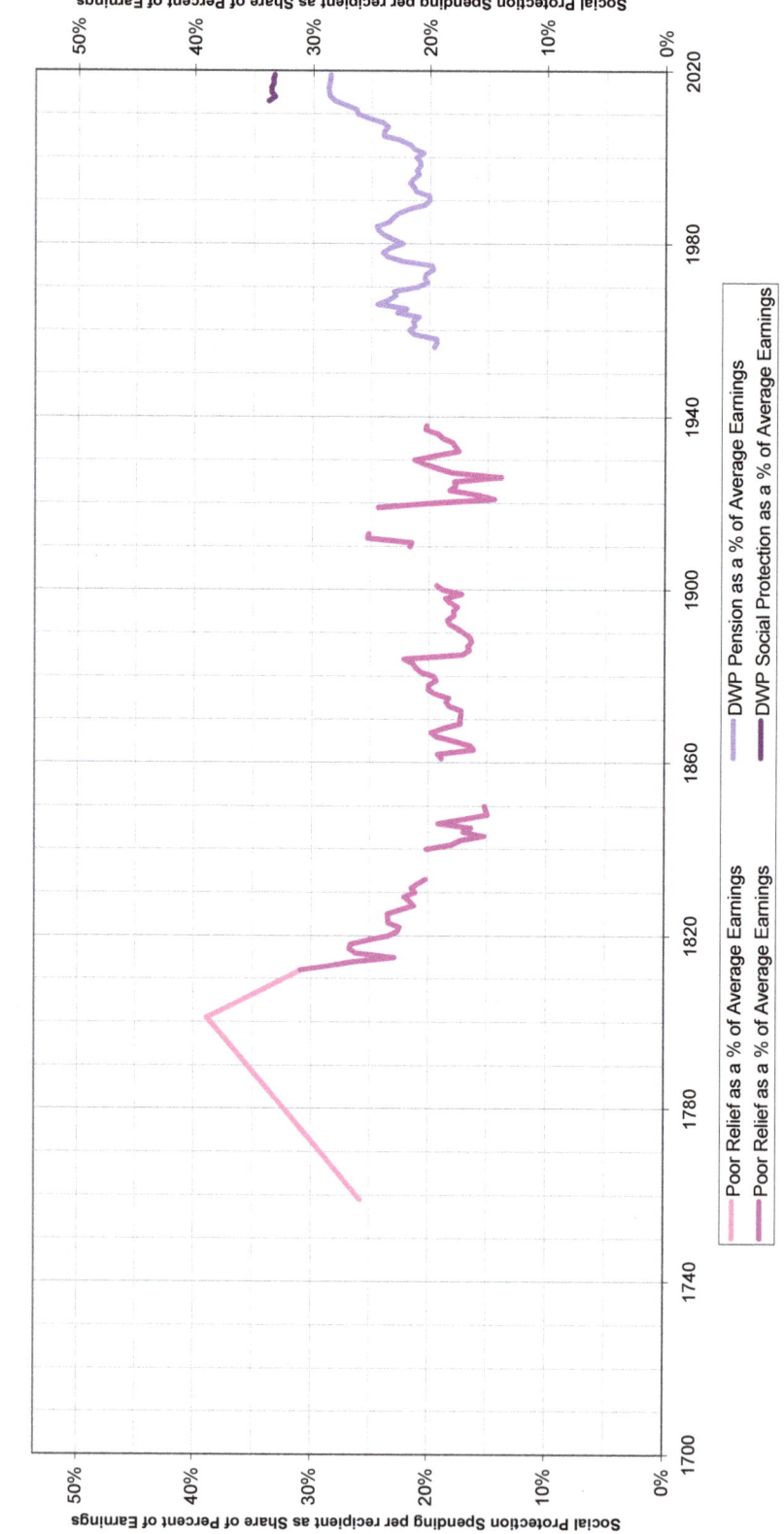

Average spending on benefits and tax credits at different ages in 2010-11 (DWP/ONS/OBR) in £'000

Part of a series - see also:

- UK Economic & Social Change – 1700-2019 – Three centuries of progress
- UK Economy – 1700-1913 – An economy in transition
- UK Economy – 1900-2019 – Growth of the state & world war
- UK Economy – 1990-2019 – Quarter of a century of new changes
- UK Economy – 1990-2019 – Stable income inequality
- UK Household Expenditure – 1700-2019 – Cost of Living
- UK Housing – 1700-2019 – Growth of home ownership
- UK Pauperism, Poverty and Hardship – 1700-2019 – The Retreat of Real Poverty
- UK Pollution (Air Quality), Cars – 1970-2019 – Continuous improvement
- UK Pollution (Air Quality), Energy – 1970-2019 – Continuous improvement
- UK Population & Life Expectancy – 1970-2019 – Continuous Improvement

UK Economy

1700-1913 or nine generations

An economy in transition

UK Population & Life Expectancy From 1700-1913

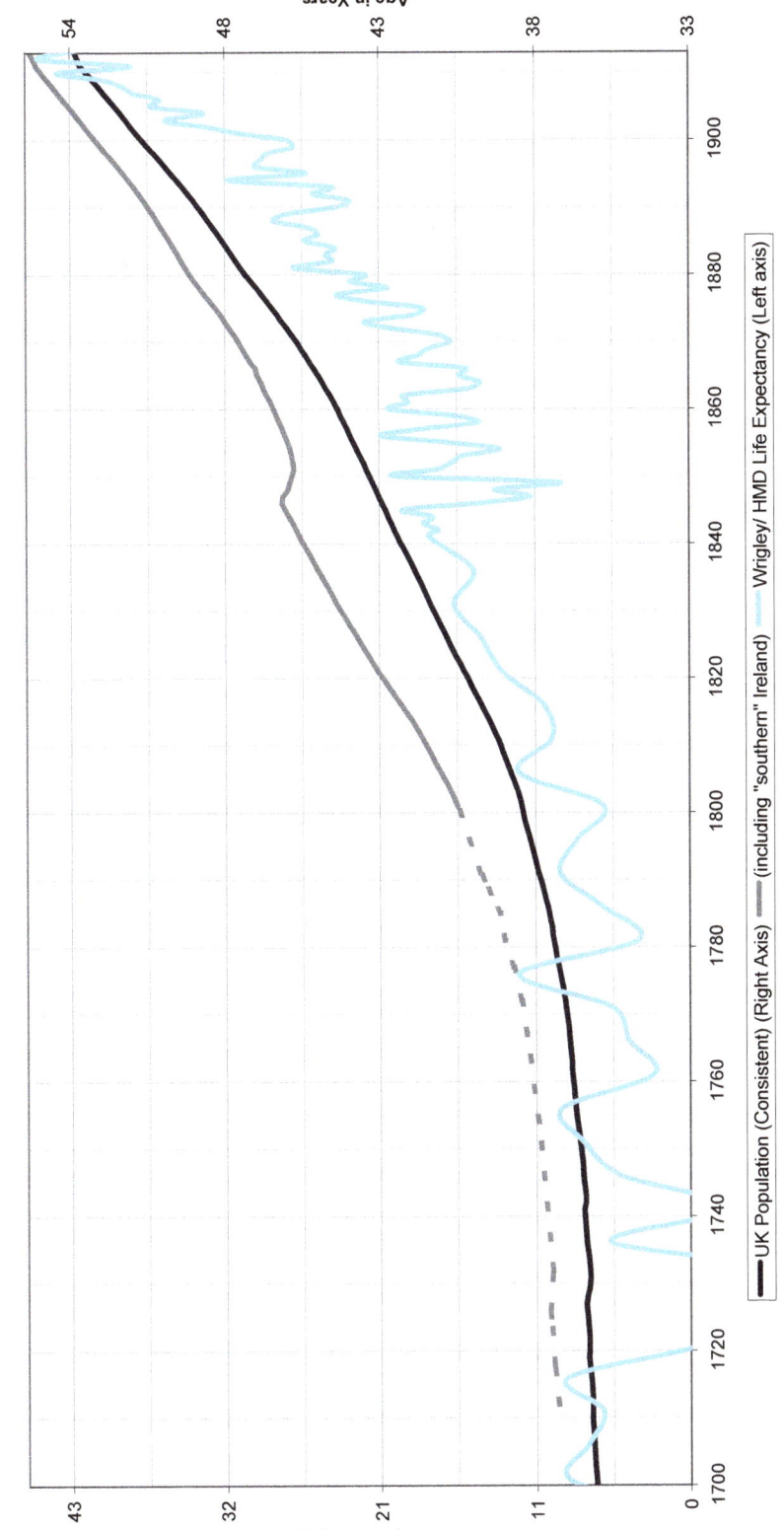

A "state" of war

Limited role of the state
(military and administrative)

& the resulting National Debt

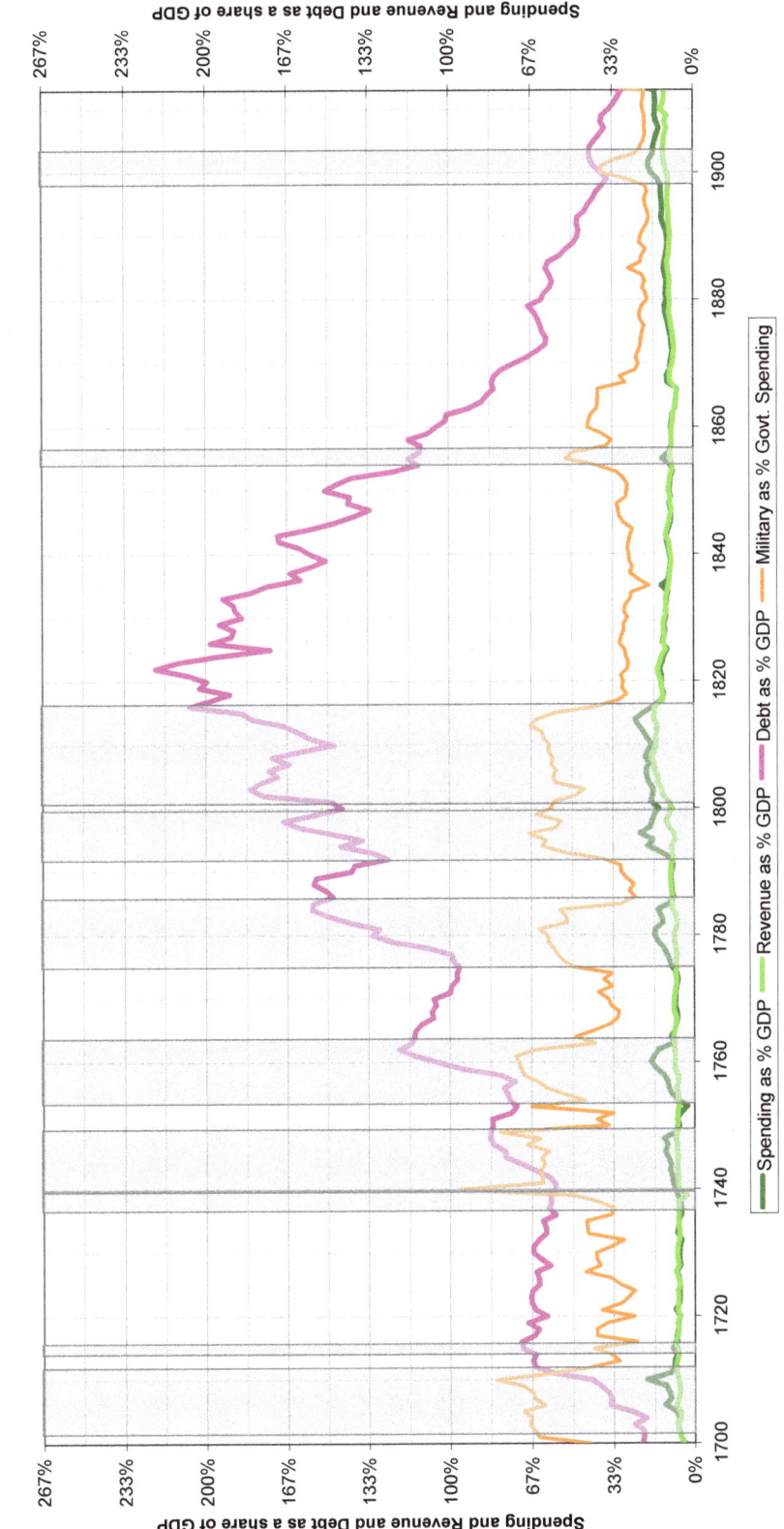

A new "state" of awareness

Early growth of the state & social spending (education, welfare etc.)

From the mid-1860's

UK Nominal Government Spending and Revenue (£ Million)

Growth of the Economy & Population

The Industrial Revolution

& "Real" earnings per recipient

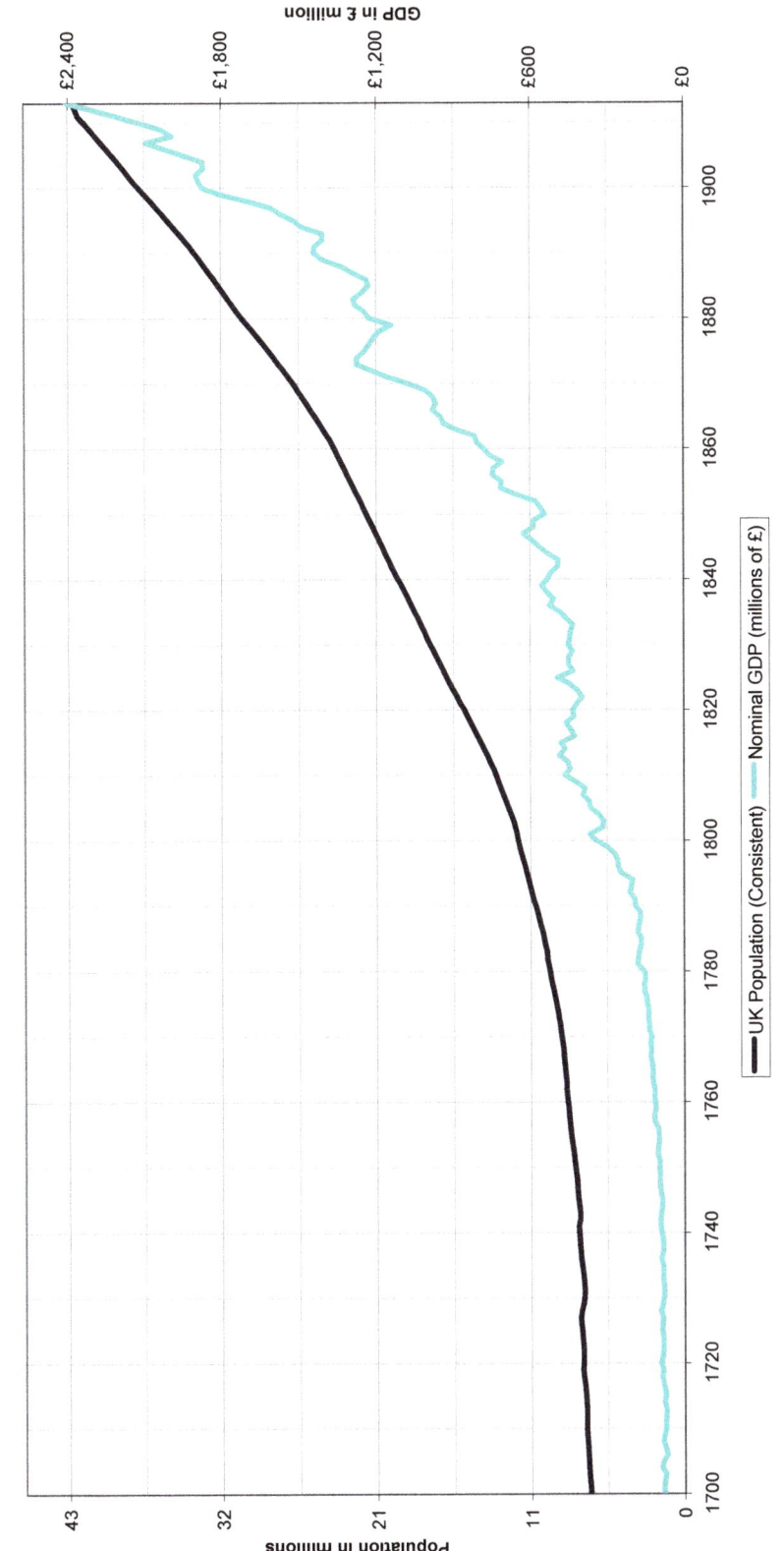

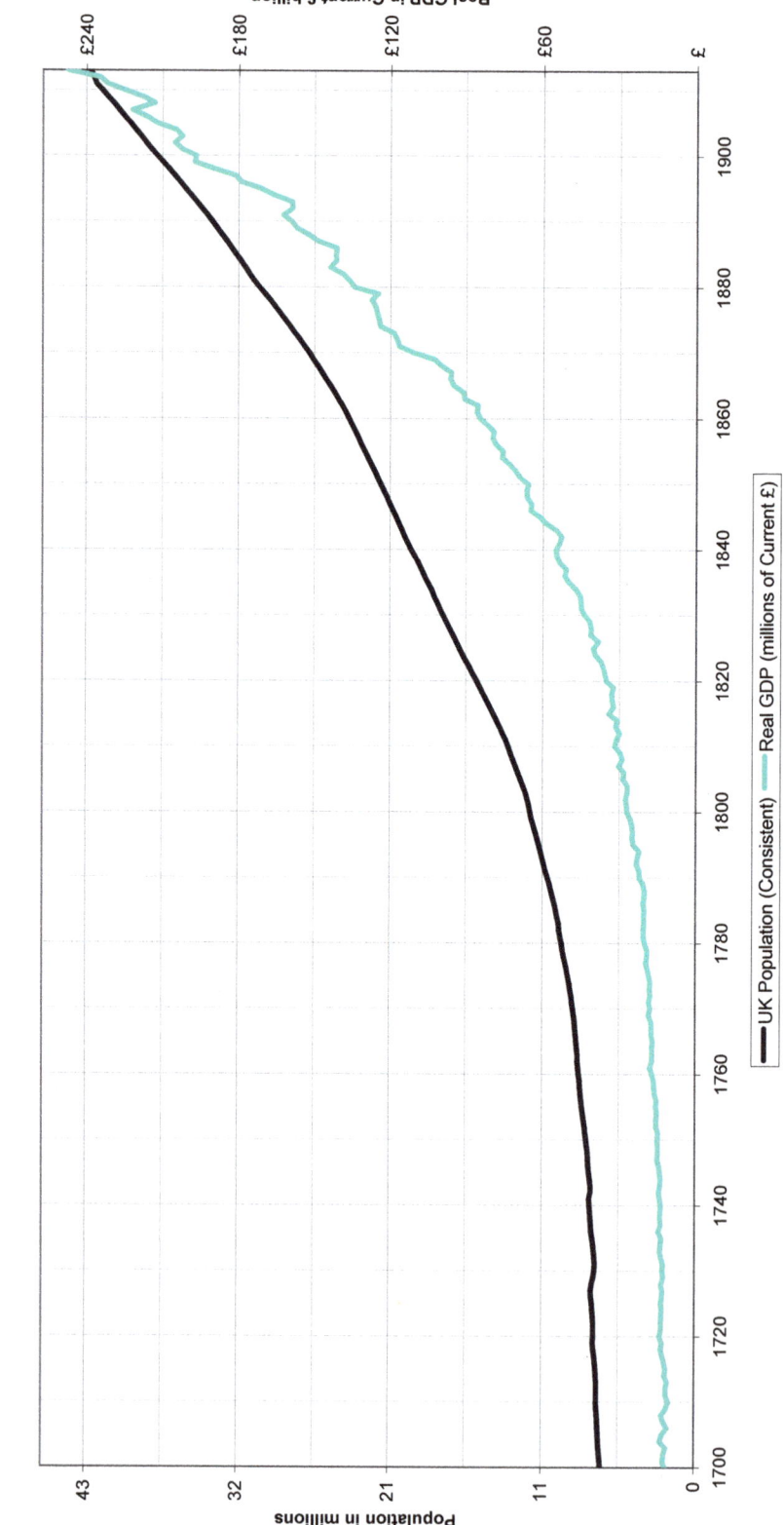

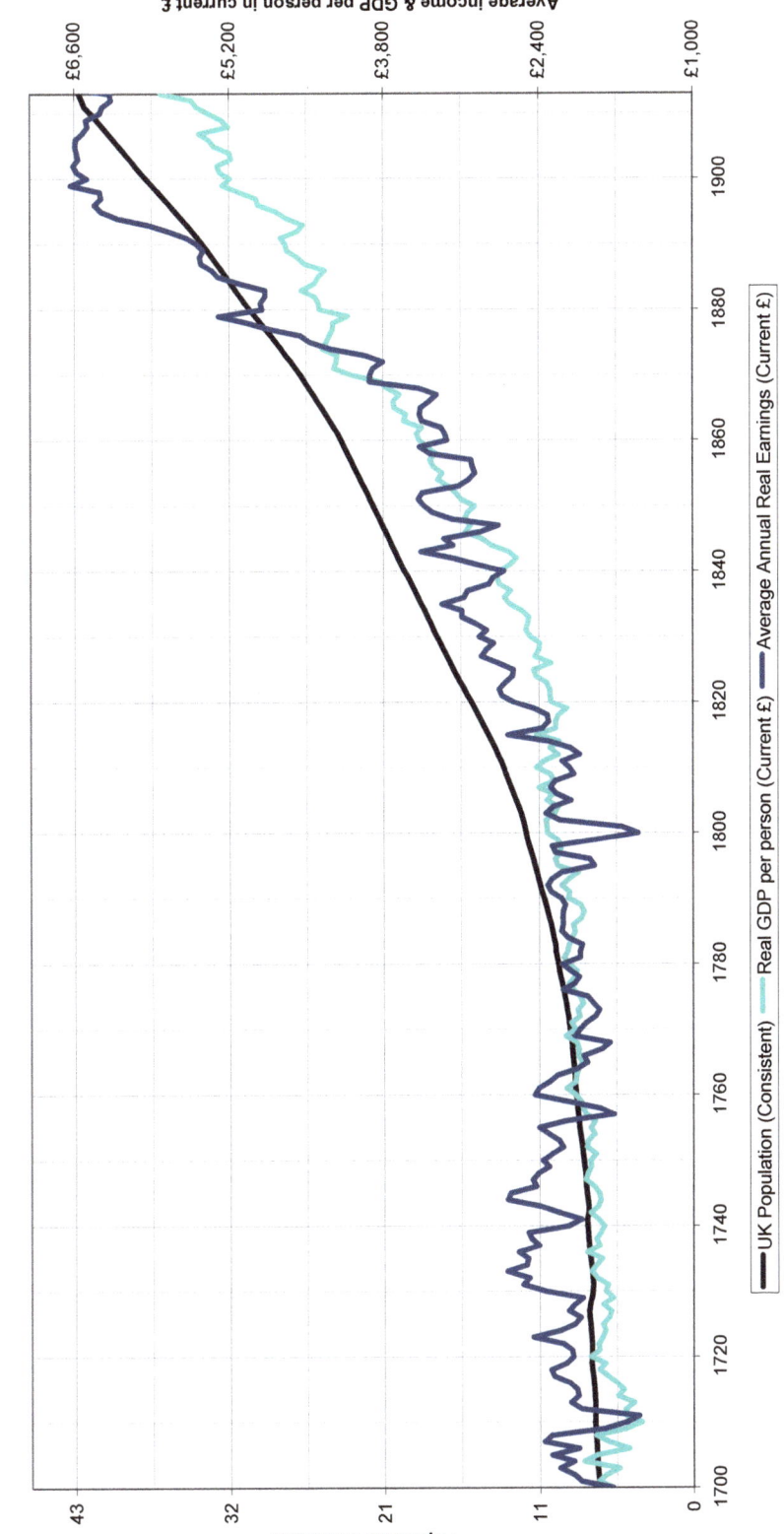

The decline of Agriculture
&
the growth of Industry
as
components of the Economy

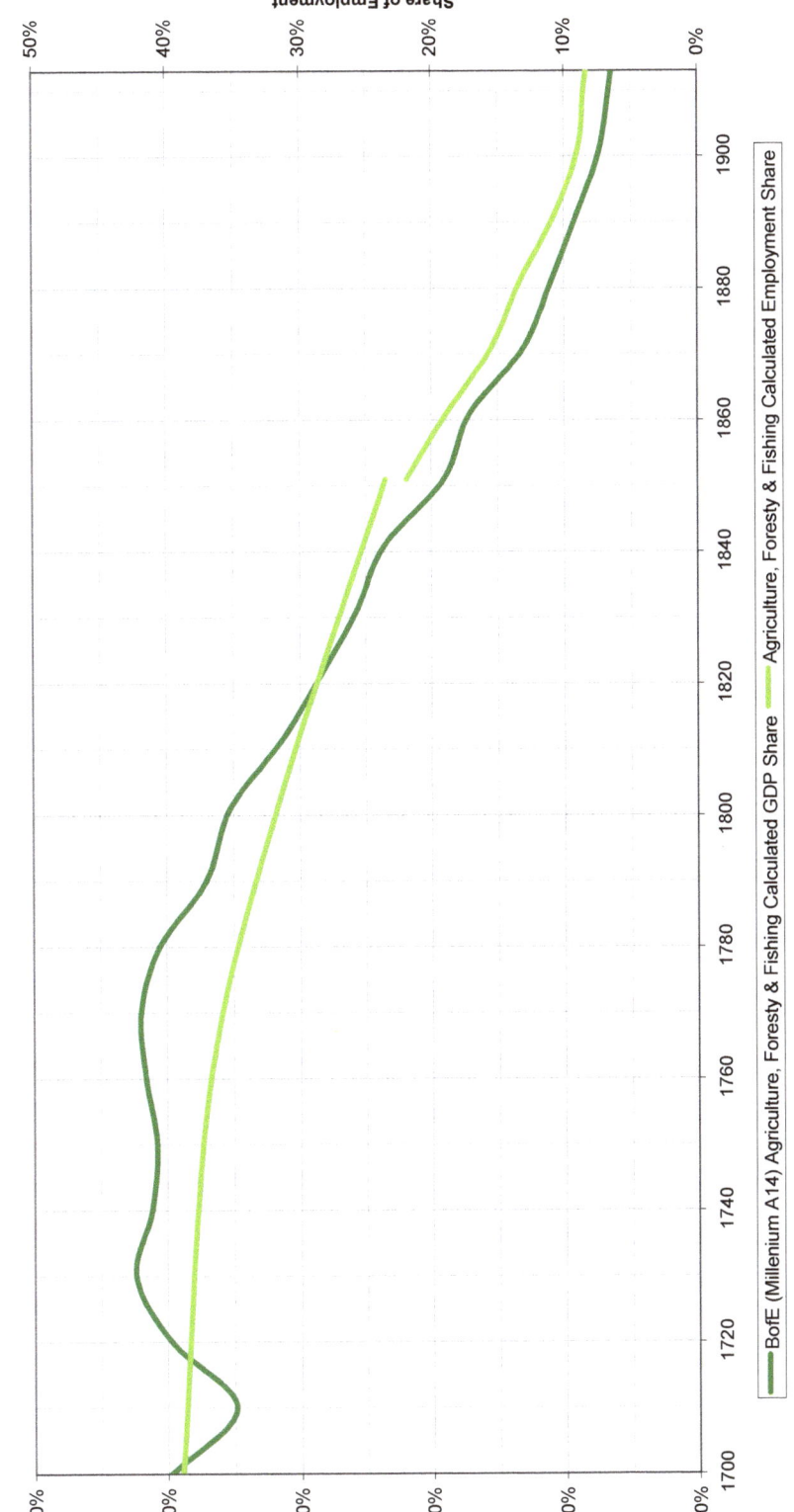

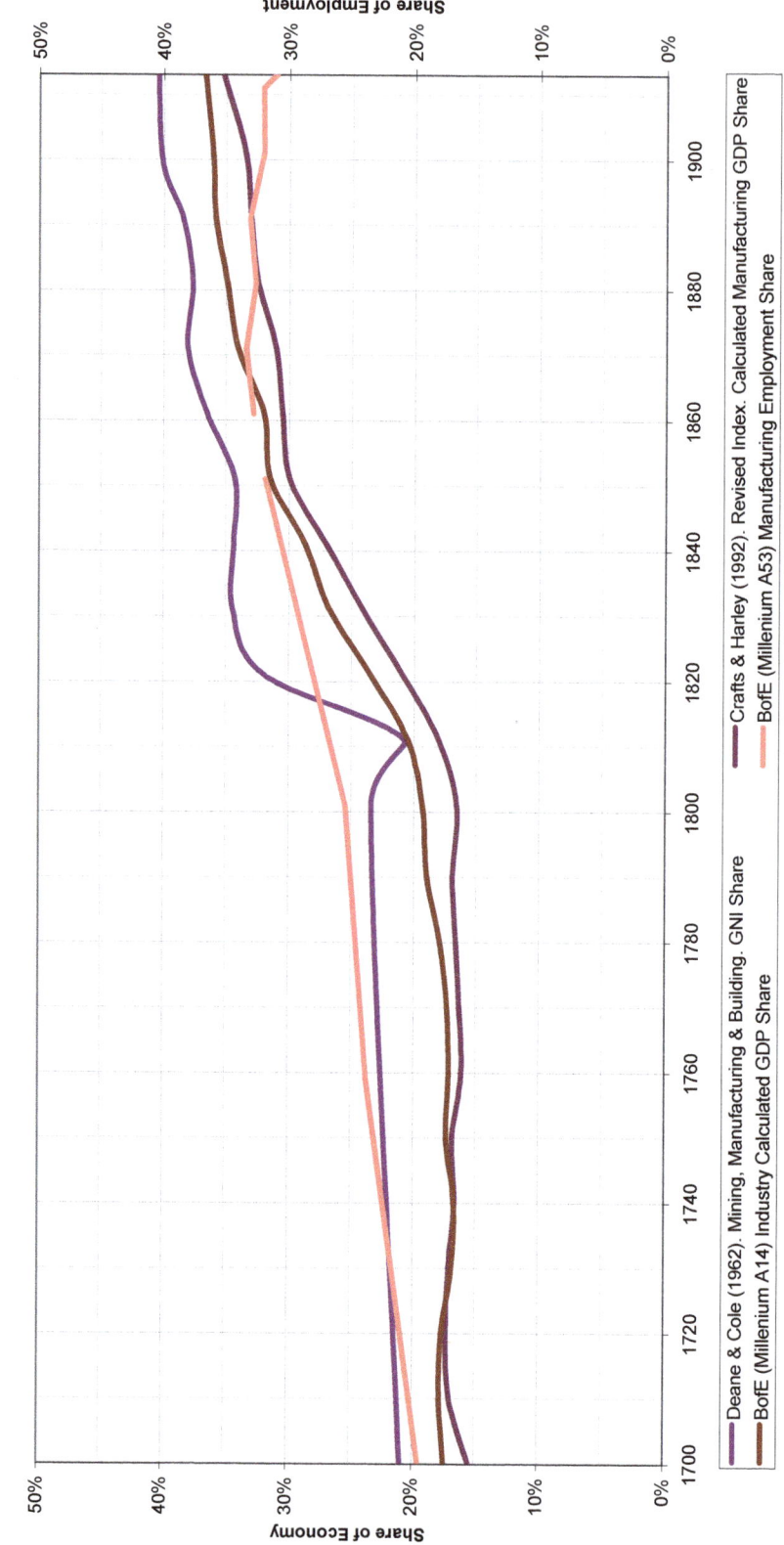

Inequality and Income Distribution

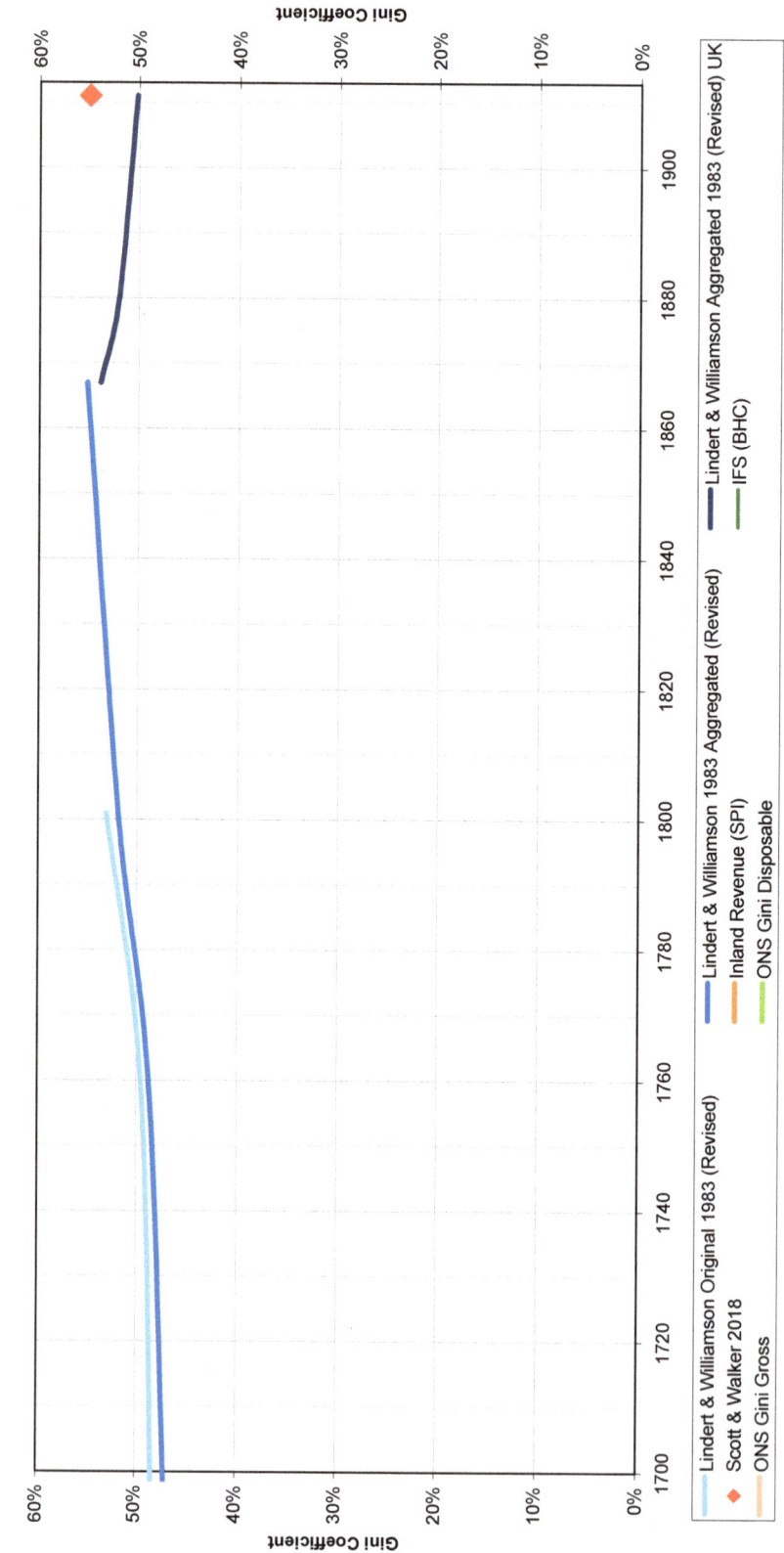

Analysis of Share of population and income by defined "Class"

By Robert Allen

2016

"Revising England's Social Tables Once Again"

Followed by 19th century to-date from various

Share of population and income by class – 1688

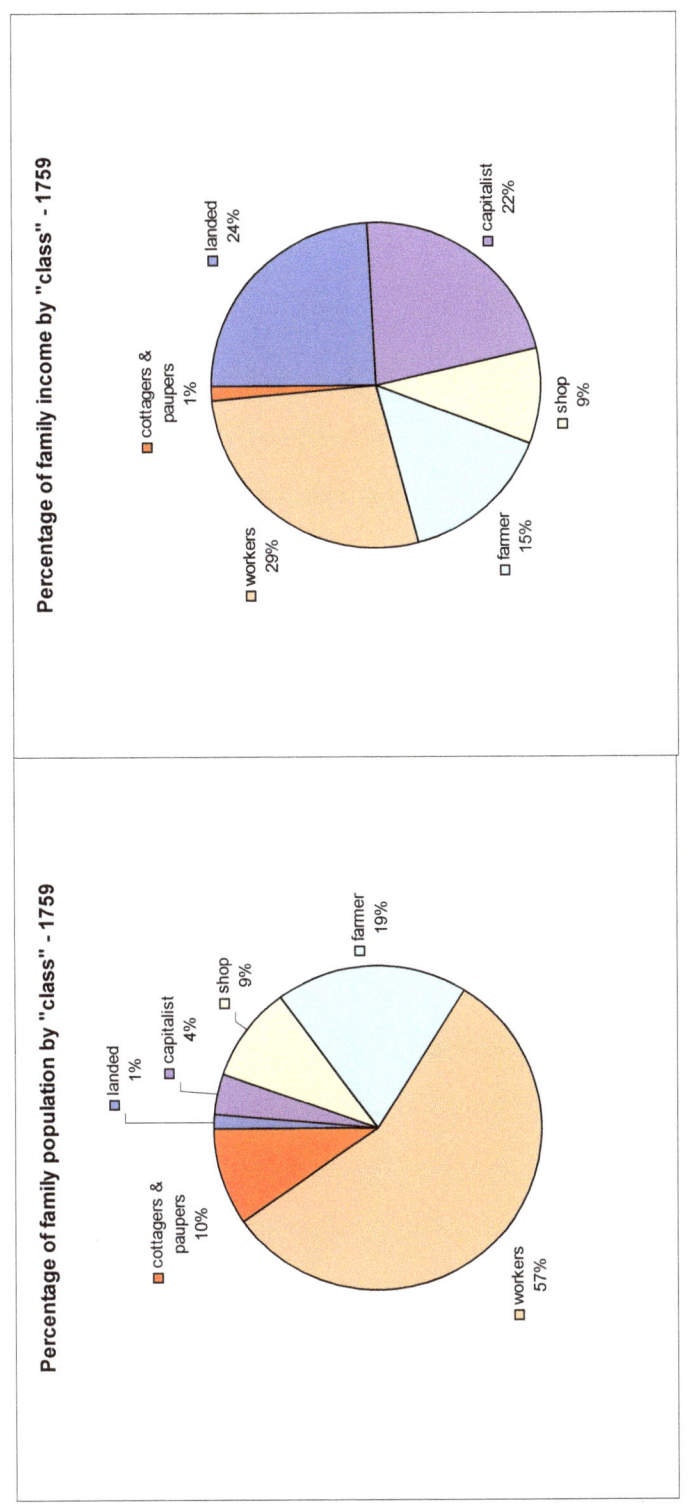

Share of population and income by class – 1798 (1801/1803)

Share of population and income by class – 1846

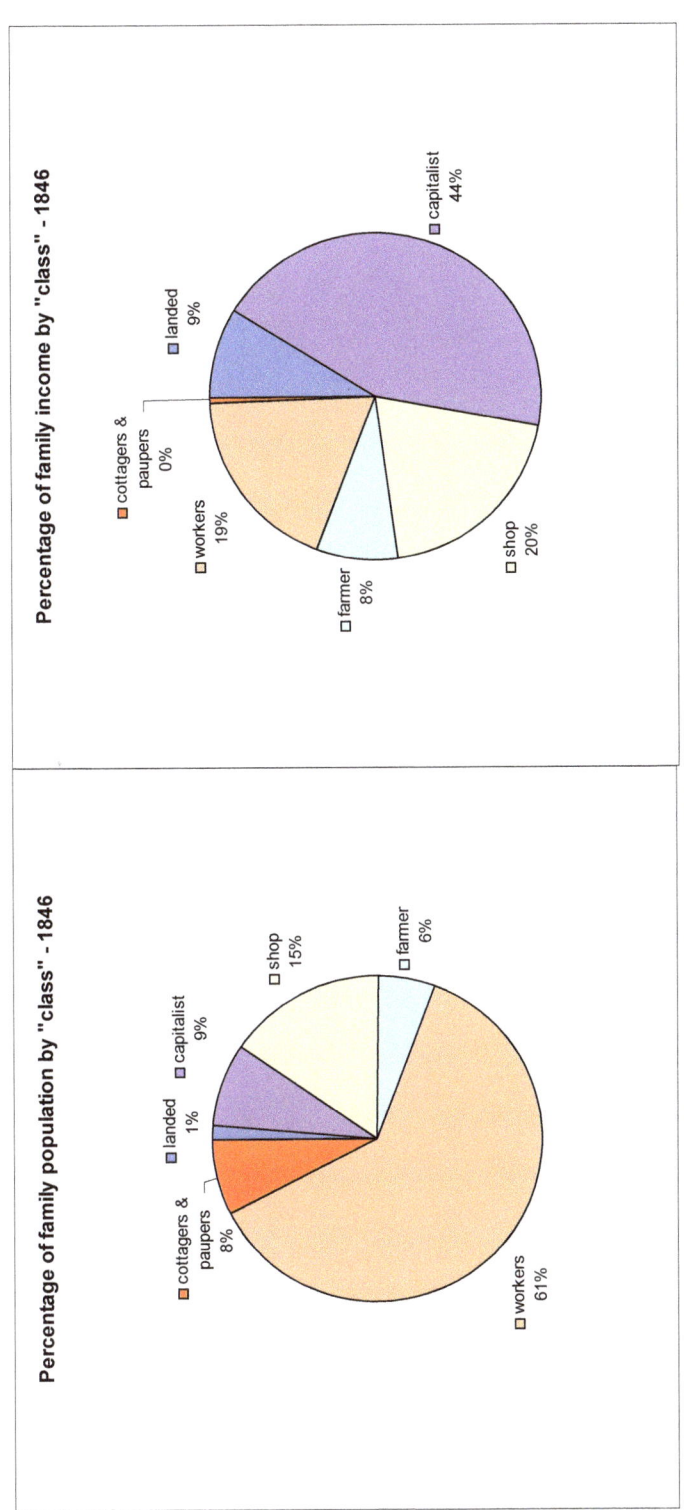

Compare real earnings/income distribution (CPI)
1867 (Baxter/Lindert '98 UK) - Gini 58.0
1911 (Scott & Walker 2018/Lindert '88) - Gini 54.9

Wages, prices & retail/cost indices

Cost of living instability & wheat/bread prices

Effect of the decline of
relative agricultural economic importance

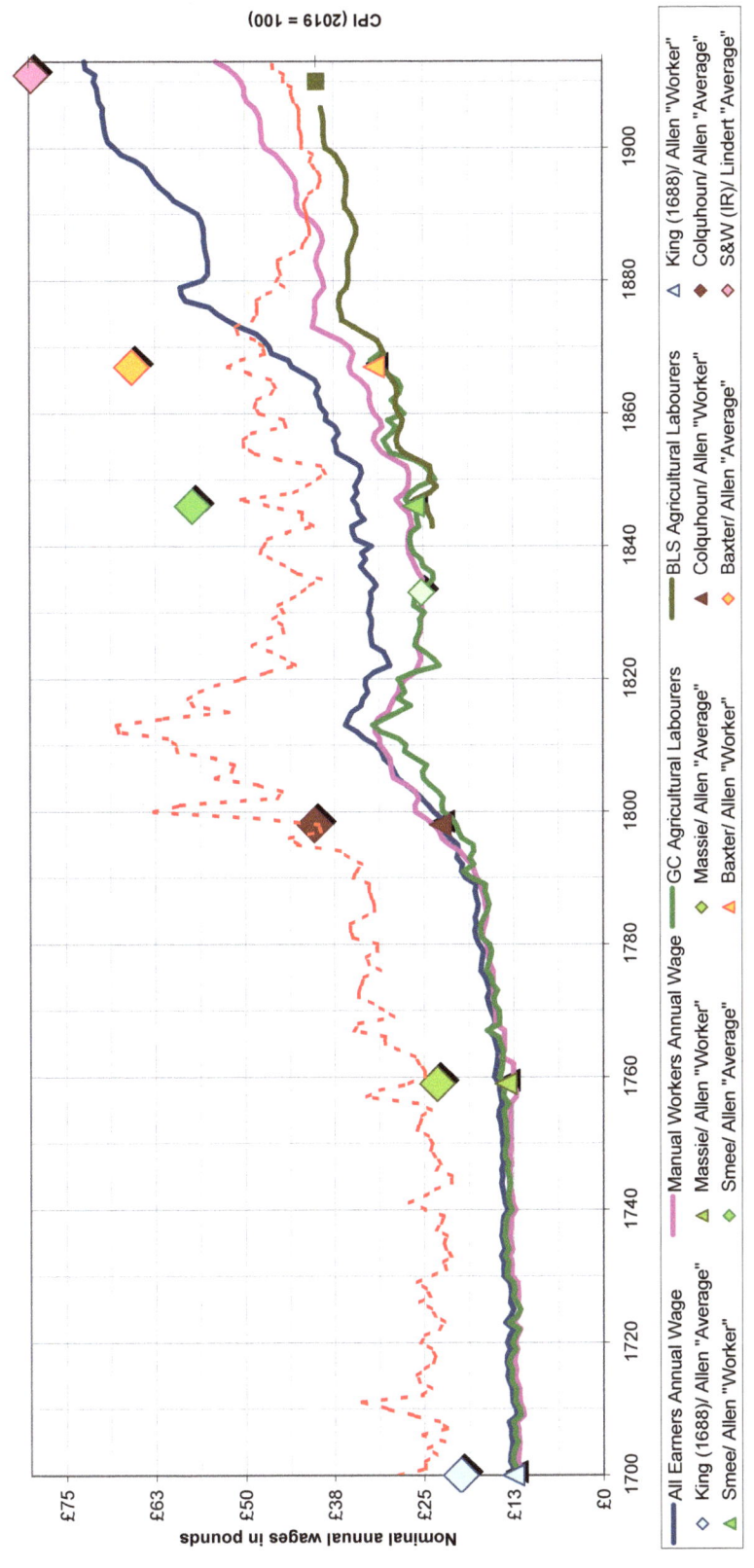

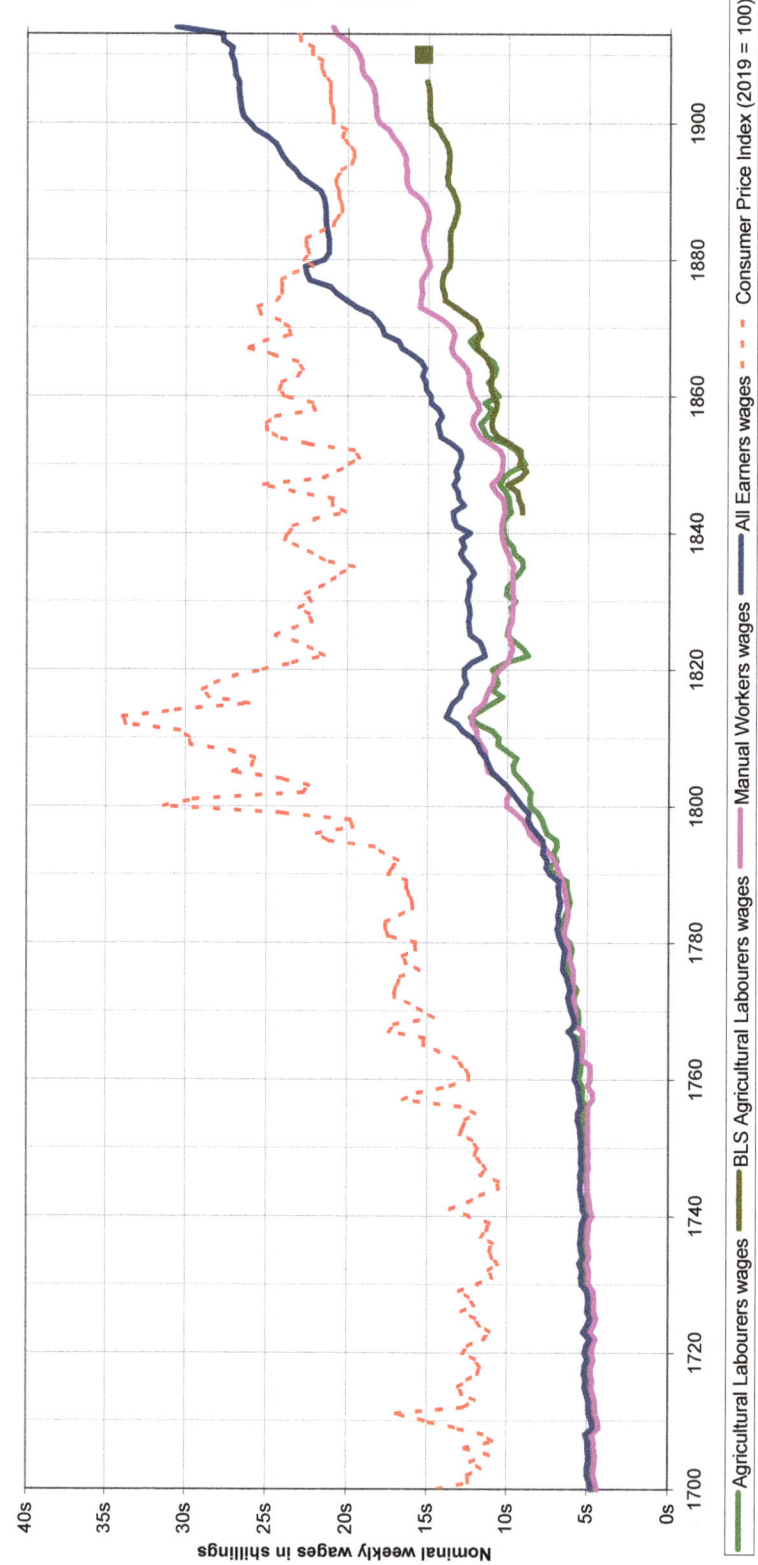

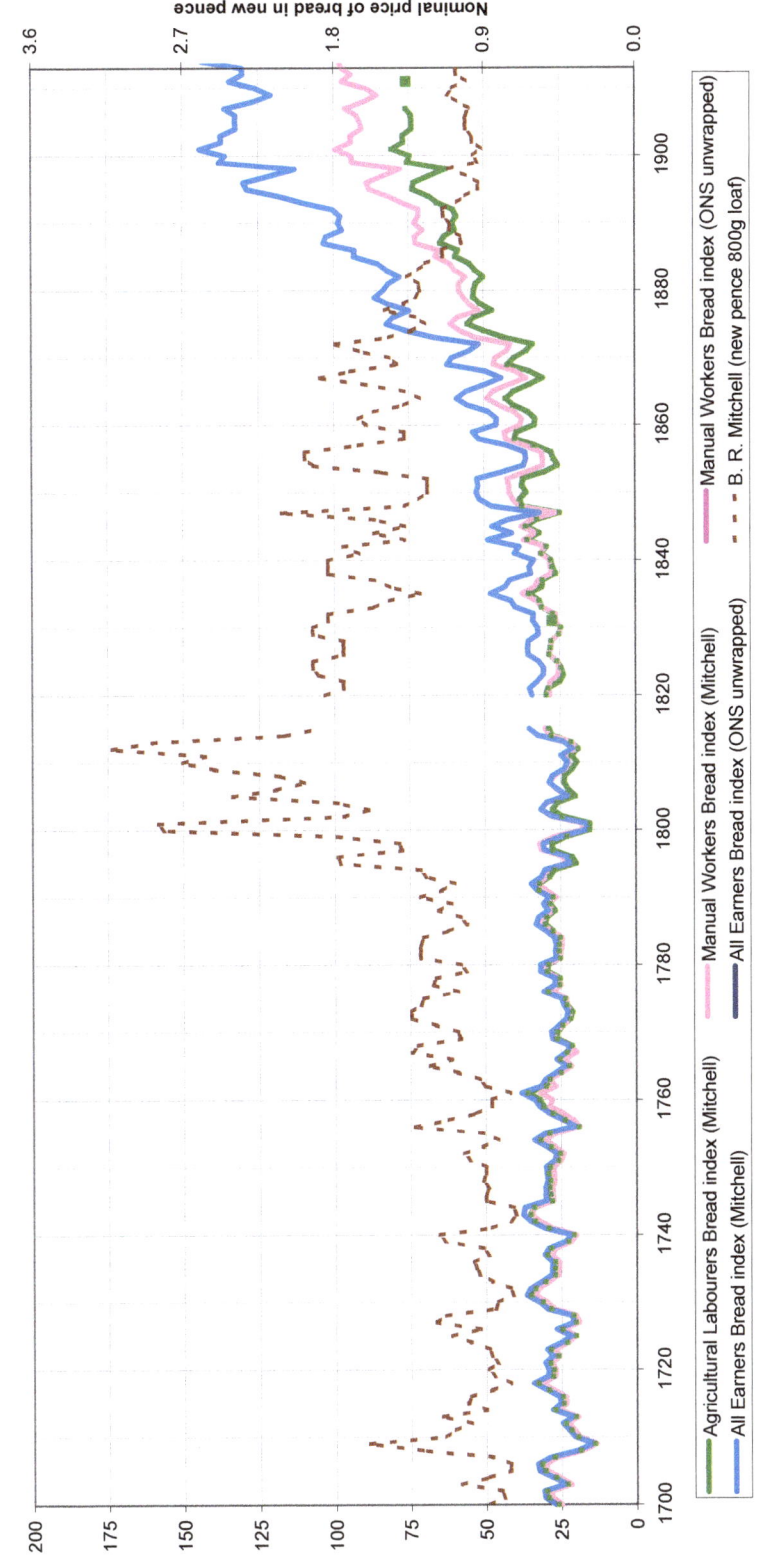

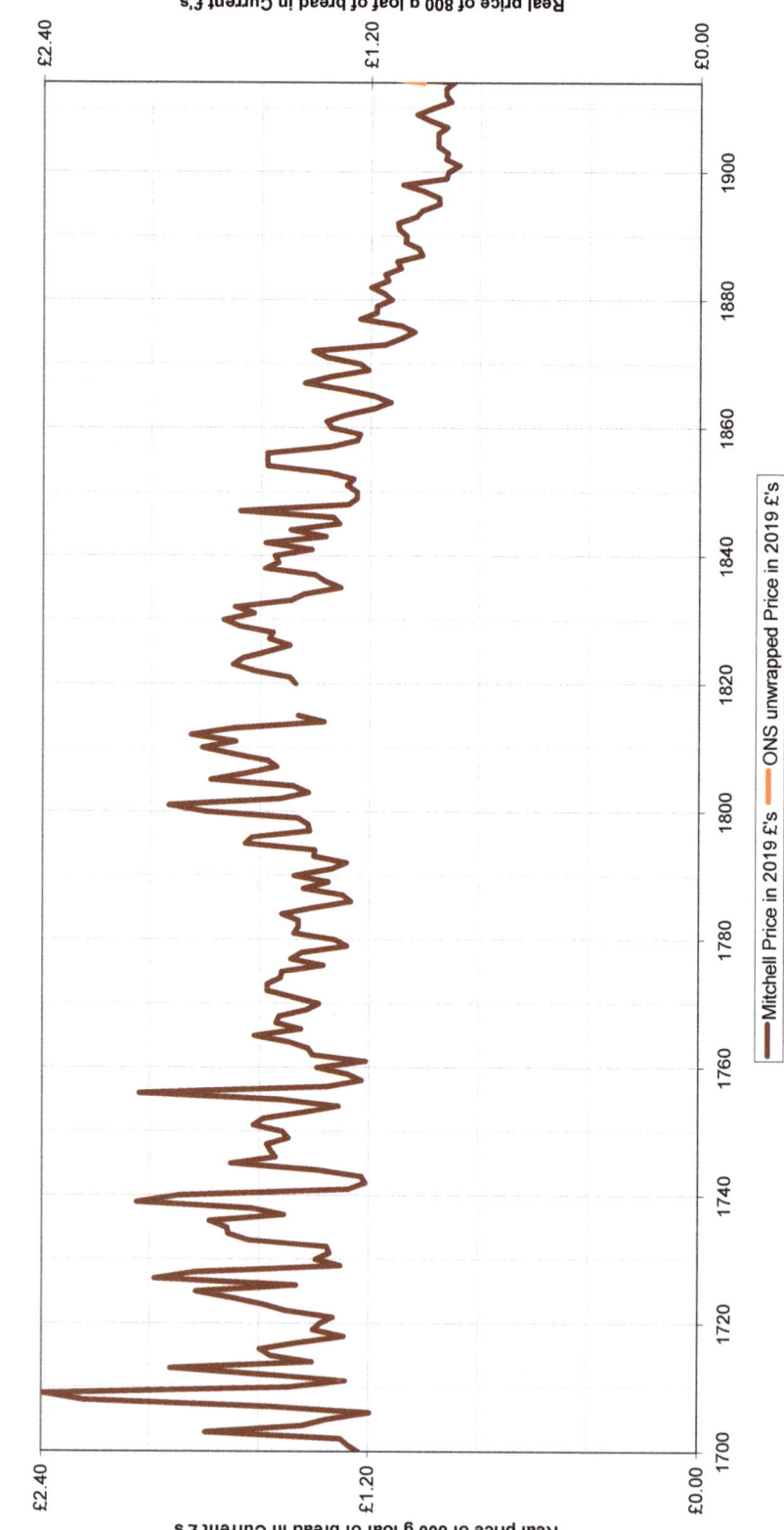

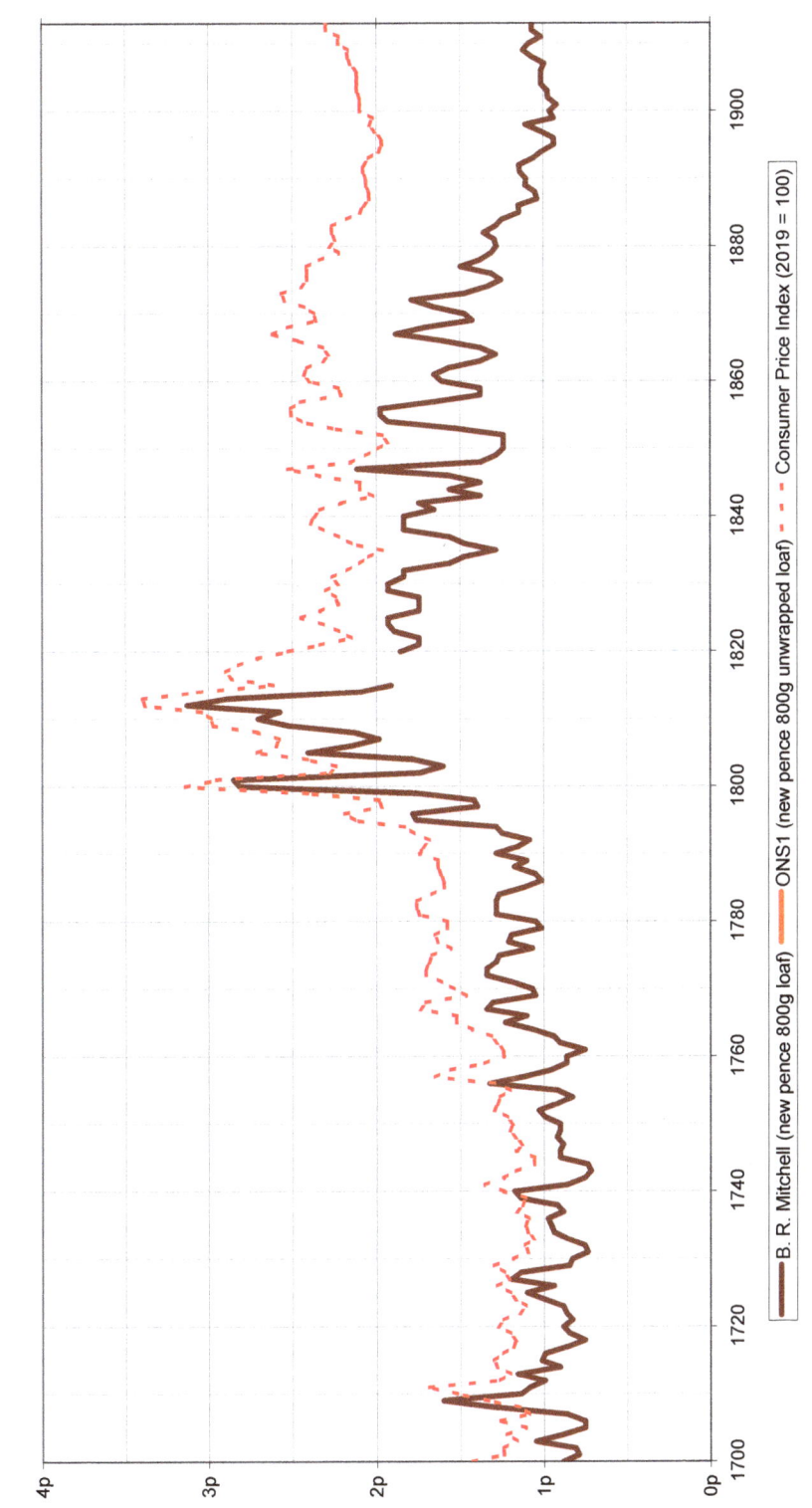

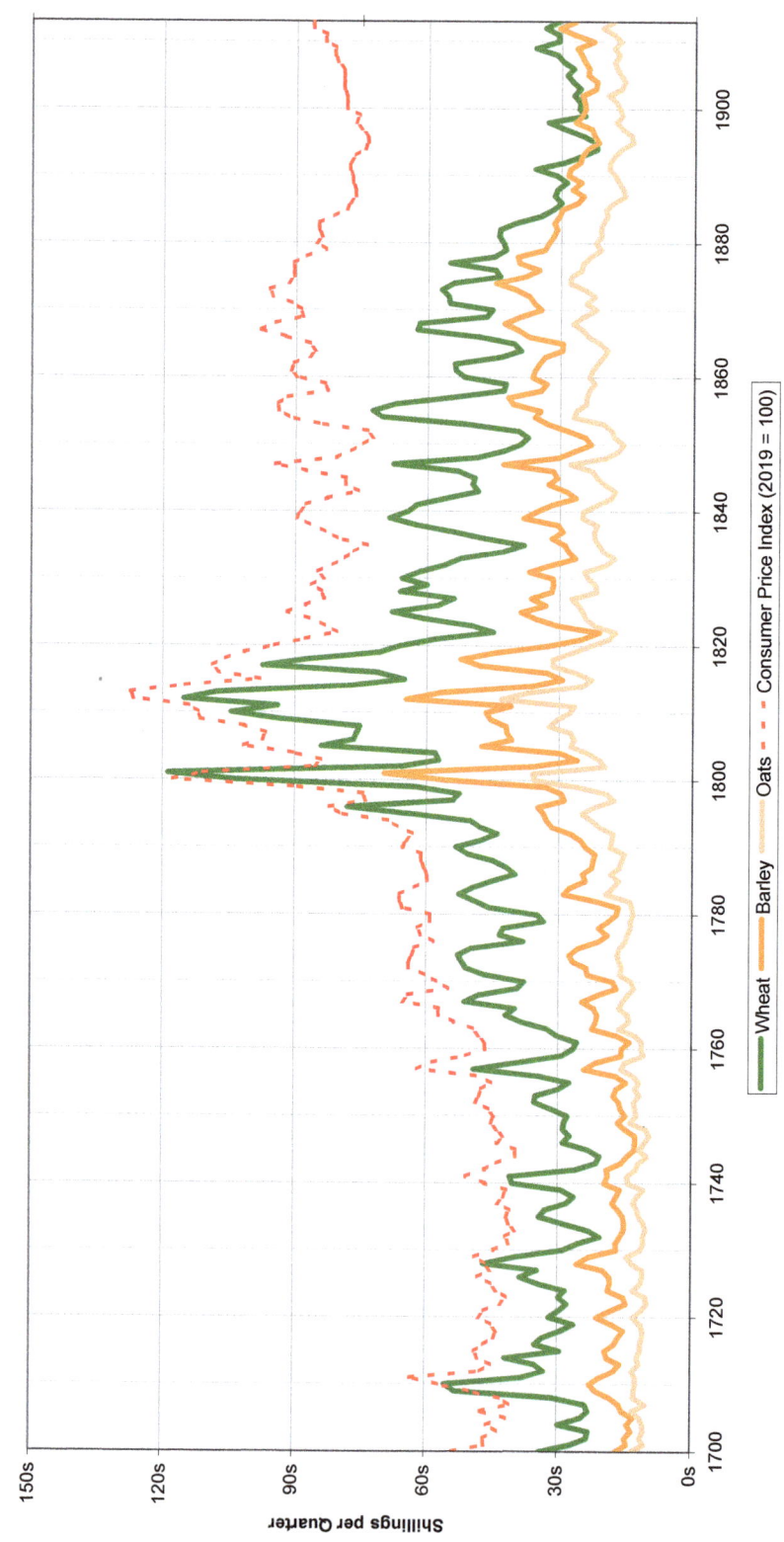

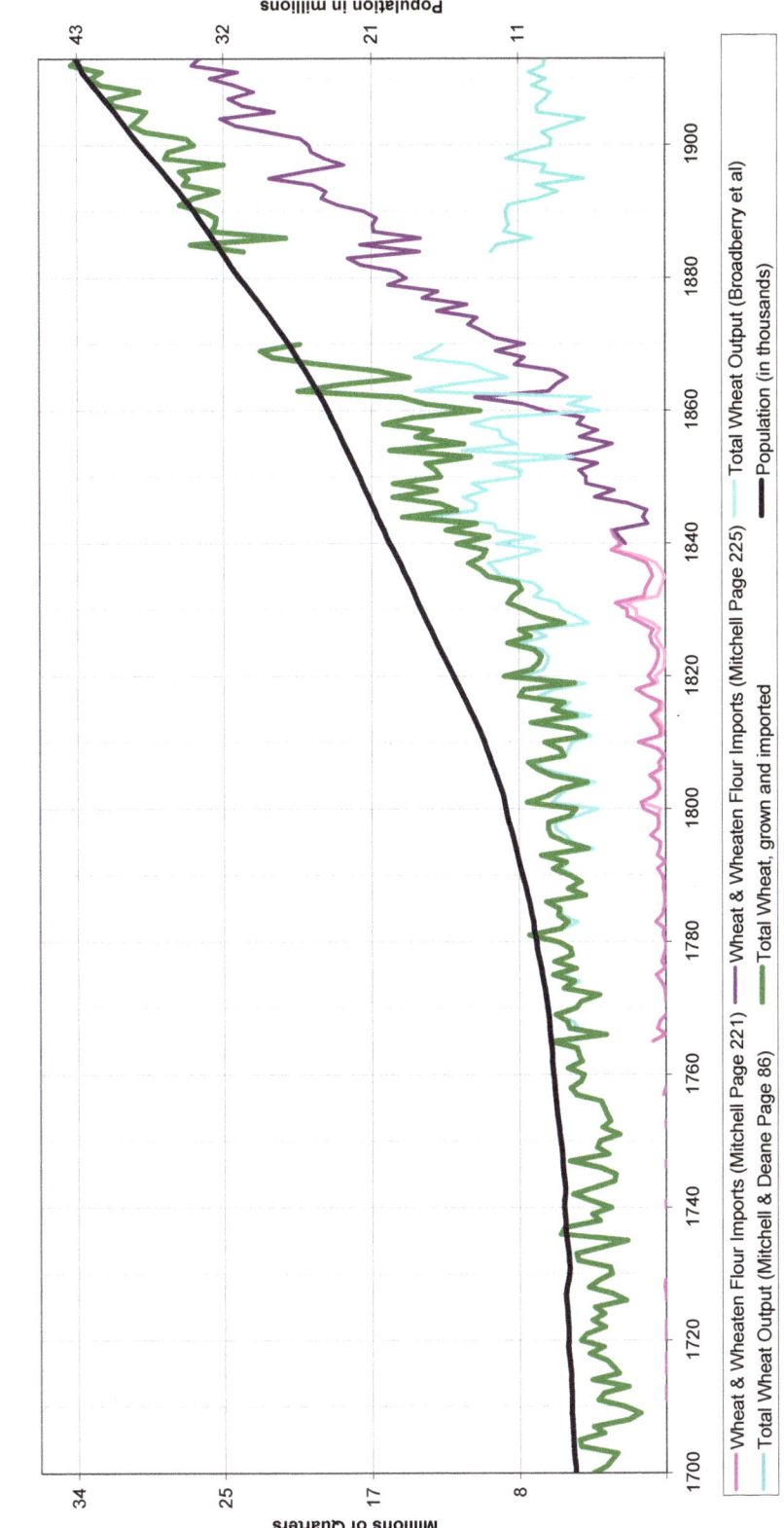

Part of a series - see also:

- UK Economic & Social Change – 1700-2019 – Three centuries of progress
- UK Economy – 1700-1913 – An economy in transition
- UK Economy – 1900-2019 – Growth of the state & world war
- UK Economy – 1990-2019 – Quarter of a century of new changes
- UK Economy – 1990-2019 – Stable income inequality
- UK Household Expenditure – 1700-2019 – Cost of Living
- UK Housing – 1700-2019 – Growth of home ownership
- UK Pauperism, Poverty and Hardship – 1700-2019 – The Retreat of Real Poverty
- UK Pollution (Air Quality), Cars – 1970-2019 – Continuous improvement
- UK Pollution (Air Quality), Energy – 1970-2019 – Continuous improvement
- UK Population & Life Expectancy – 1970-2019 – Continuous Improvement

UK Economy

1900-2019 or five generations

Growth of the state & world war

UK Population & Life Expectancy From 1900-2019

UK population (millions) and Life Expectancy at Birth (Years)

— Wrigley/ HMD Life Expectancy (Left axis) — UK Population (Consistent) (Right Axis)

UK Economy

The growth of the state

Government Spending and Revenue

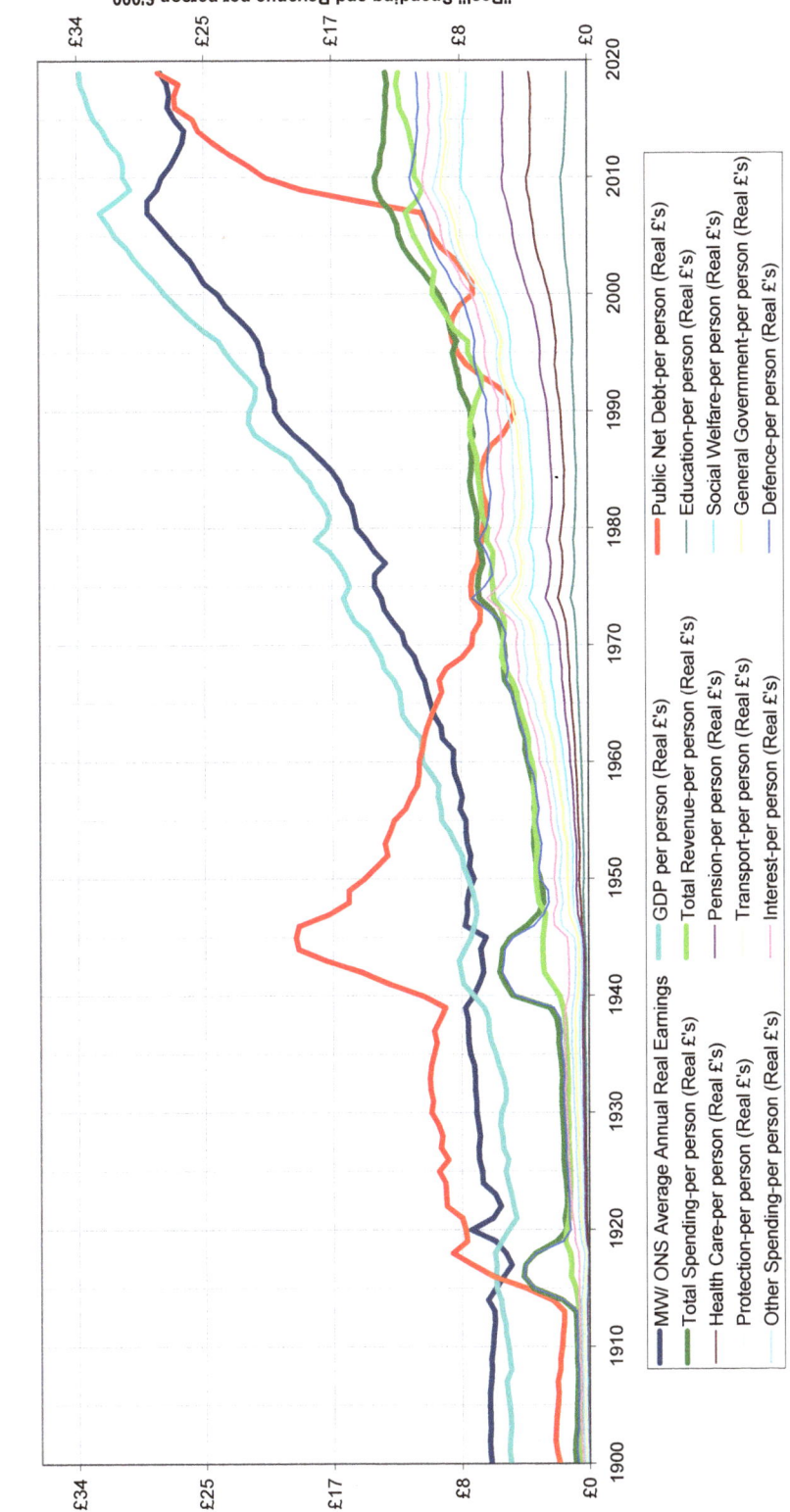

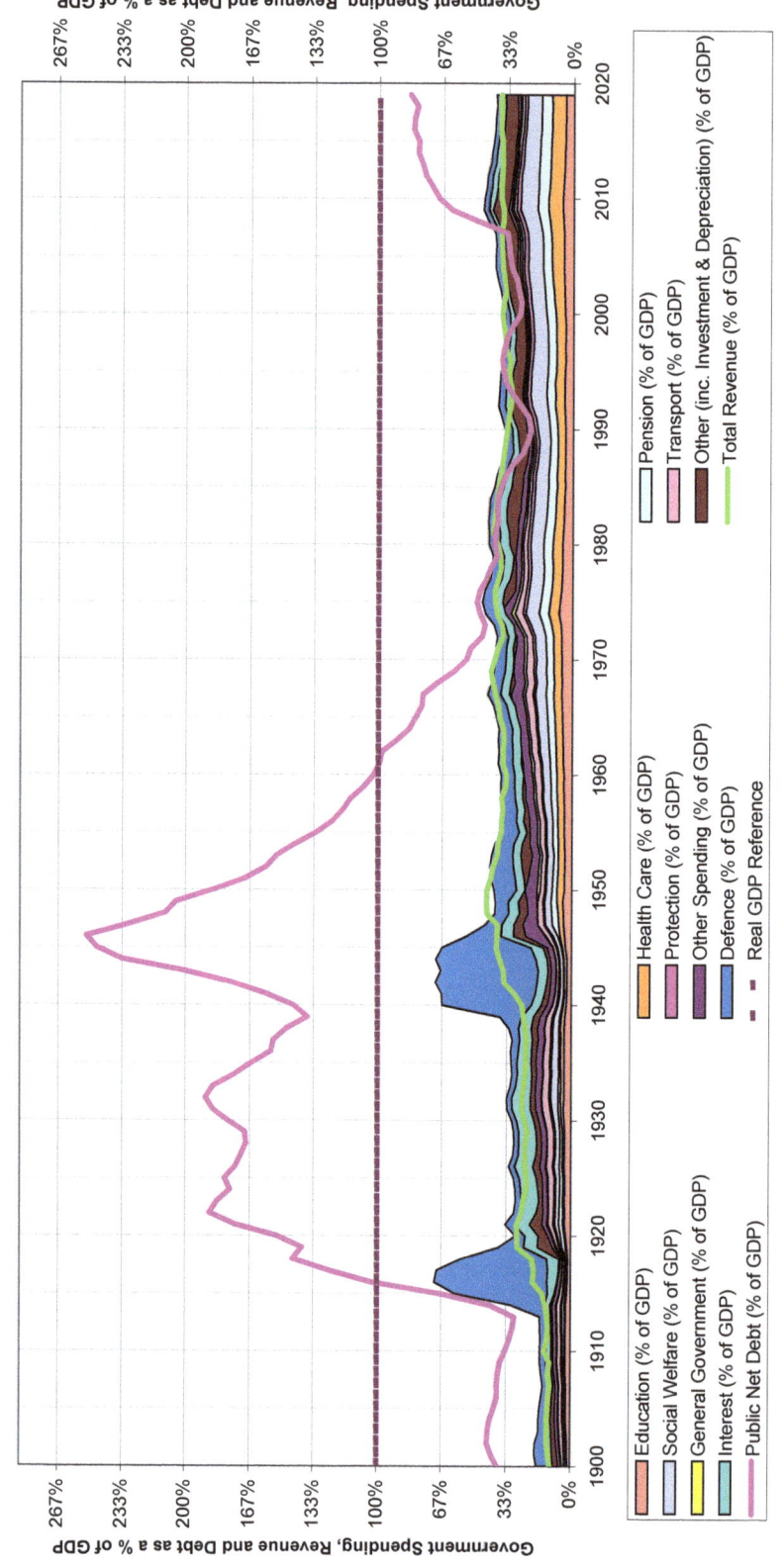

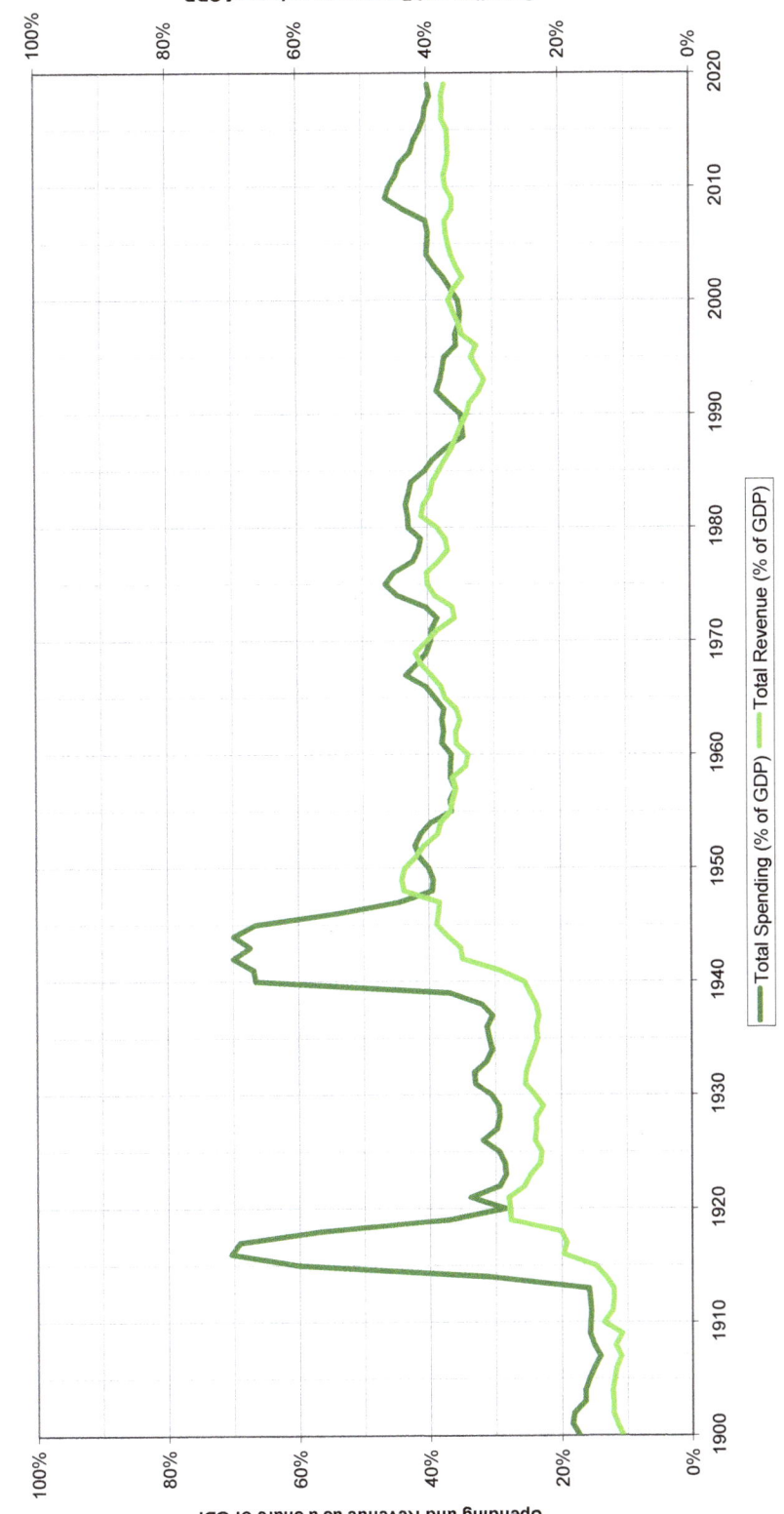

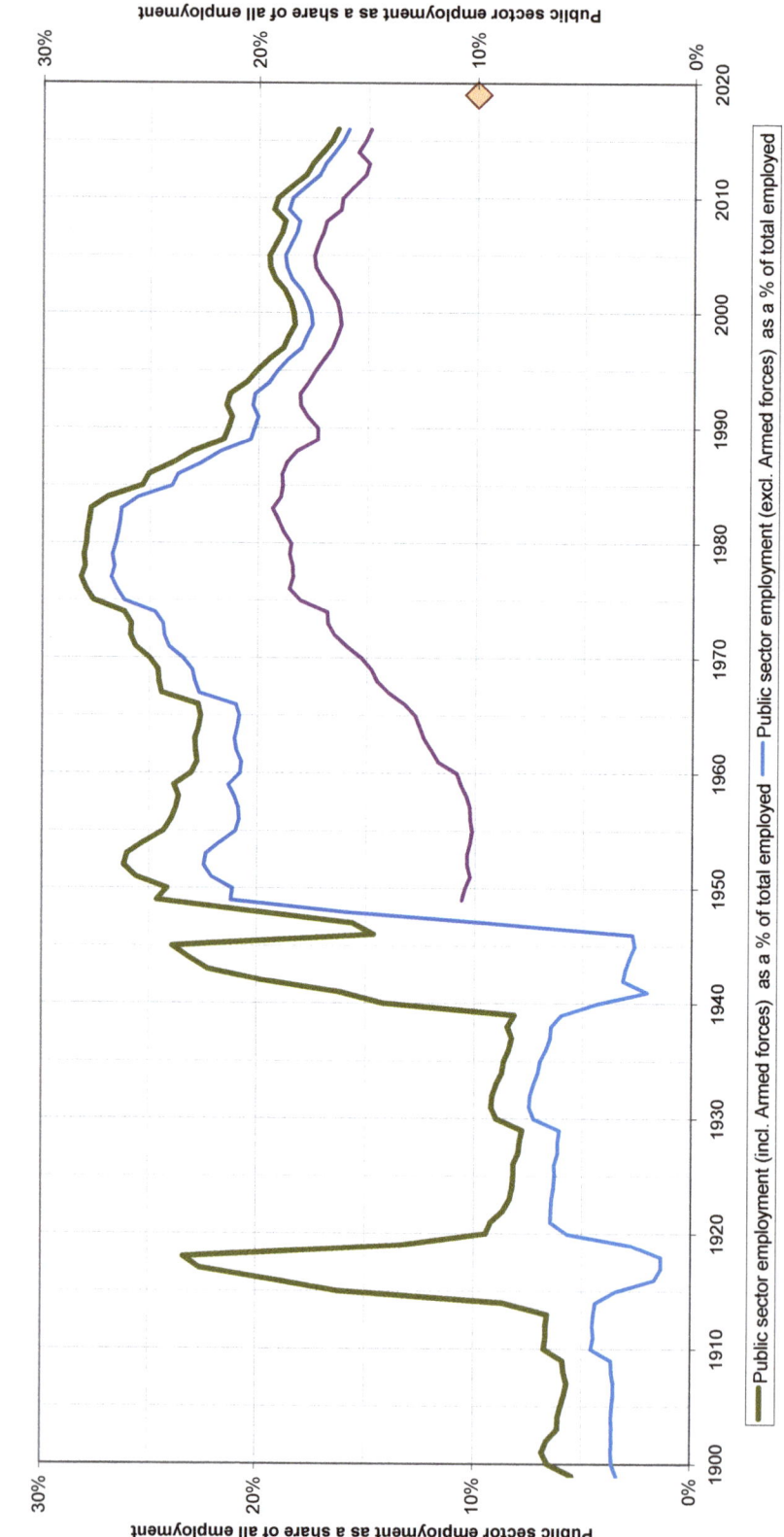

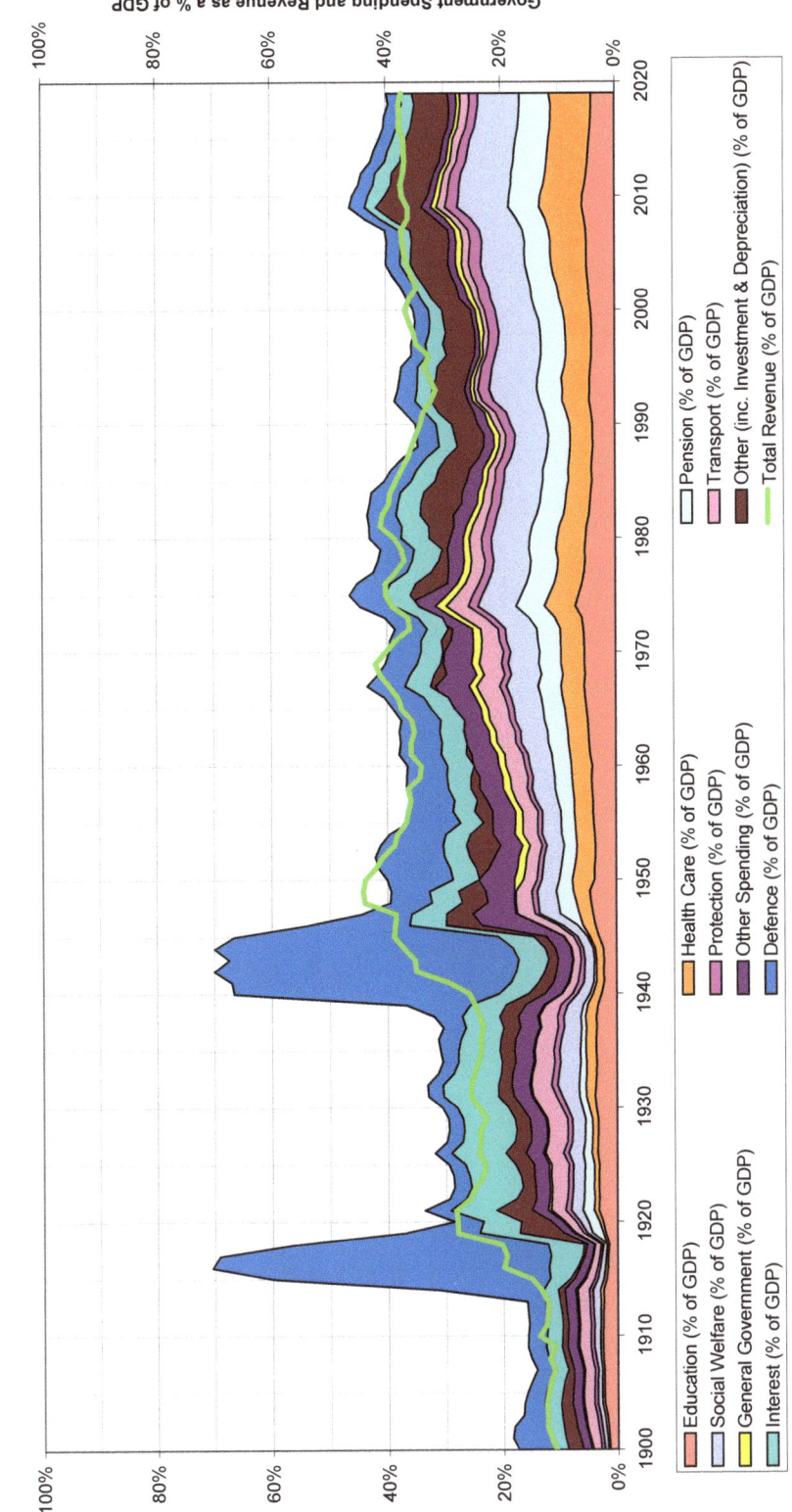

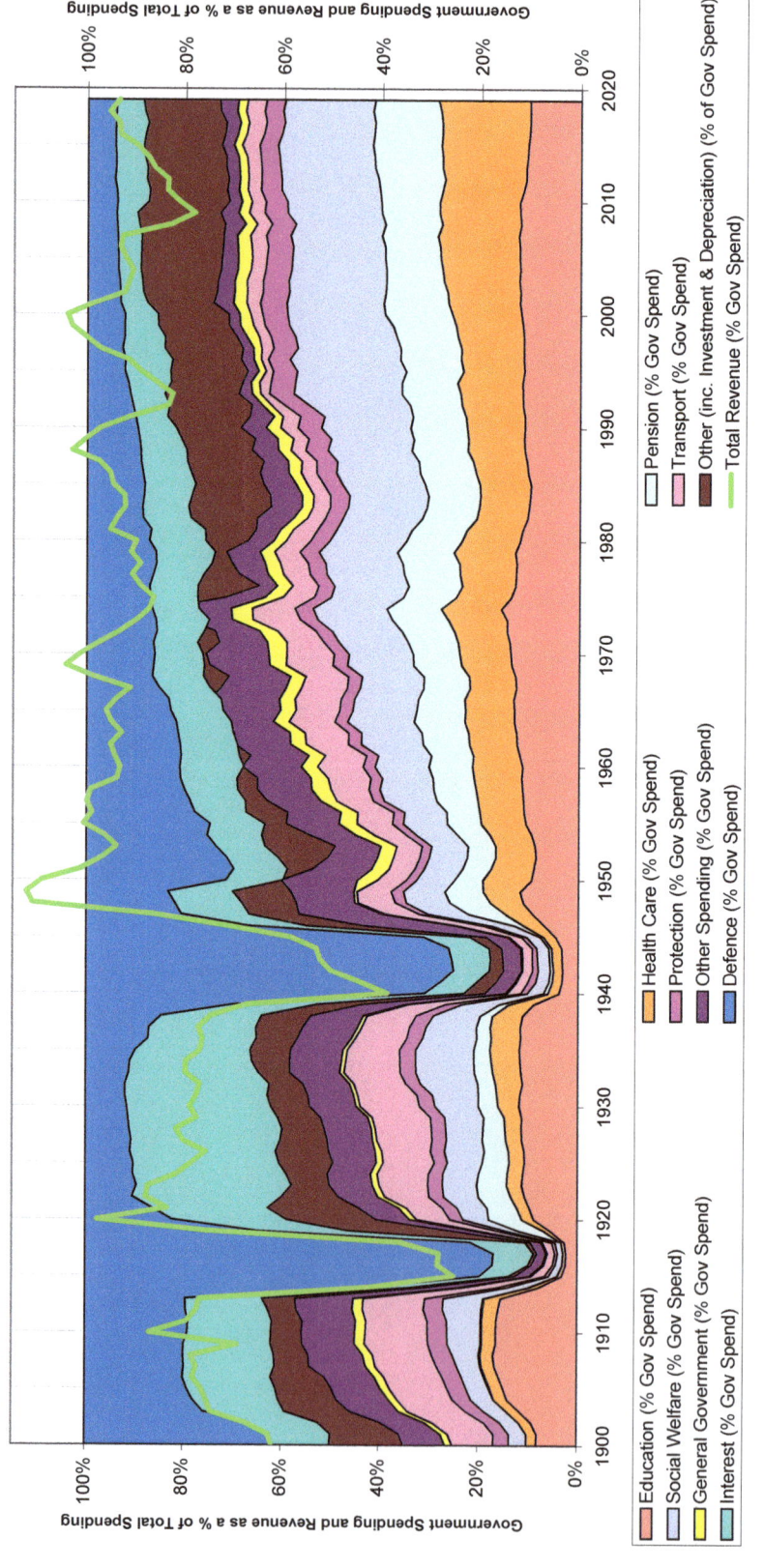

Specific Areas

Of

Government Spending

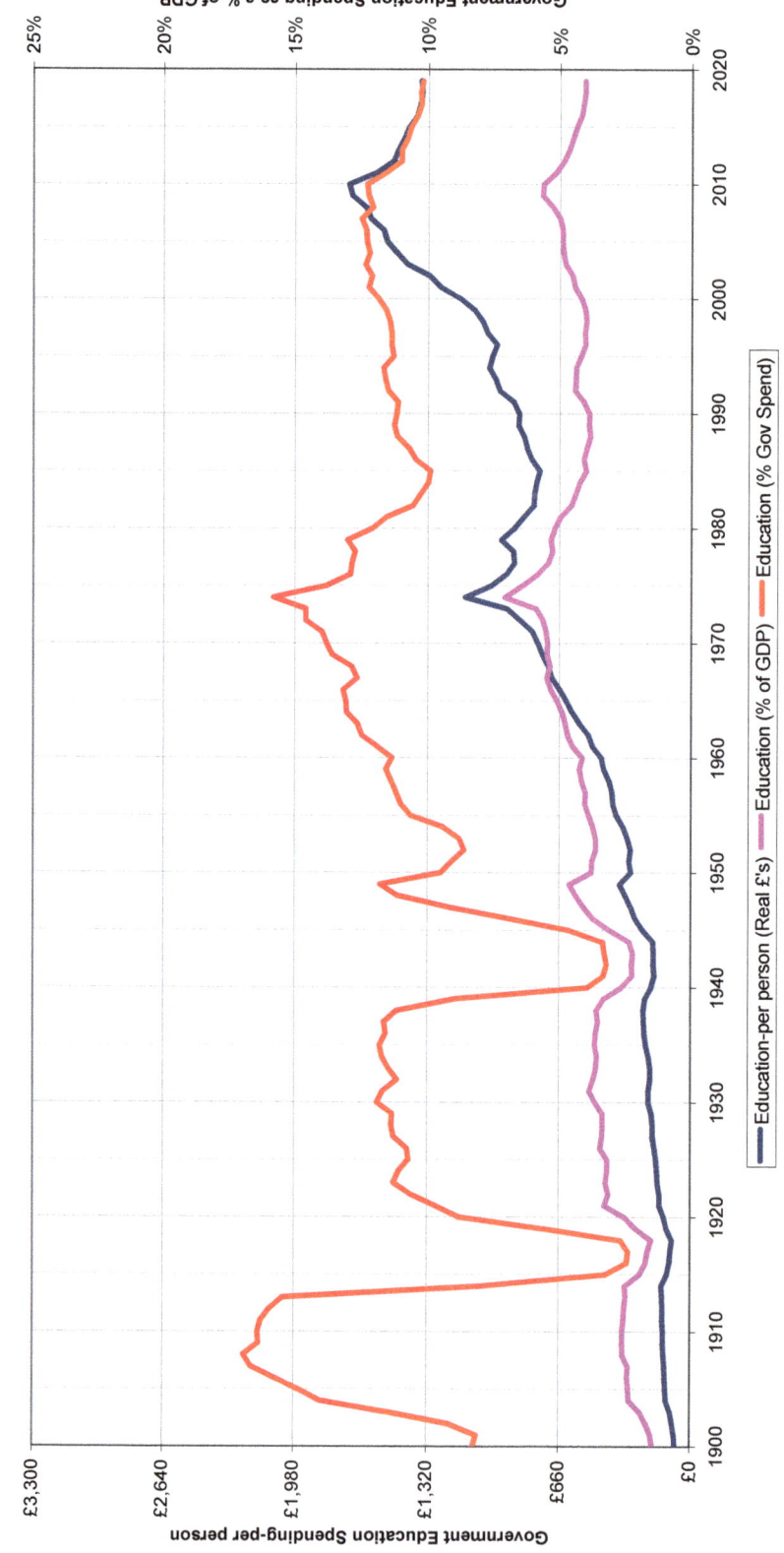

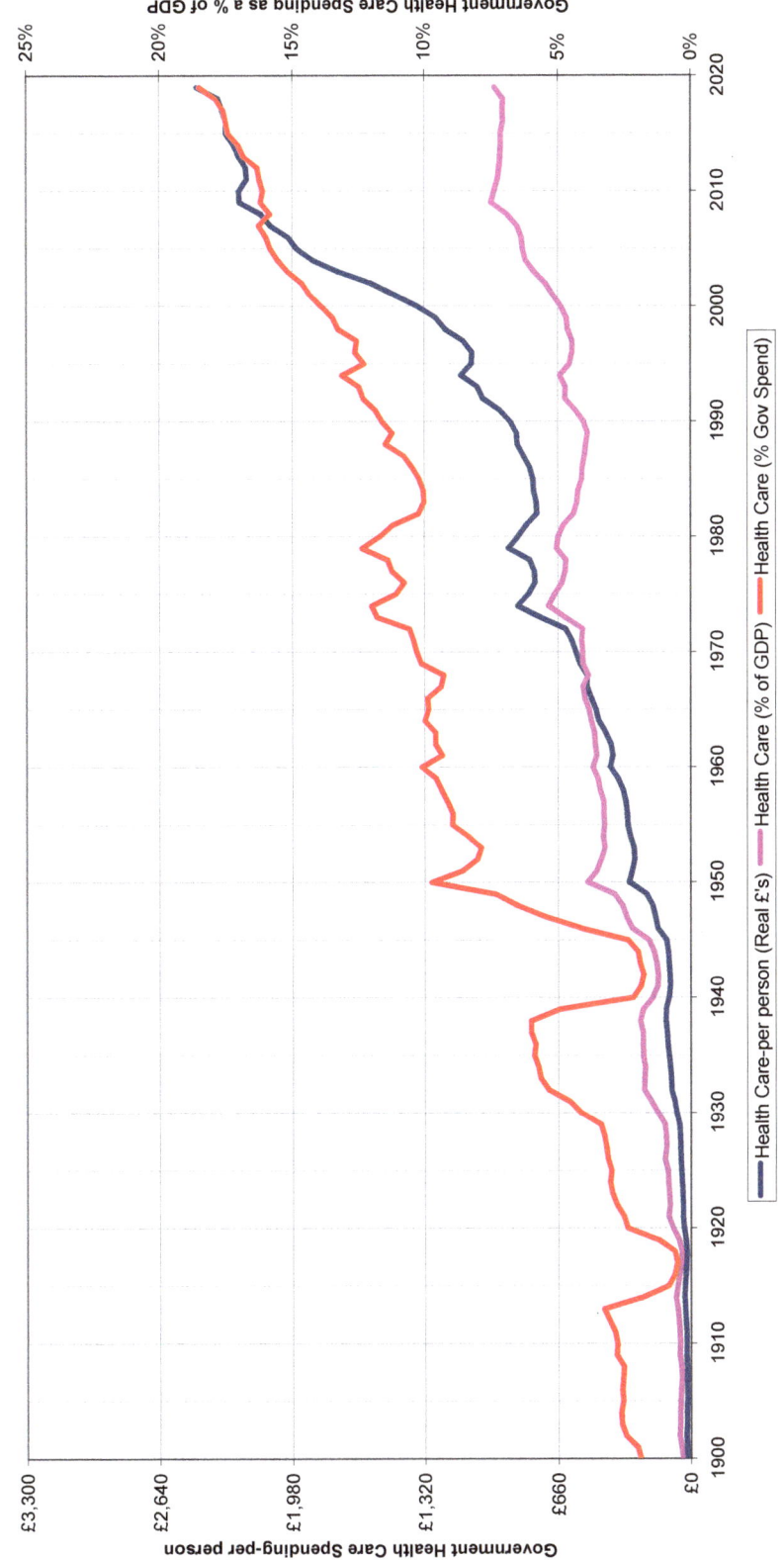

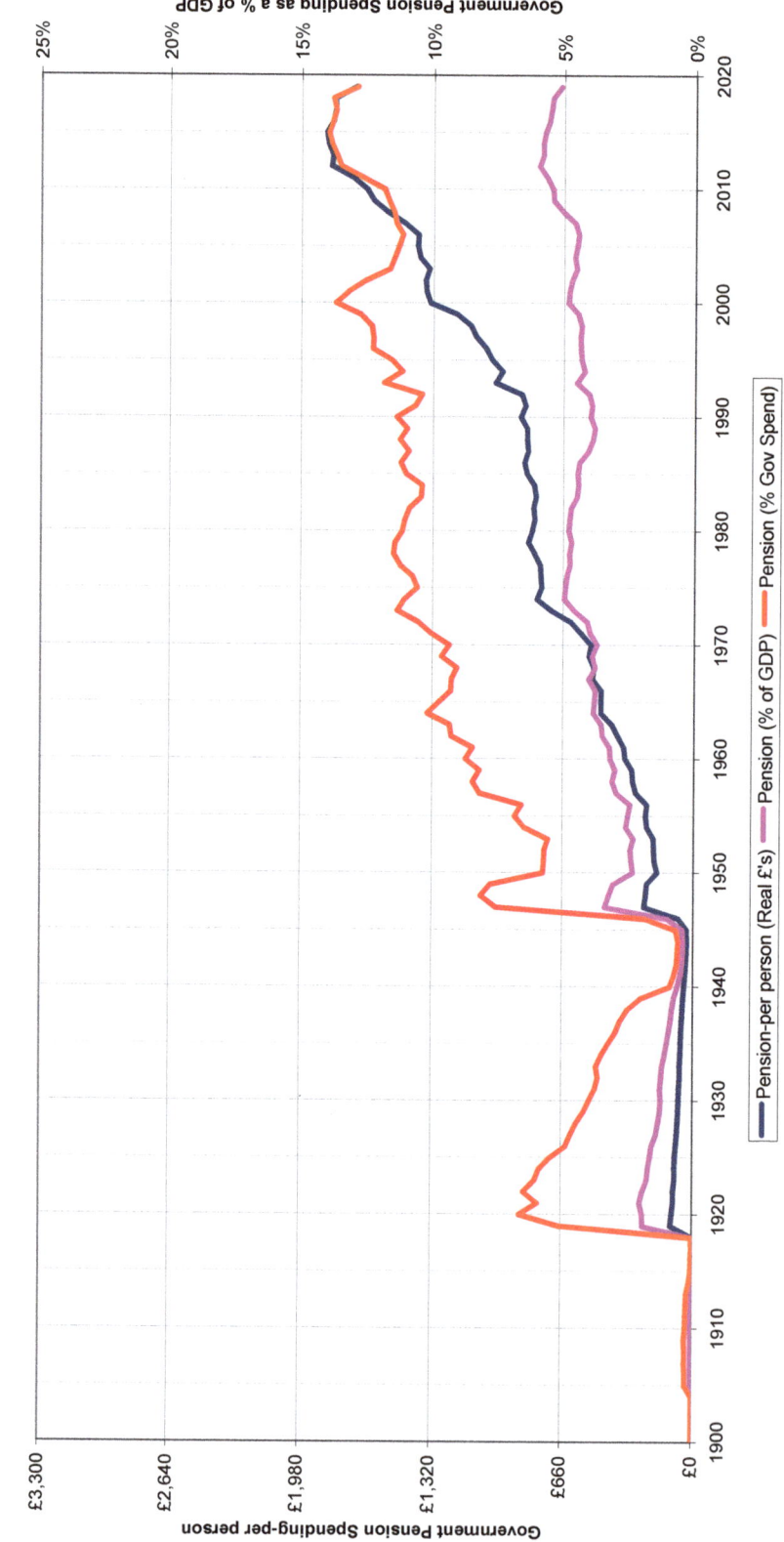

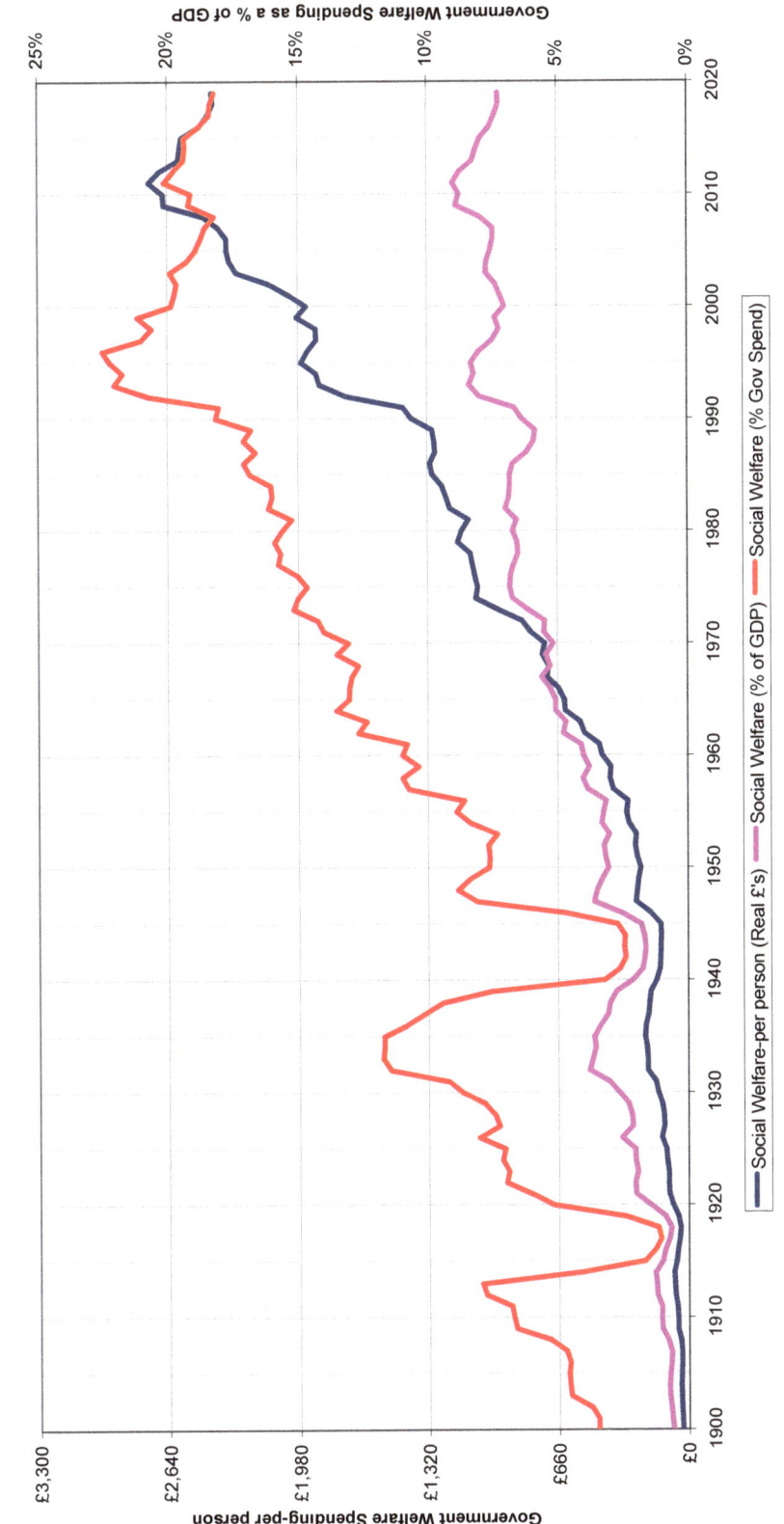

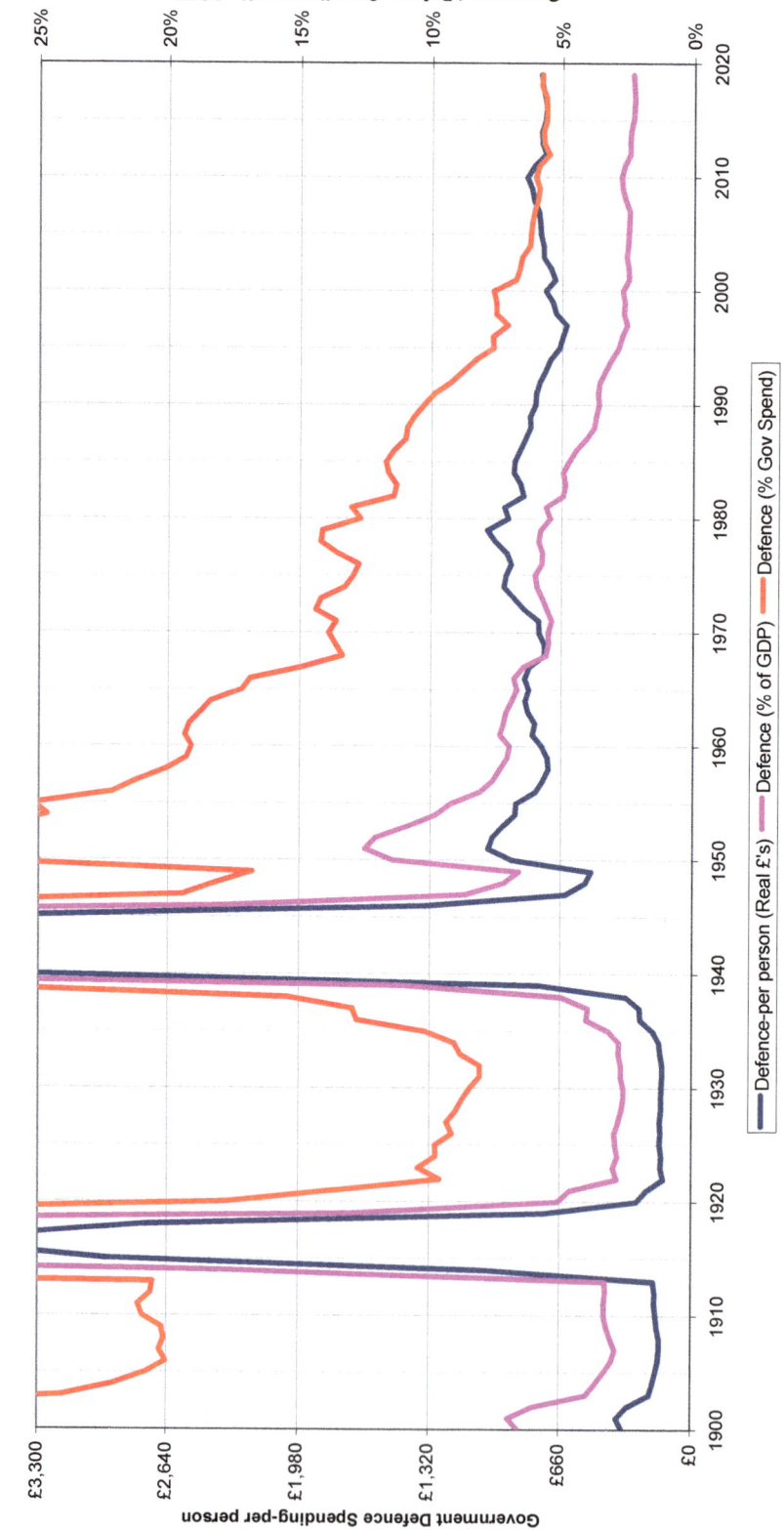

The new transition to a Service Economy

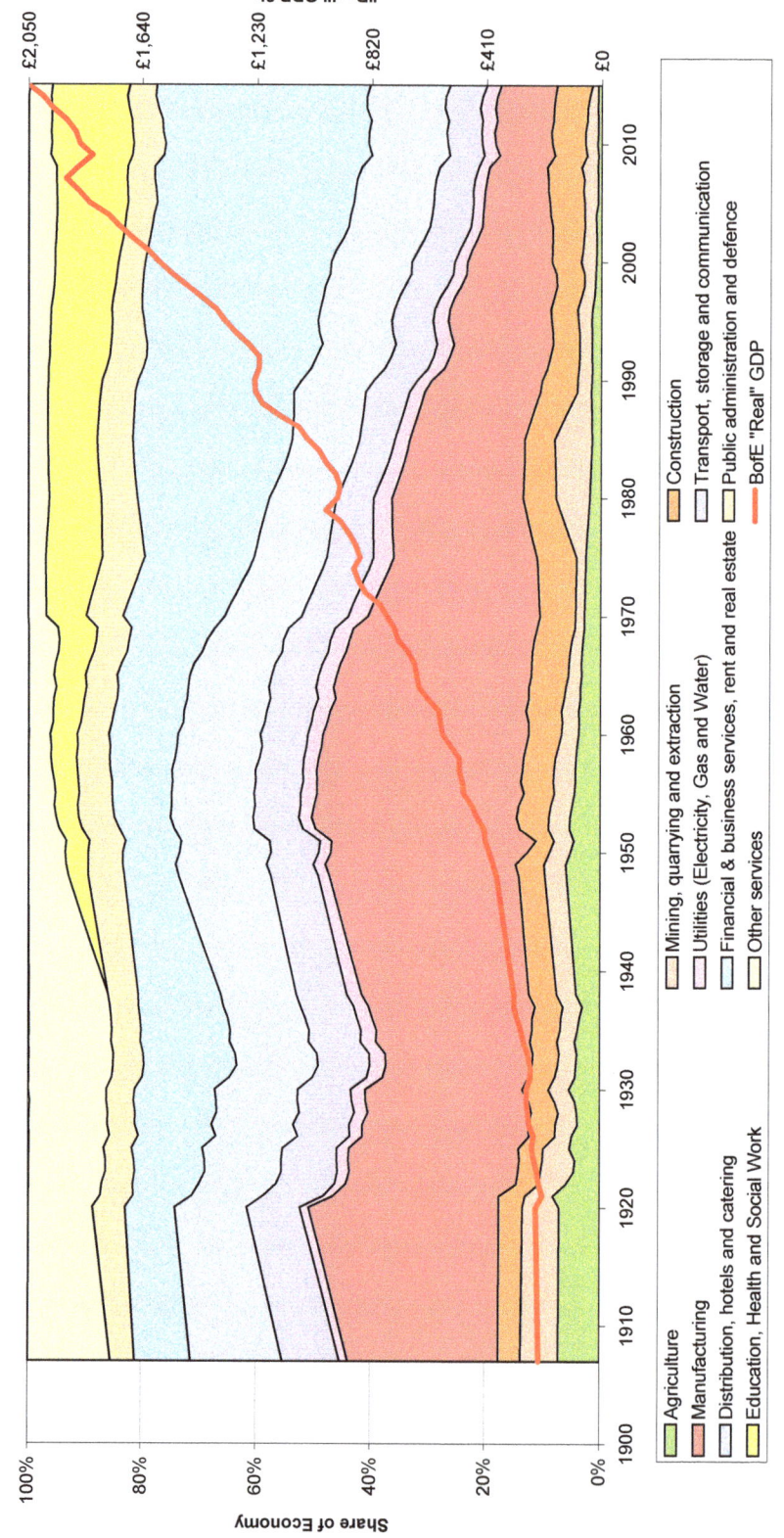

Inequality

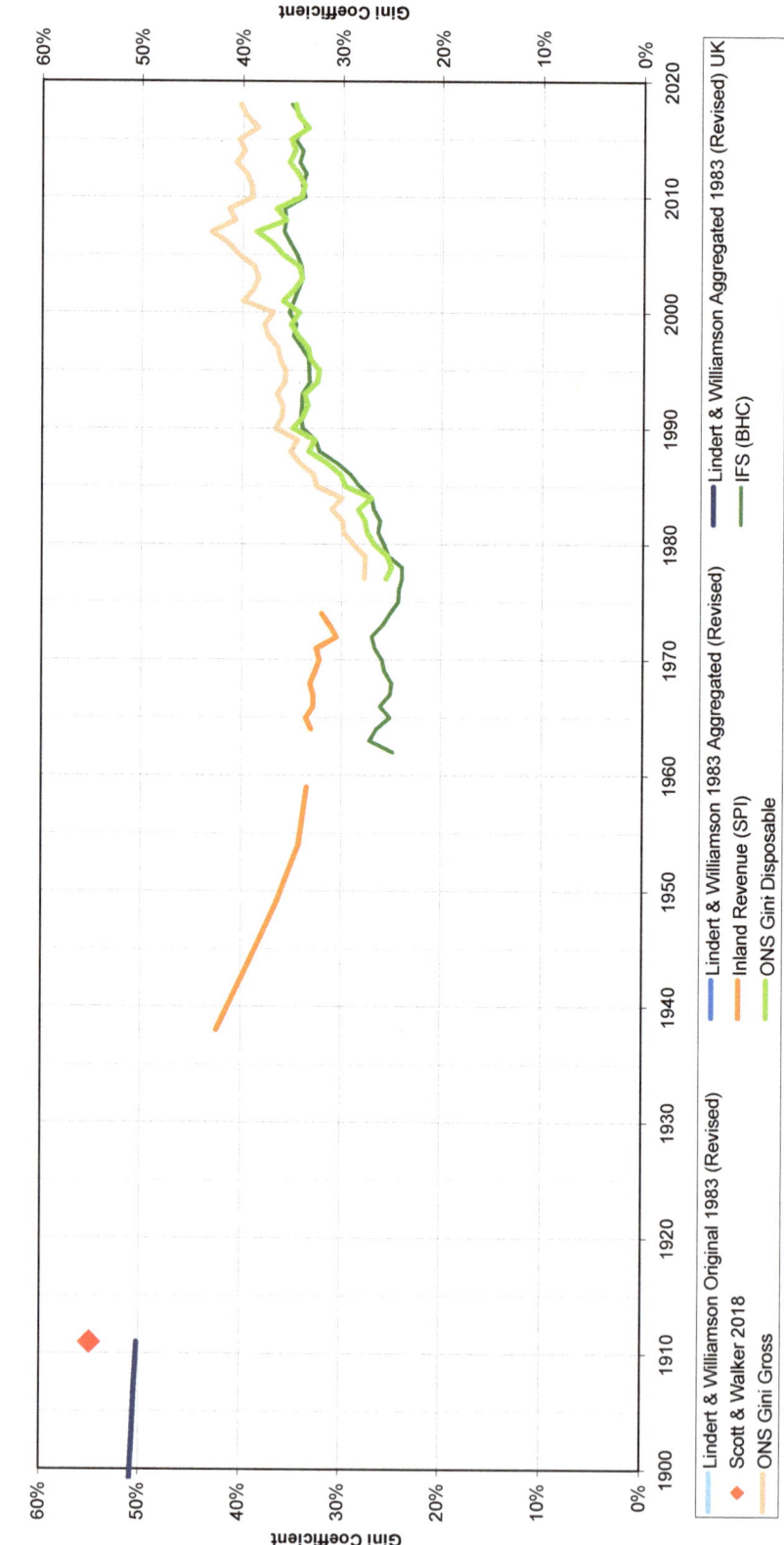

Guide to Inequality in England, GB and UK using the top 1% and 10% shares of income

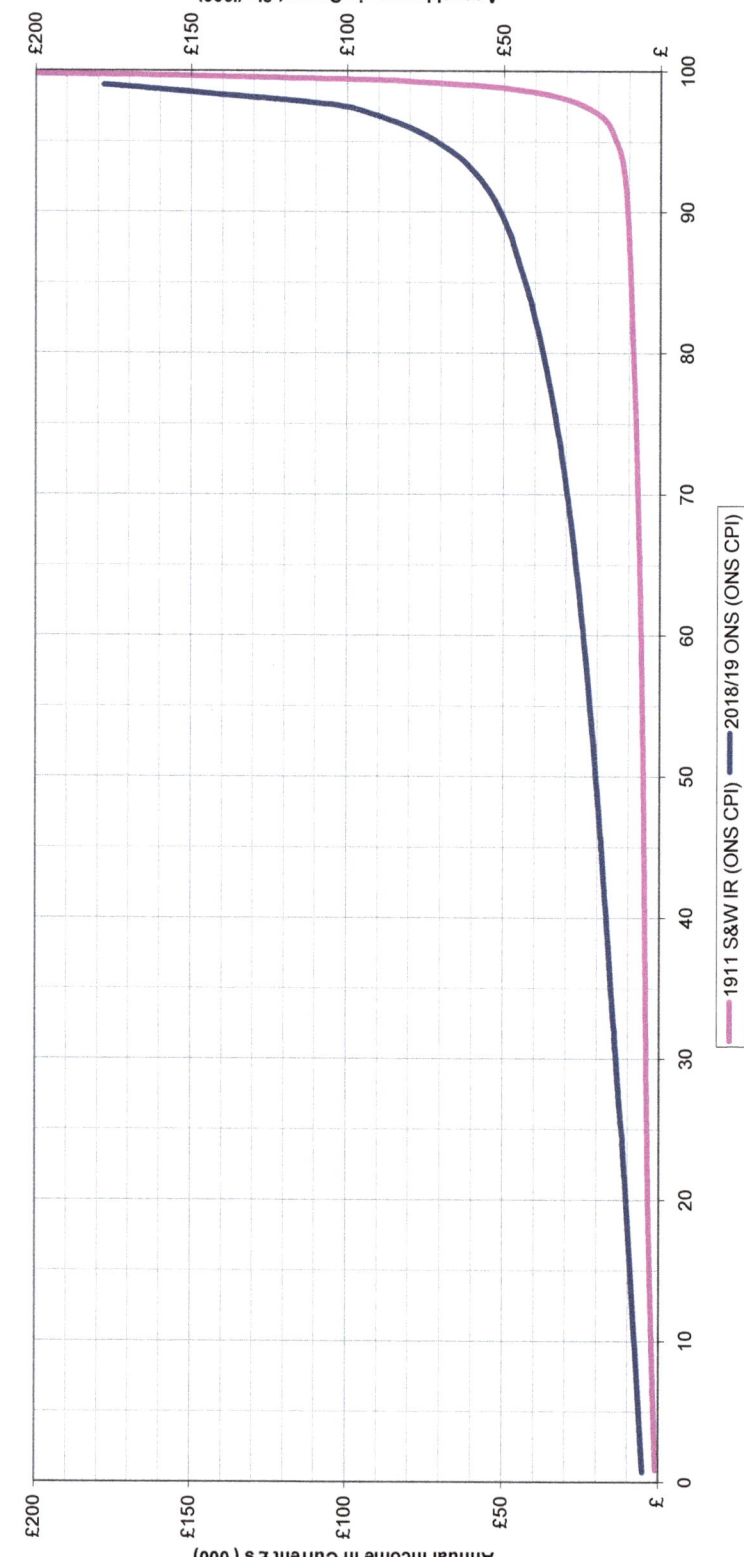

Compare real earnings/income distribution (CPI)
1949 (Scott & Walker 2018/IR) - est. Gini 41.1
2018/19 (SPI - factored for estimated non-taxpayers) - ONS Gross Gini 40.2

— 1949 S&W IR (ONS CPI) — 2018/19 ONS (ONS CPI)

115

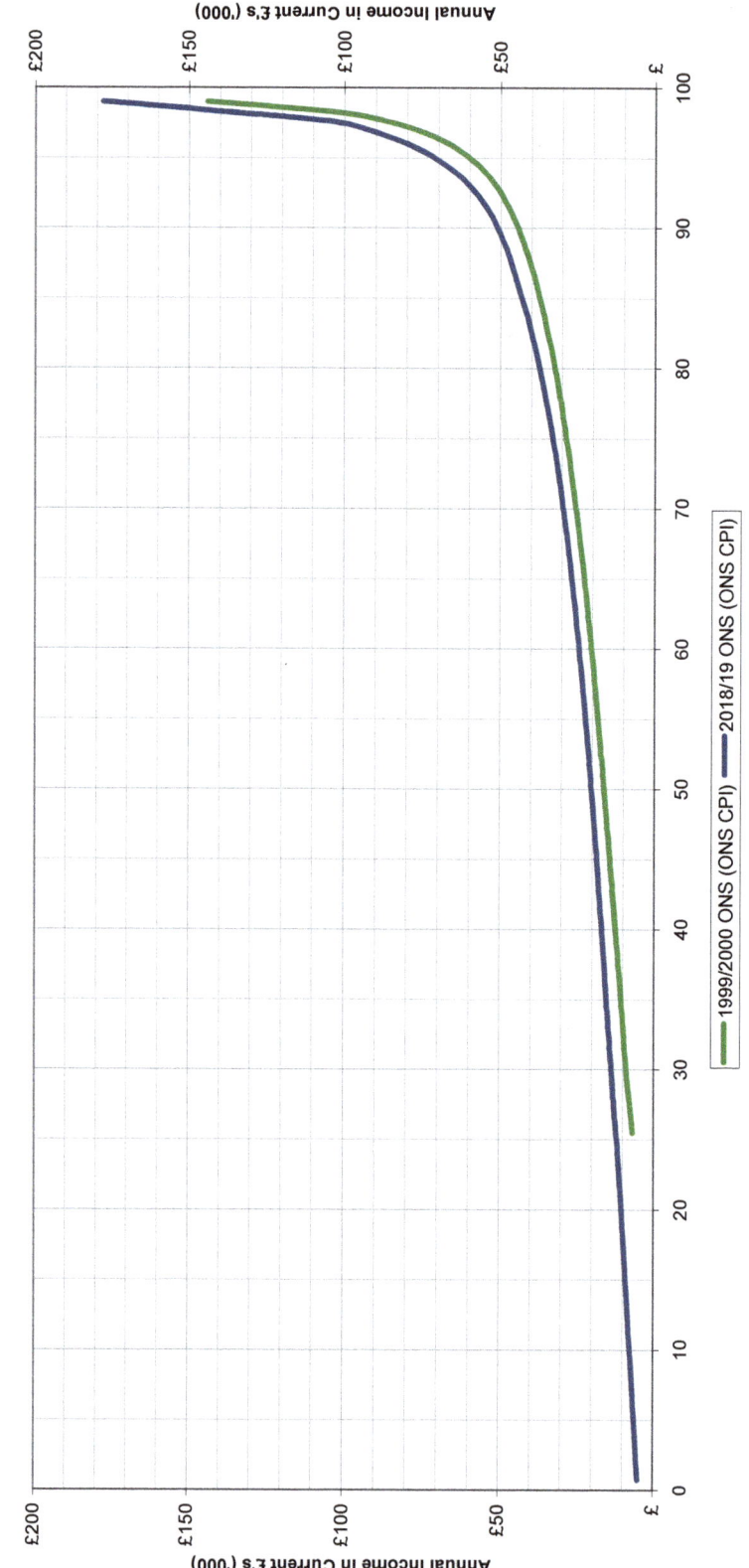

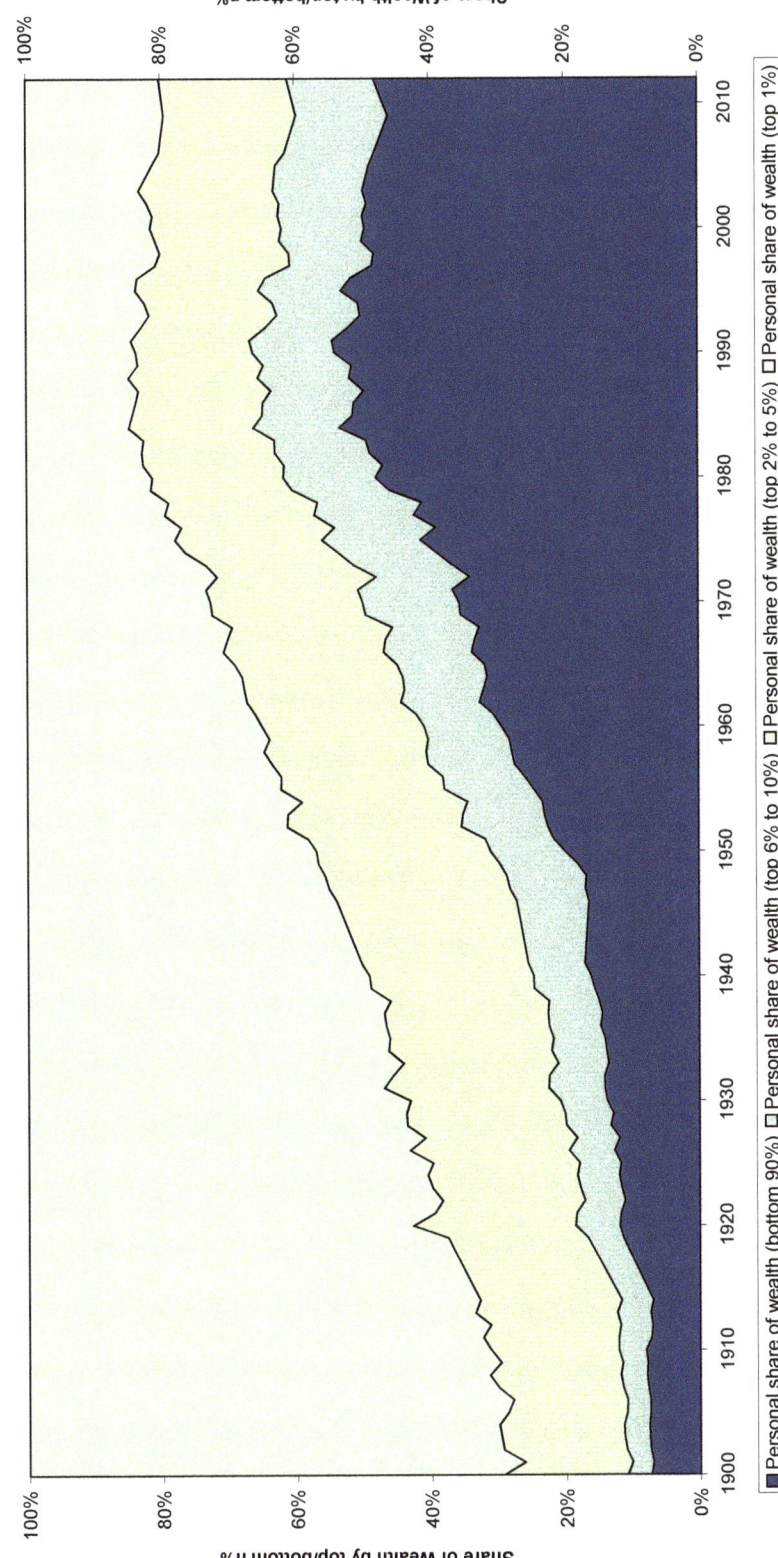

Part of a series - see also:

- UK Economic & Social Change – 1700-2019 – Three centuries of progress
- UK Economy – 1700-1913 – An economy in transition
- UK Economy – 1900-2019 – Growth of the state & world war
- UK Economy – 1990-2019 – Quarter of a century of new changes
- UK Economy – 1990-2019 – Stable income inequality
- UK Household Expenditure – 1700-2019 – Cost of Living
- UK Housing – 1700-2019 – Growth of home ownership
- UK Pauperism, Poverty and Hardship – 1700-2019 – The Retreat of Real Poverty
- UK Pollution (Air Quality), Cars – 1970-2019 – Continuous improvement
- UK Pollution (Air Quality), Energy – 1970-2019 – Continuous improvement
- UK Population & Life Expectancy – 1970-2019 – Continuous Improvement

UK Economy

1990/91-2018/19 or one generation +

Quarter of a century of new changes

UK Population, Life Expectancy & Inequality

From 1990/91-2018/19

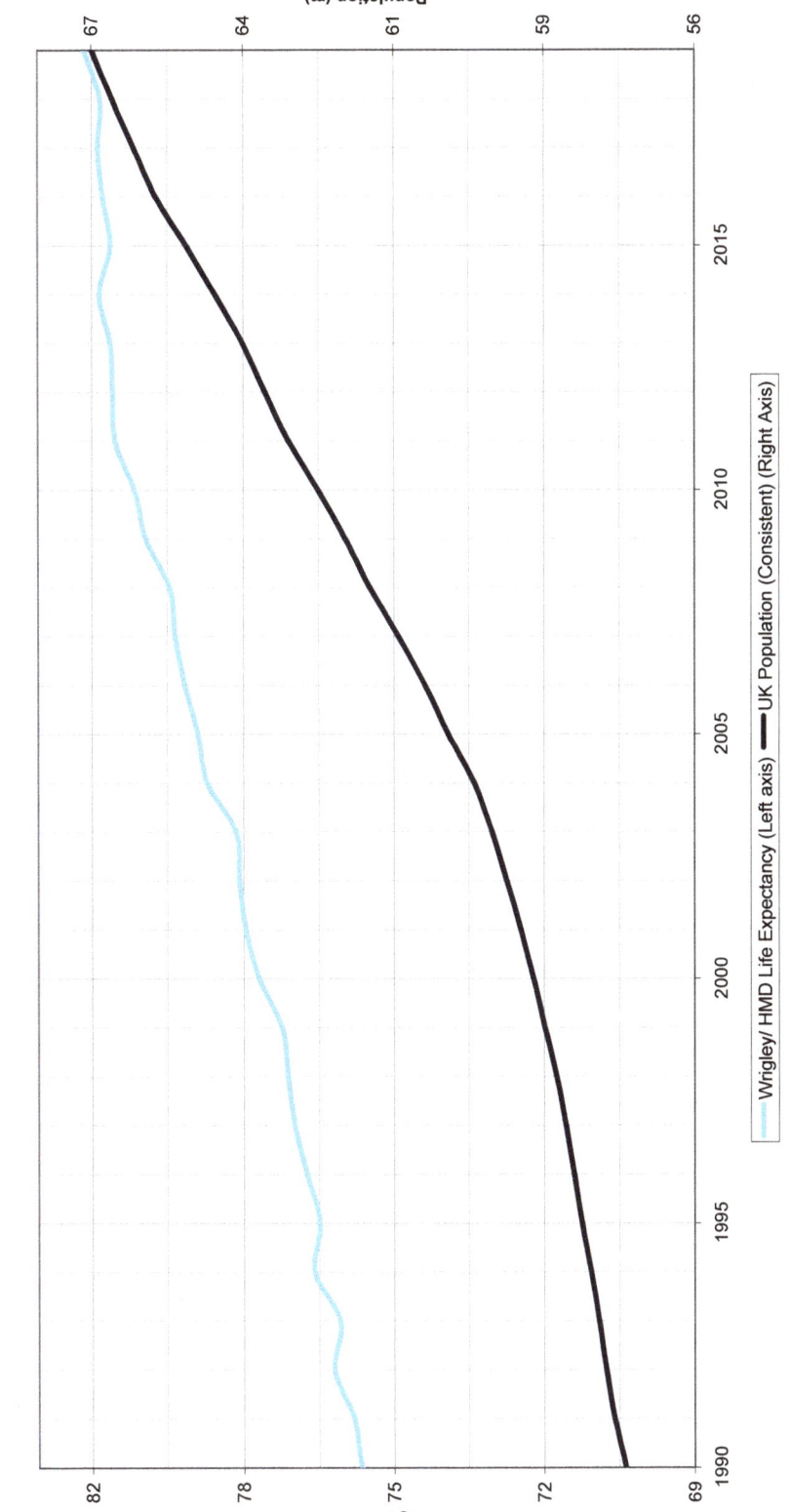

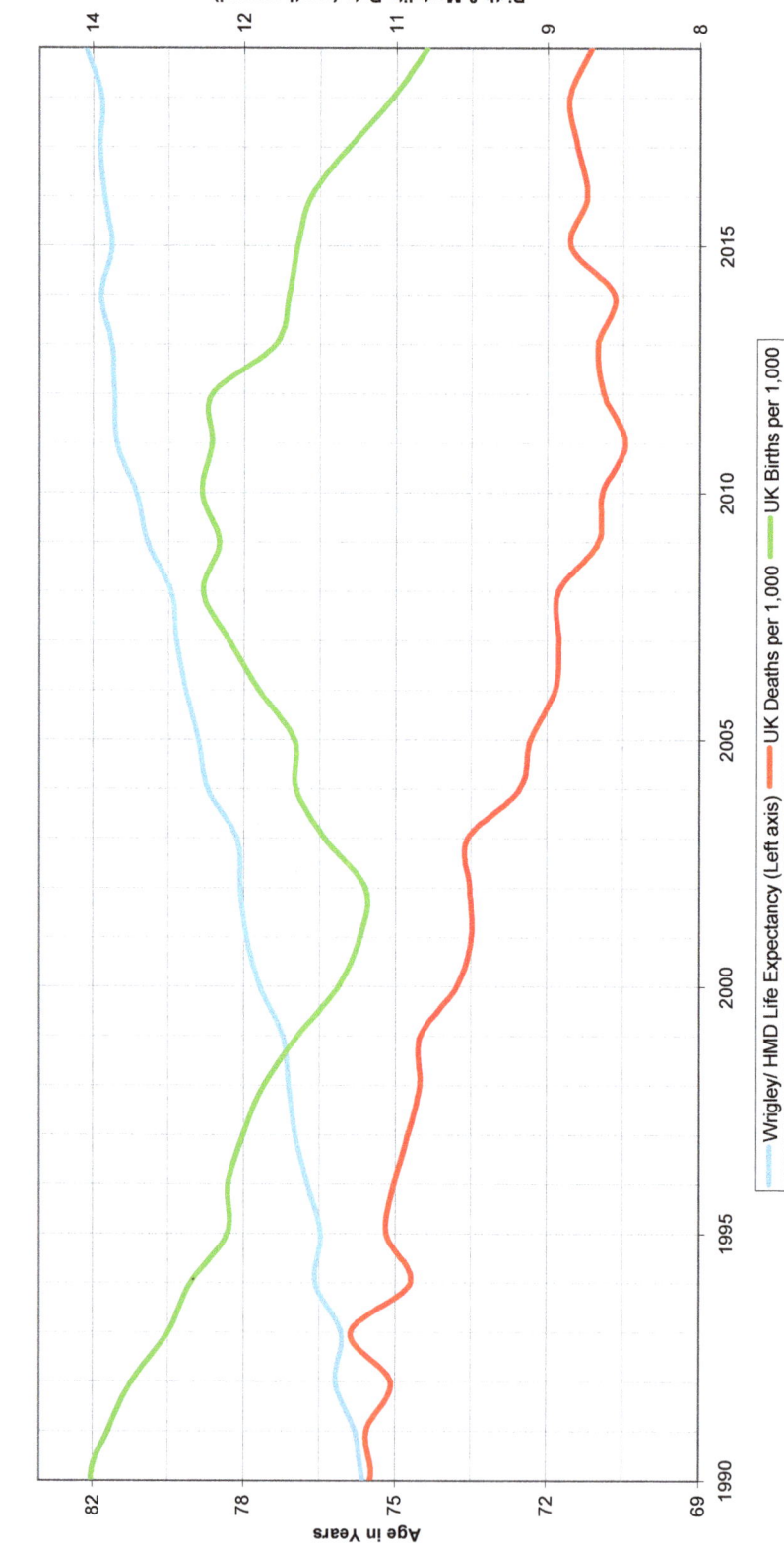

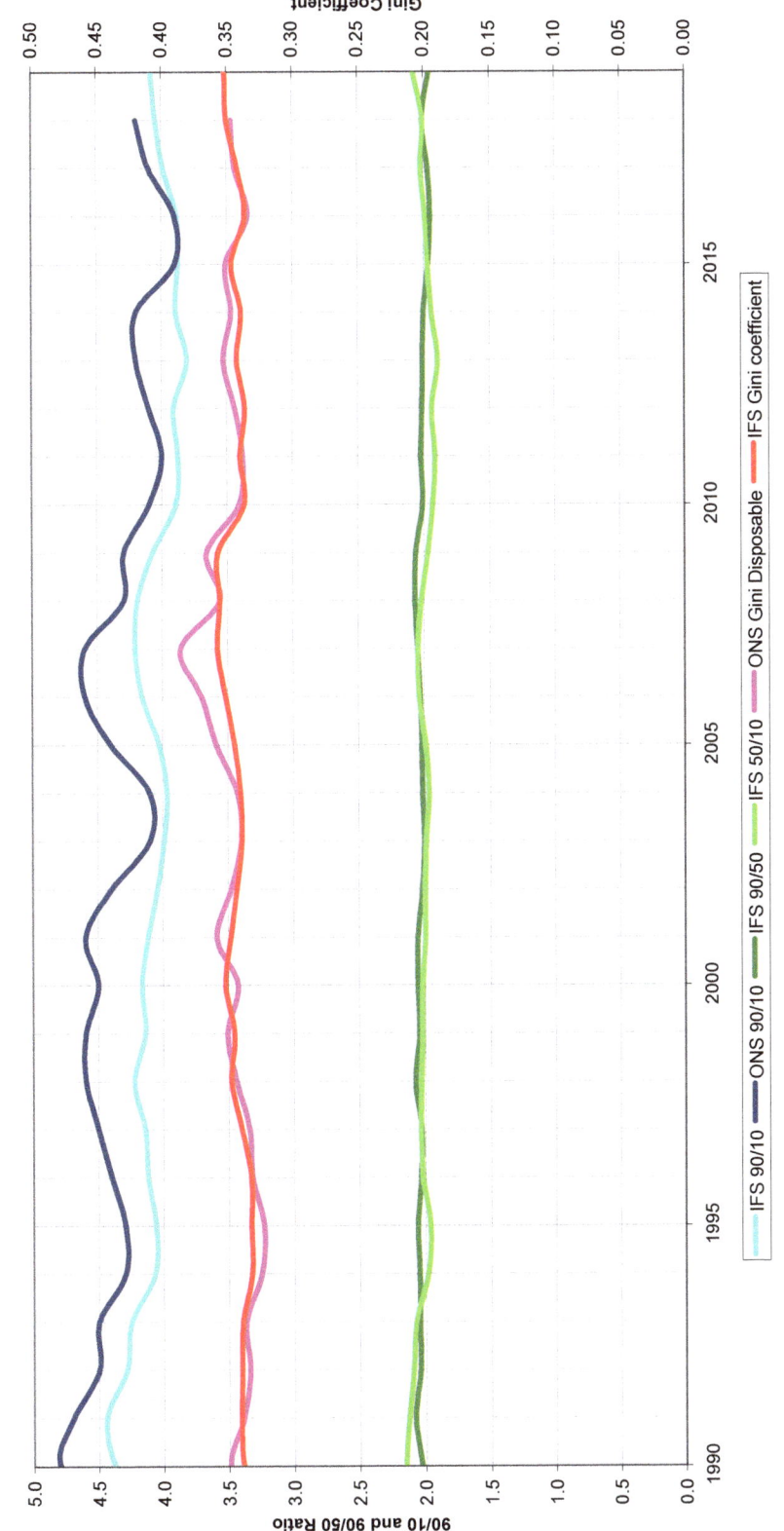

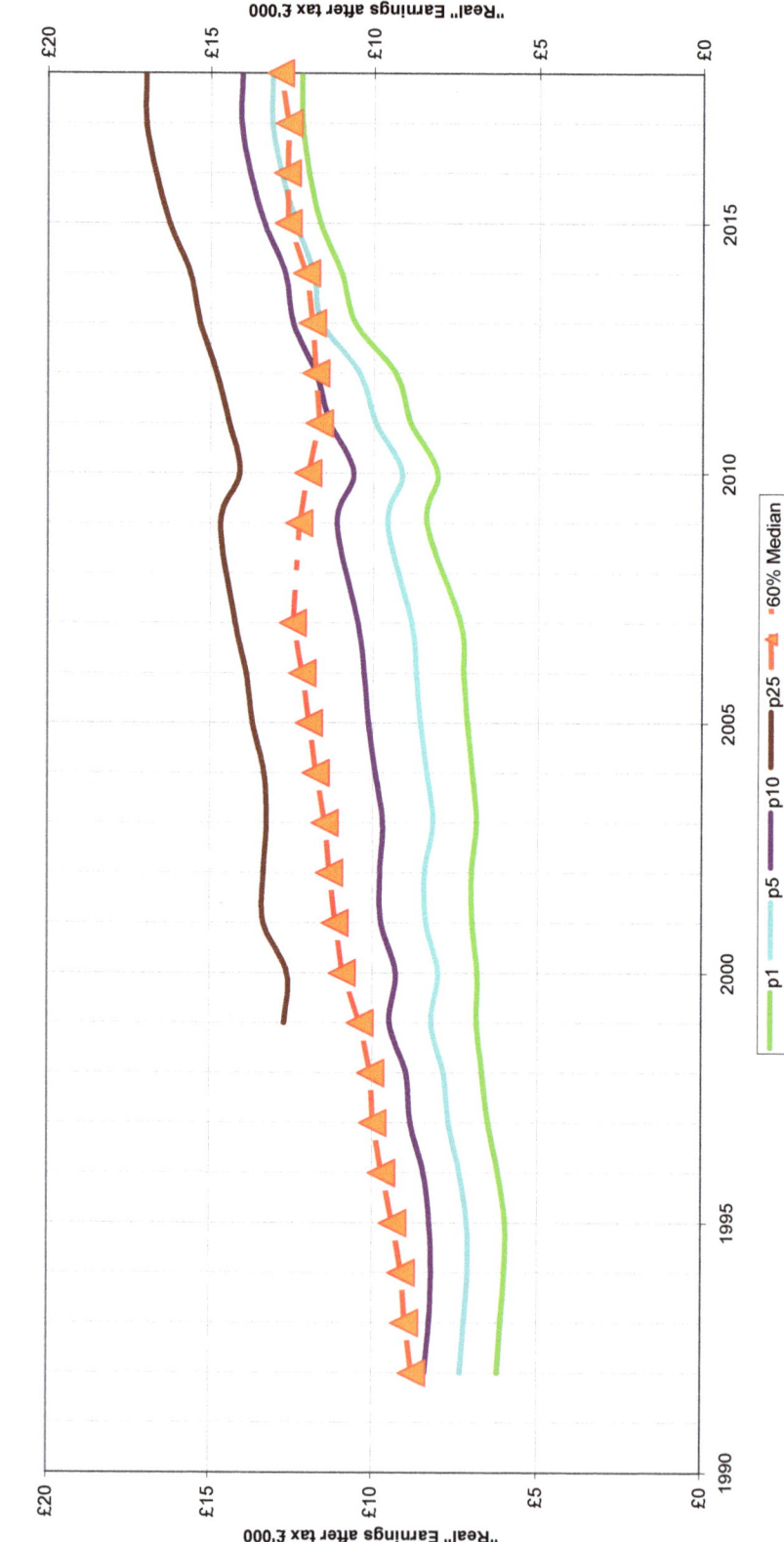
Percentiles - "Real" (in Current £'s) Taxable Income of first quartile - After Tax

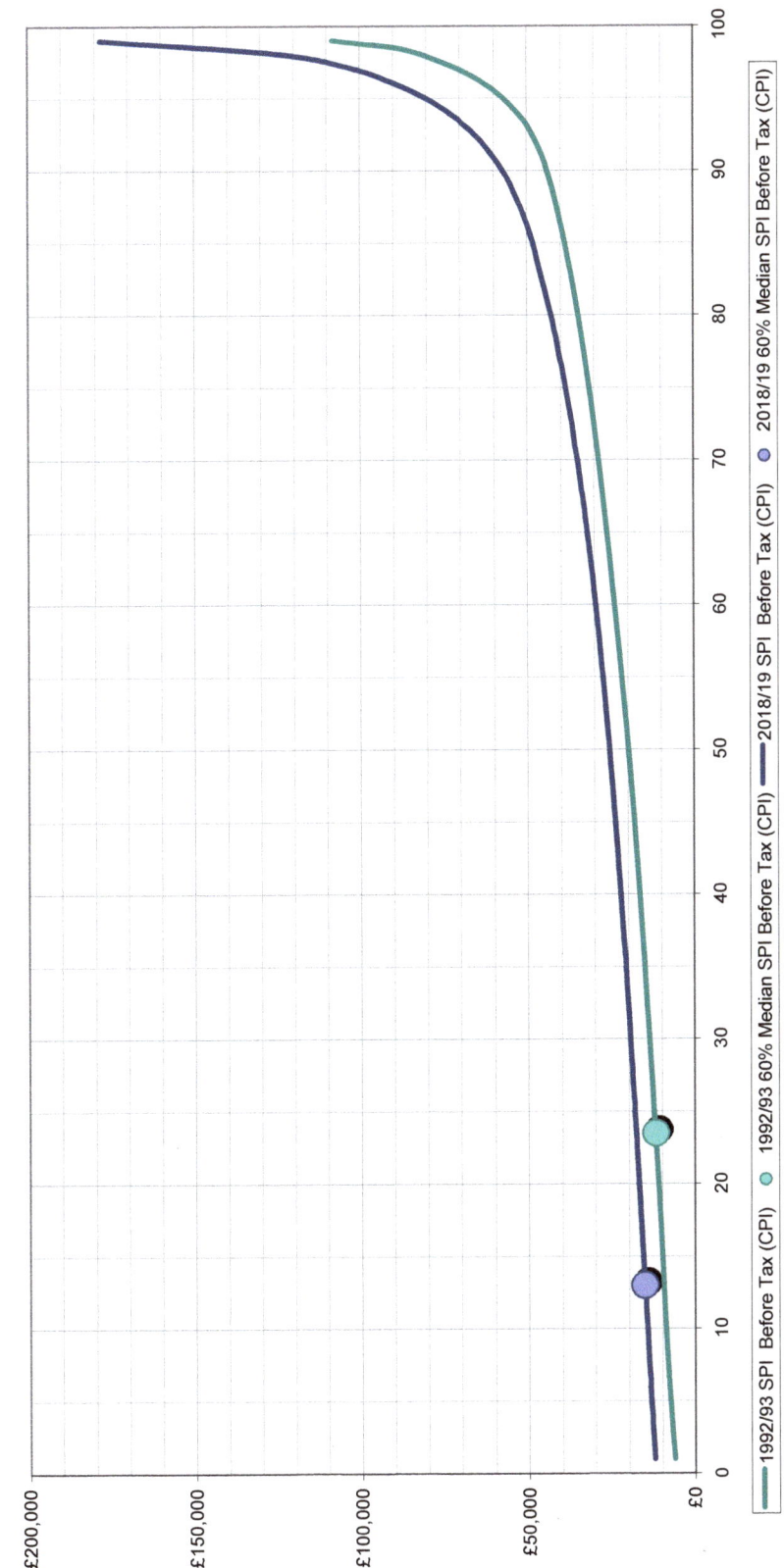

UK Economy

The last quarter century – the return of debt

1990-2019 or one generation plus

"Real" Average Full-time Earnings, Government Spending, Revenue, National GDP and National Debt per person in £'000

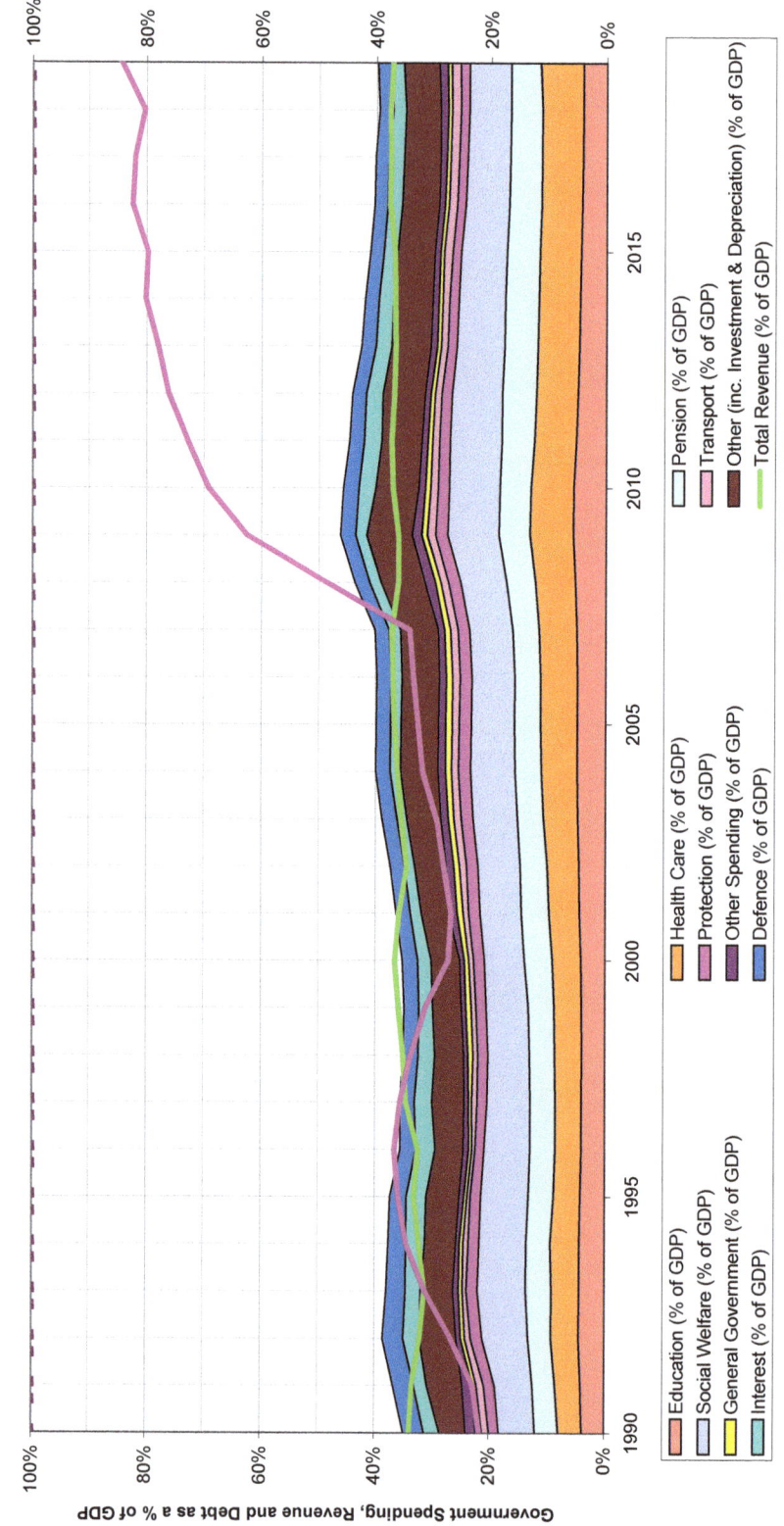

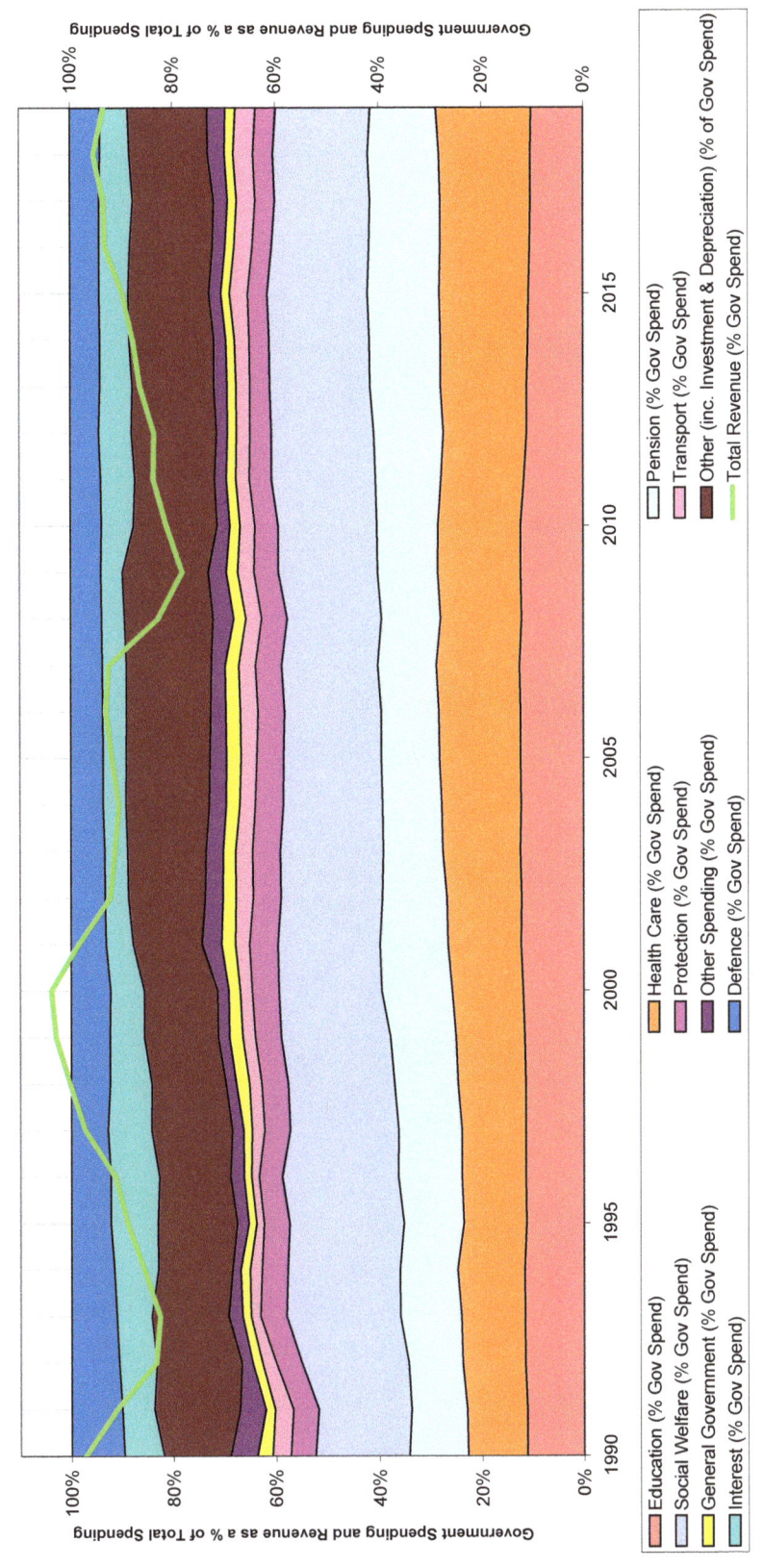

129

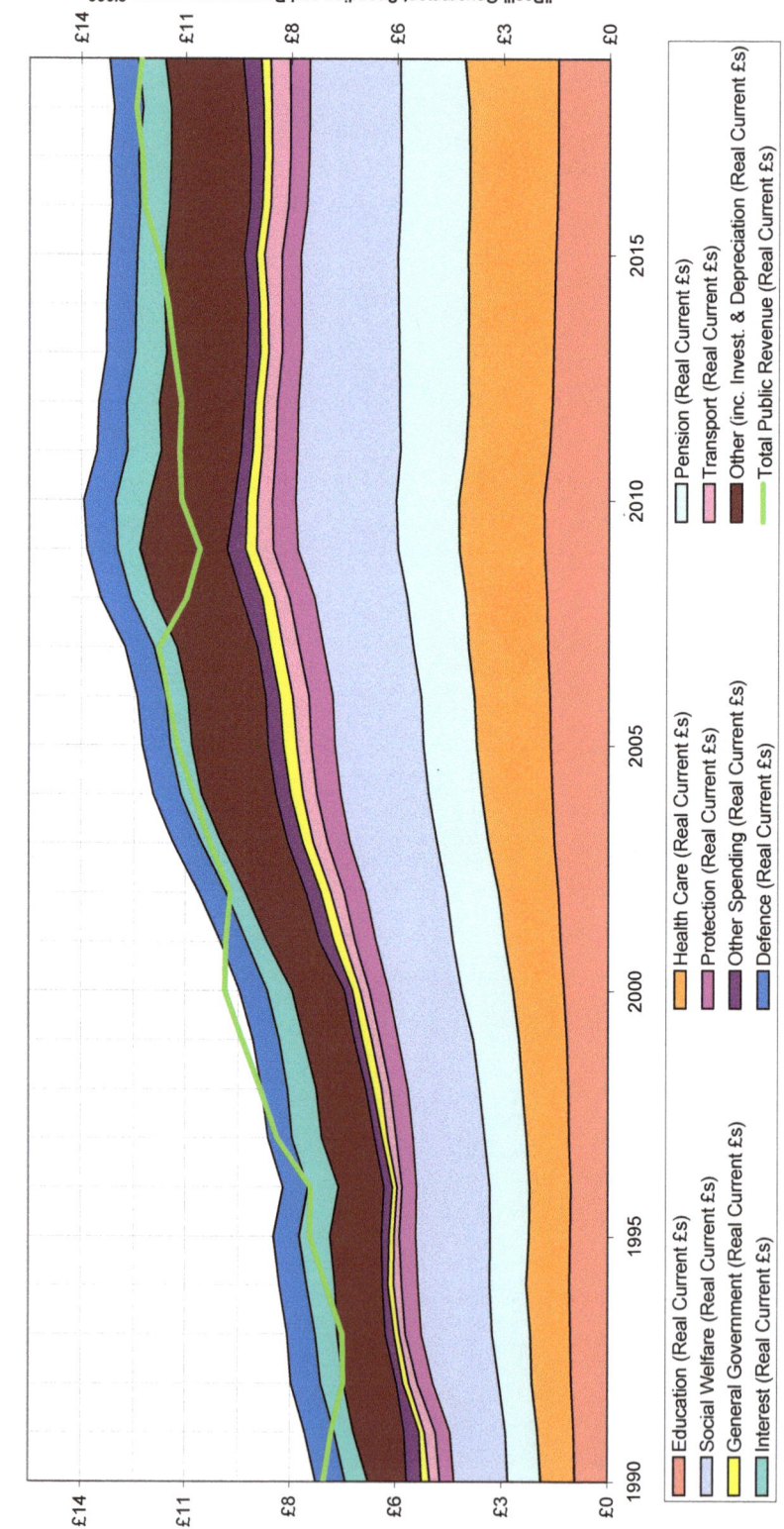

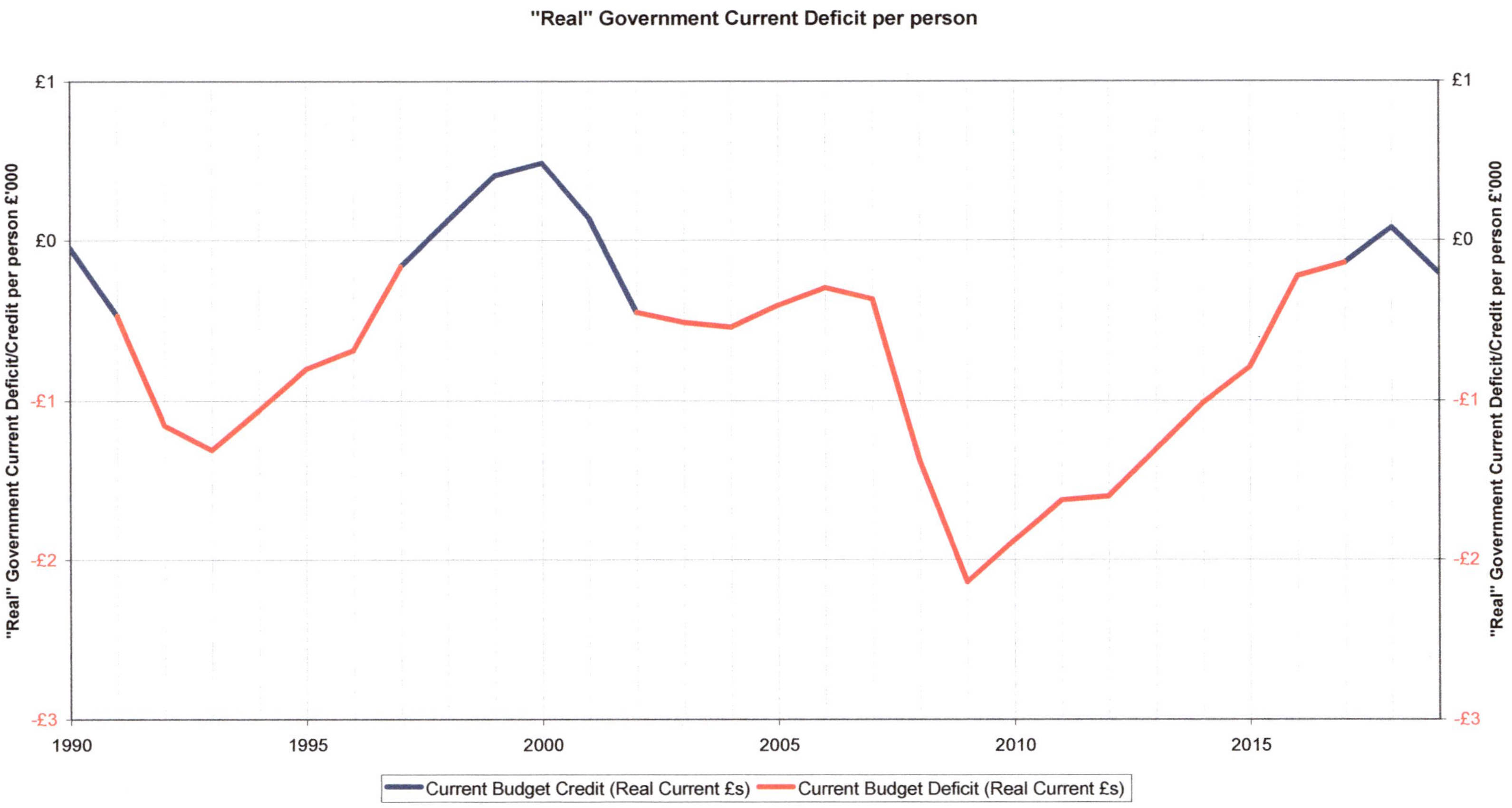
"Real" Government Current Deficit per person
£1
£0
-£1
-£2
-£3
"Real" Government Current Deficit/Credit per person £'000
1990
1995
2000
2005
2010
2015
Current Budget Credit (Real Current £s)
Current Budget Deficit (Real Current £s)

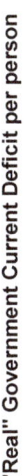

Specific Areas of Government Spending

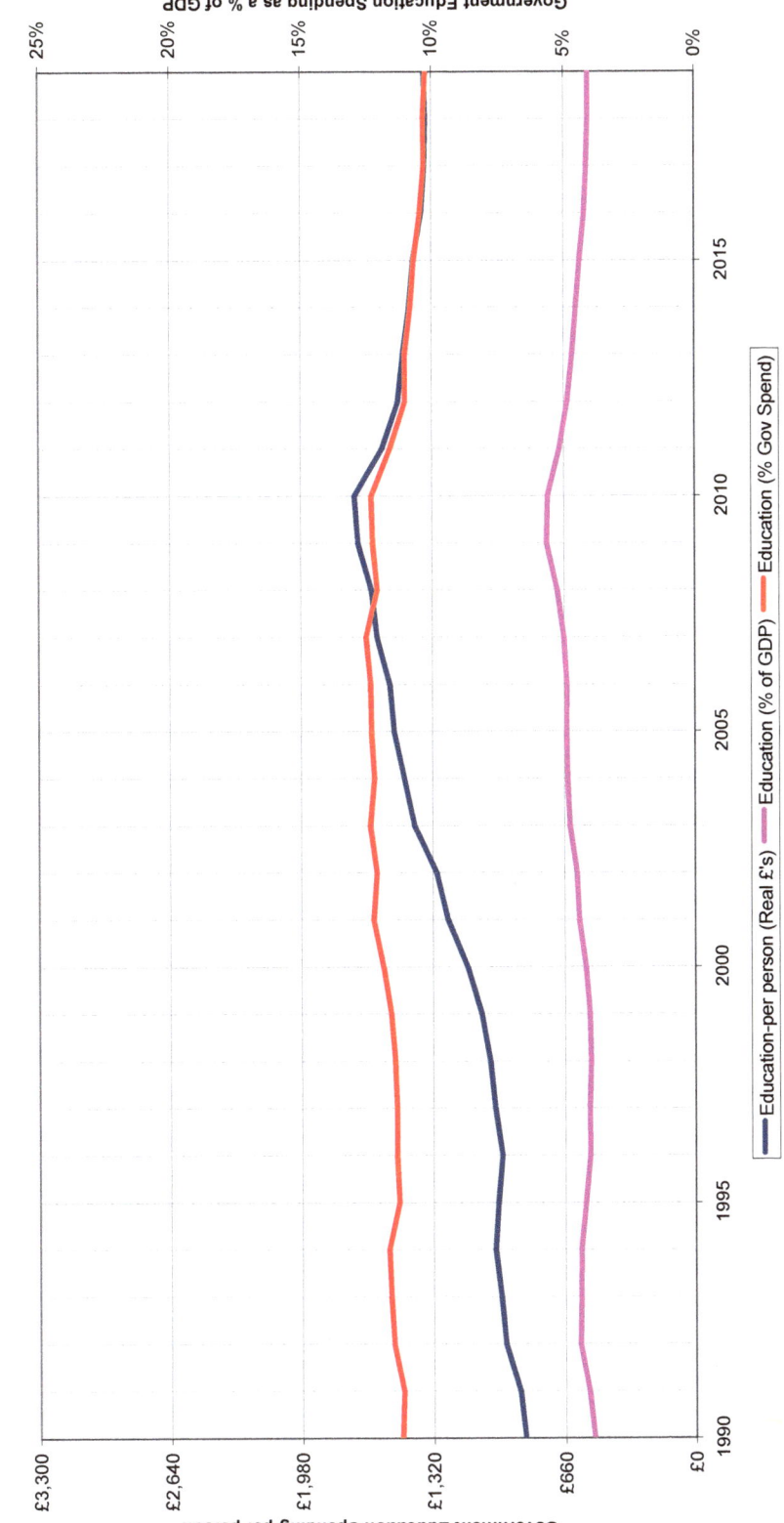

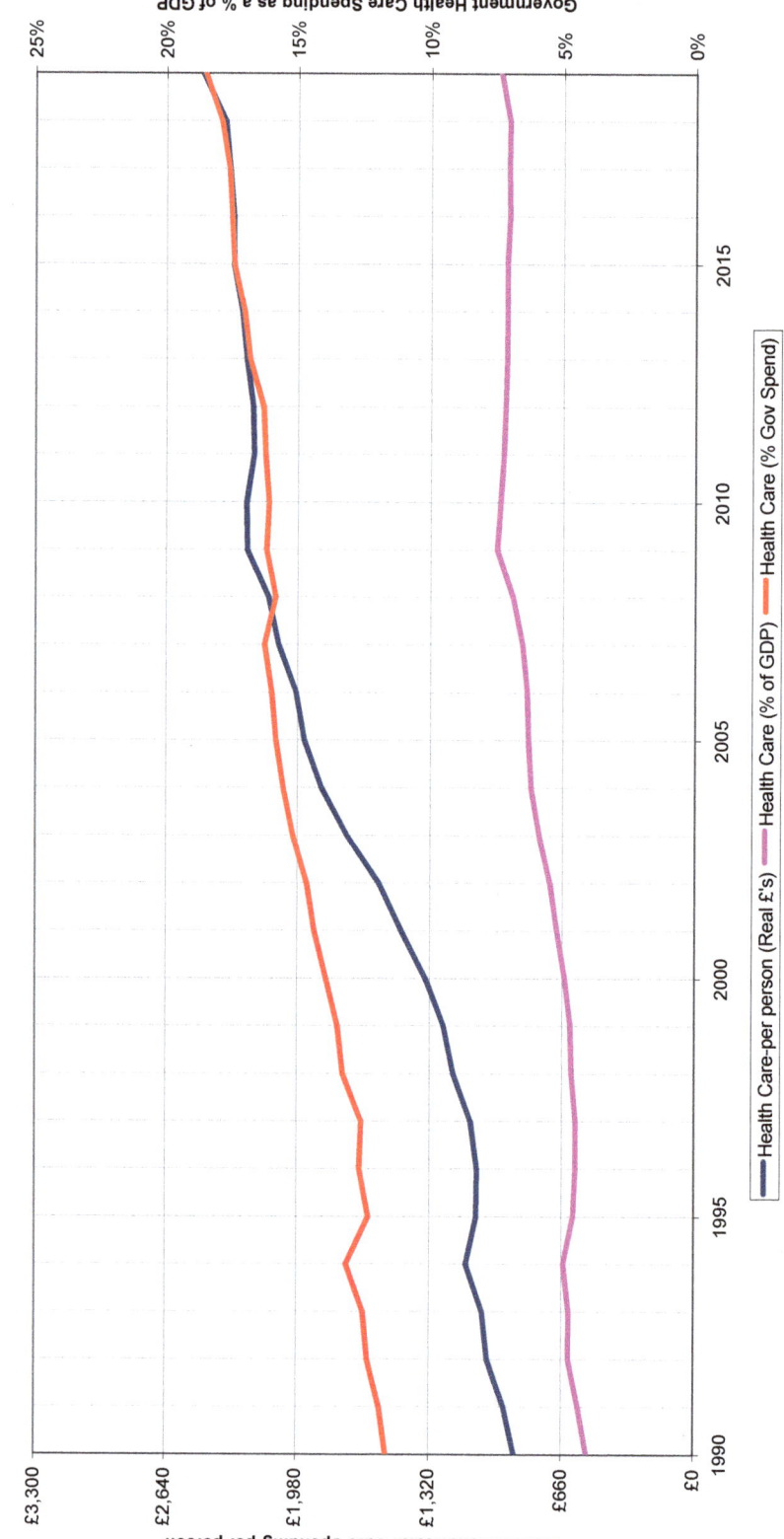

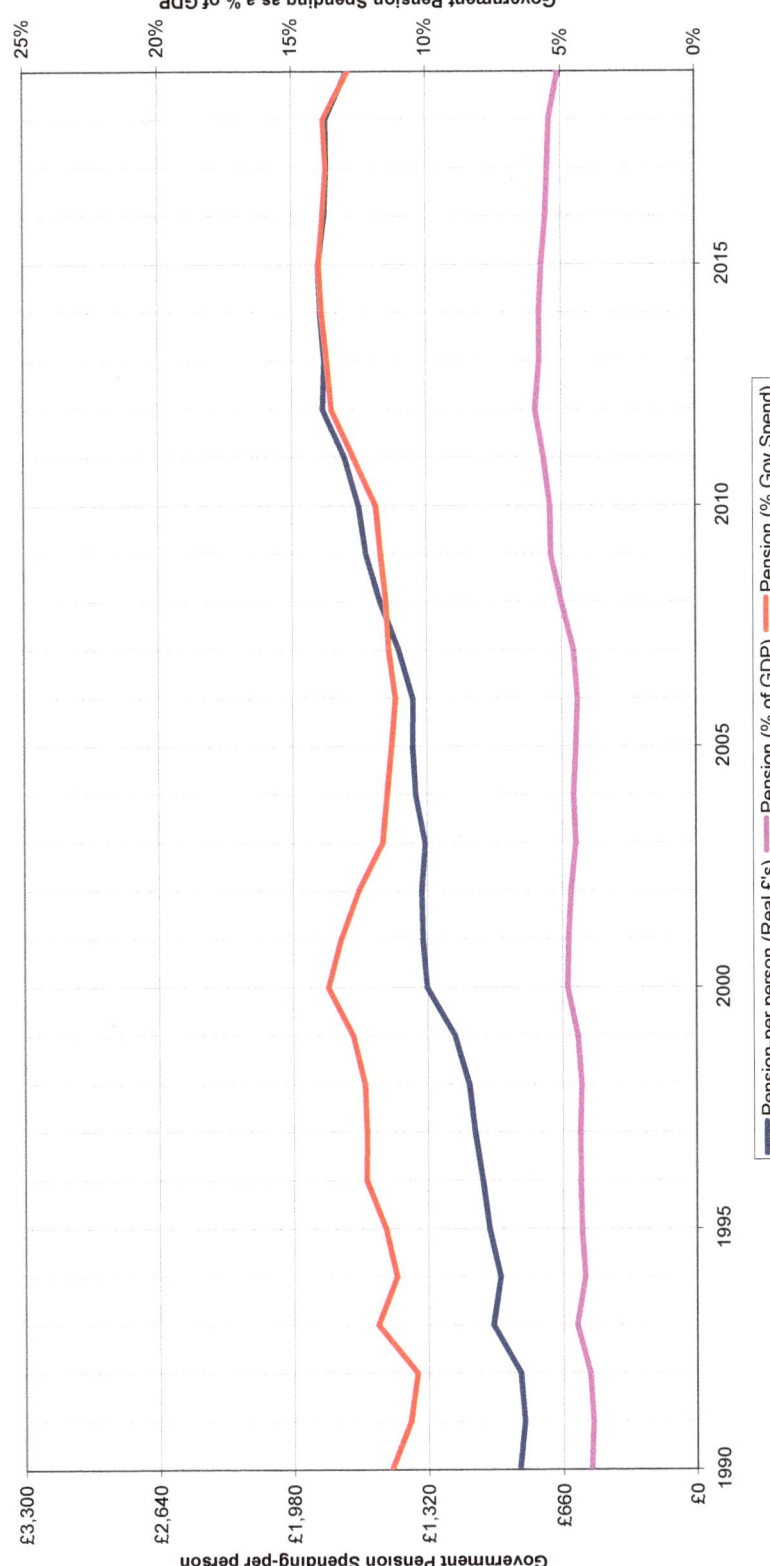

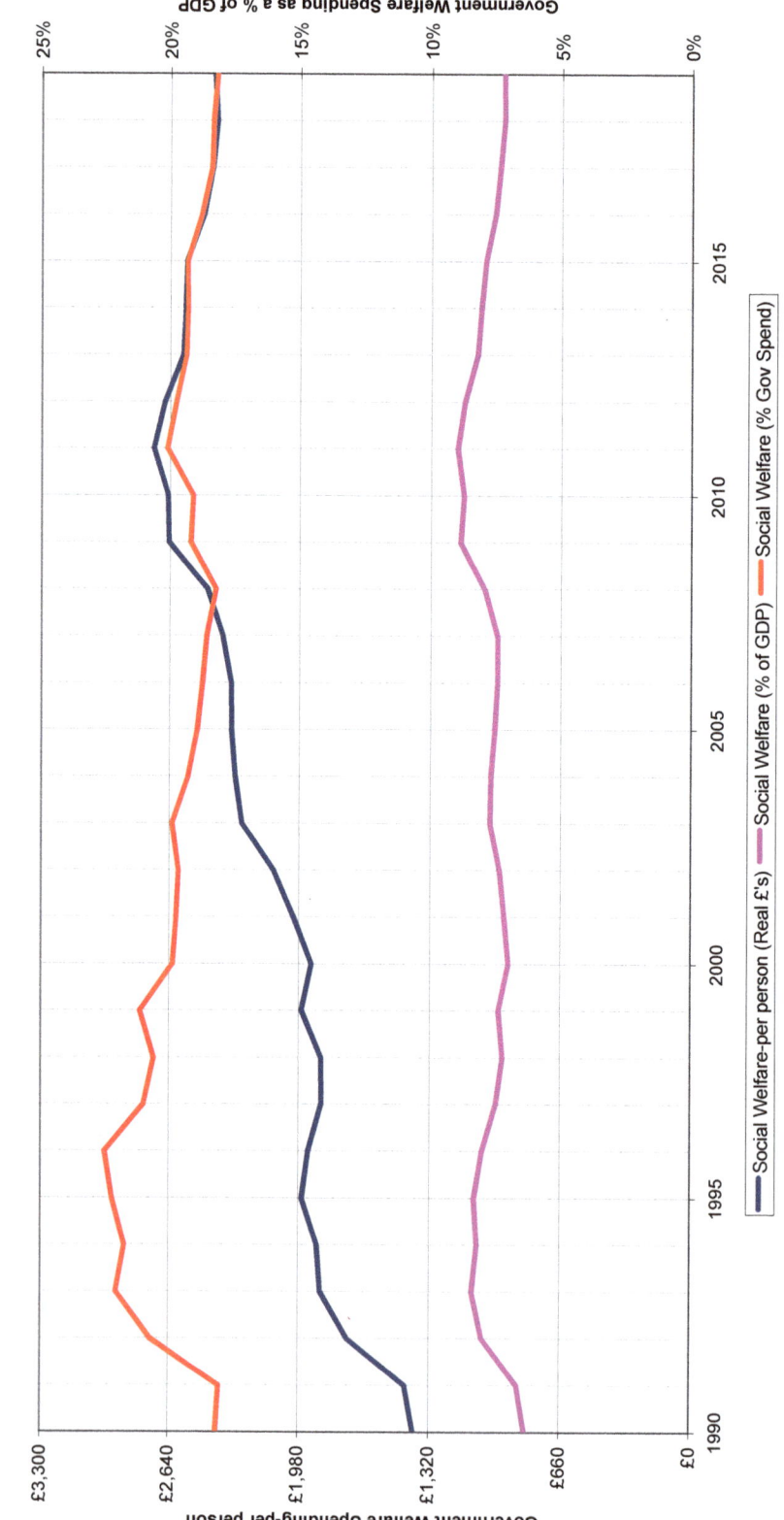

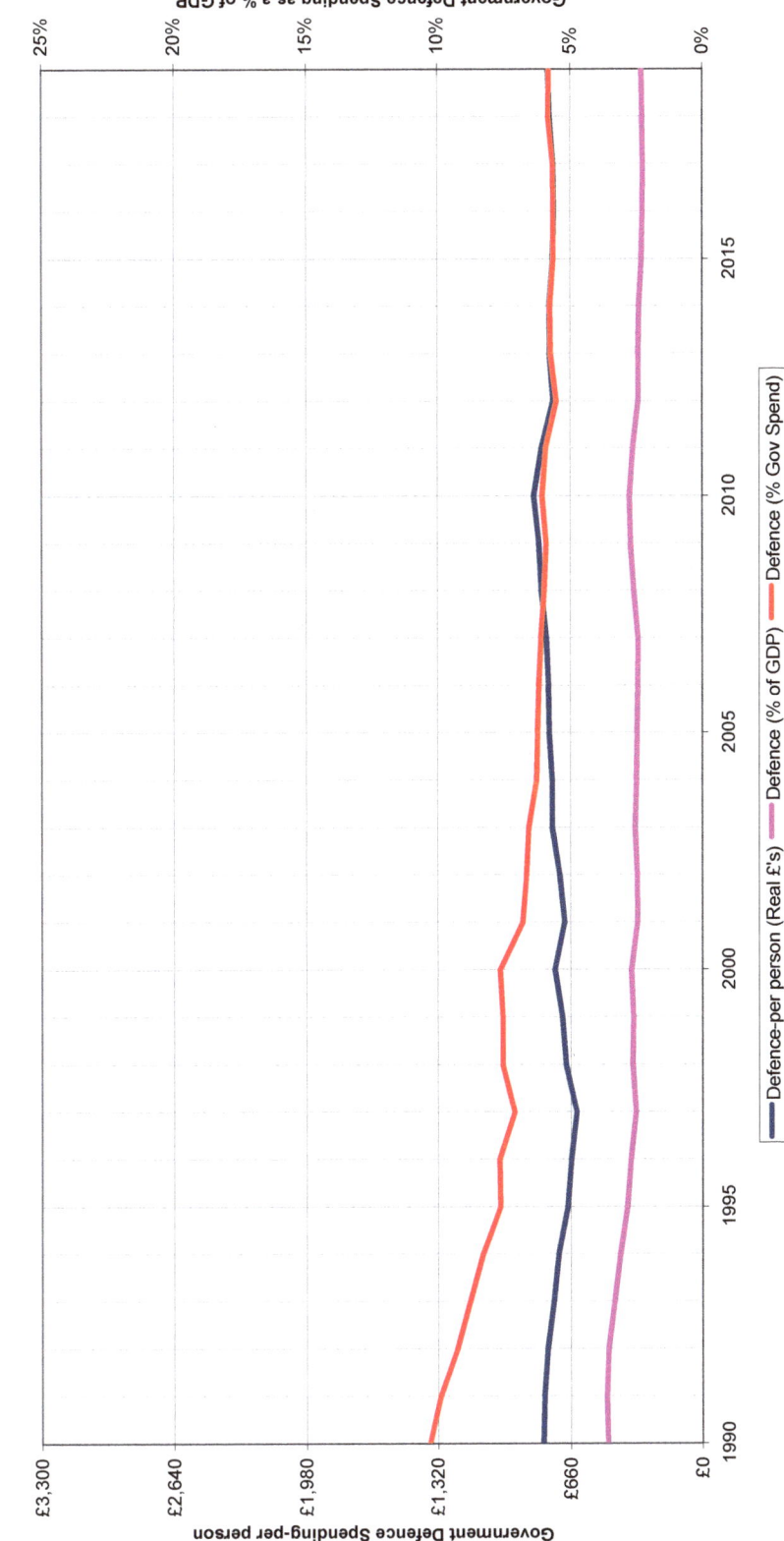

Part of a series - see also:

- UK Economic & Social Change – 1700-2019 – Three centuries of progress
  - UK Economy – 1700-1913 – An economy in transition
- UK Economy – 1900-2019 – Growth of the state & world war
- UK Economy – 1990-2019 – Quarter of a century of new changes
  - UK Economy – 1990-2019 – Stable income inequality
  - UK Household Expenditure – 1700-2019 – Cost of Living
  - UK Housing – 1700-2019 – Growth of home ownership
- UK Pauperism, Poverty and Hardship – 1700-2019 – The Retreat of Real Poverty
  - UK Pollution (Air Quality), Cars – 1970-2019 – Continuous improvement
  - UK Pollution (Air Quality), Energy – 1970-2019 – Continuous improvement
  - UK Population & Life Expectancy – 1970-2019 – Continuous Improvement

UK Economy

1990/91-2018/19 or one generation +

Stable income inequality

Inequality

Multiple years from 1992/93-2018/19

Normalised to "Real" 2018/19 pounds using CPI

UK Gini Coefficient with 90/10, 90/50 and 50/10 ratios

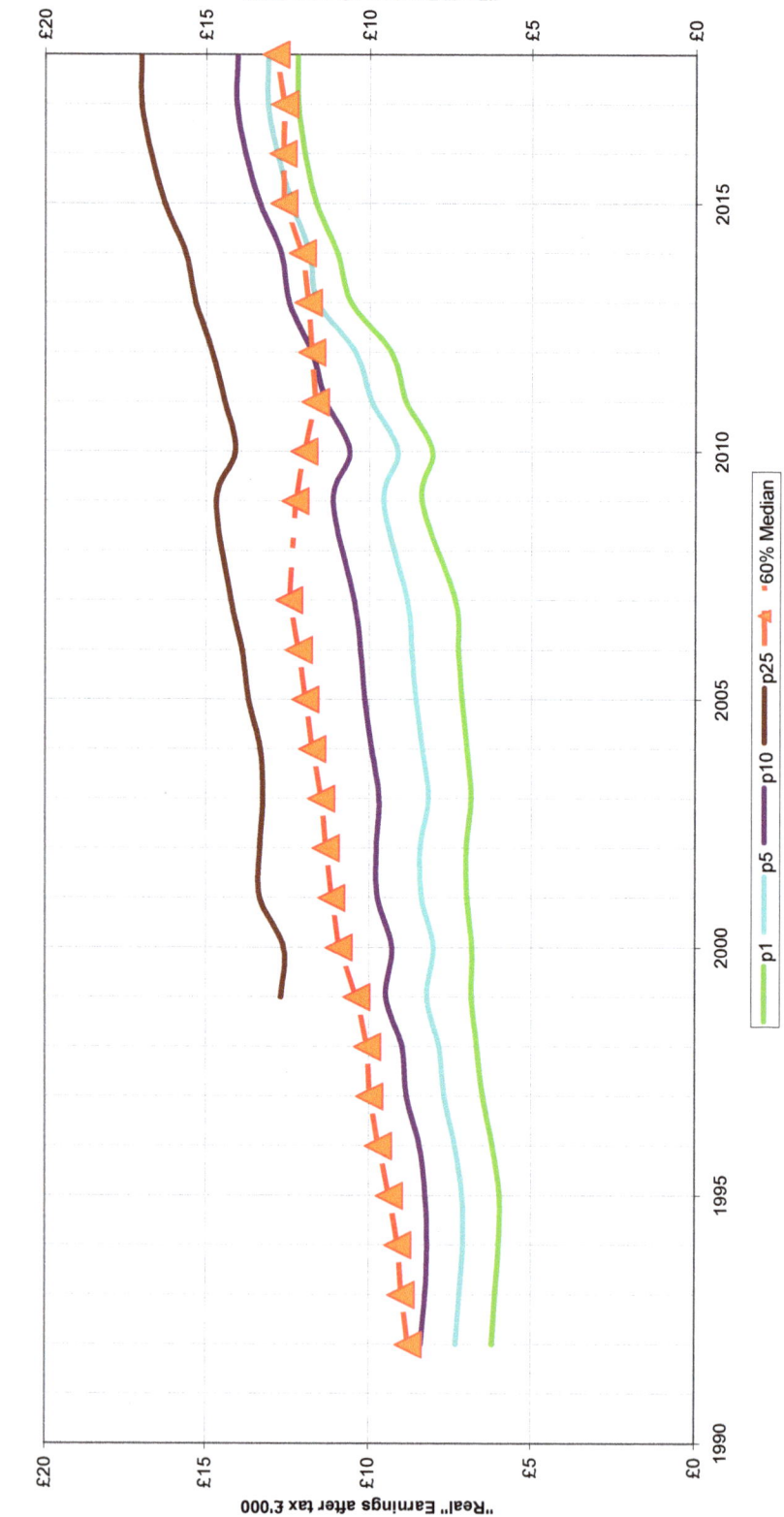

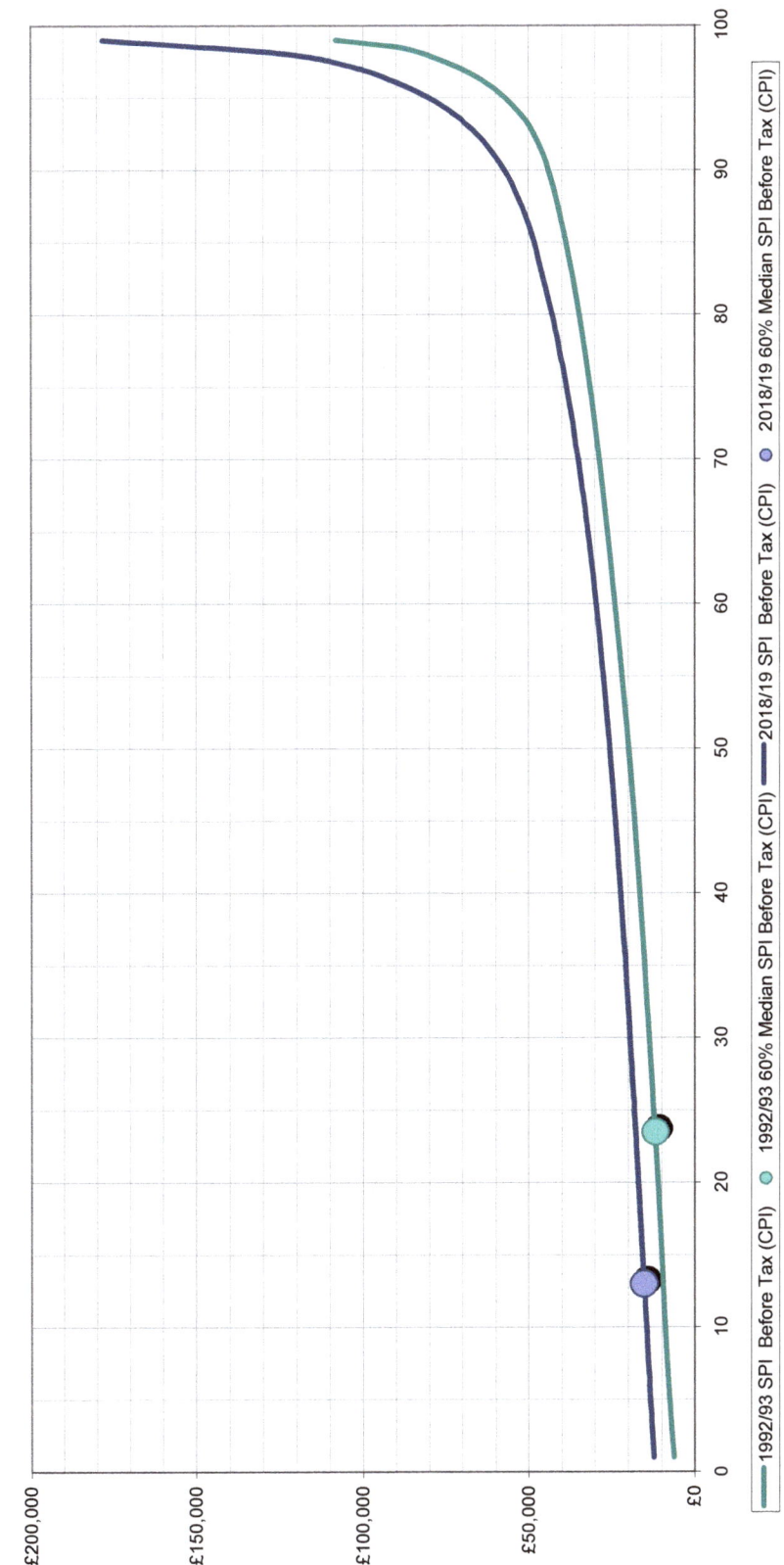

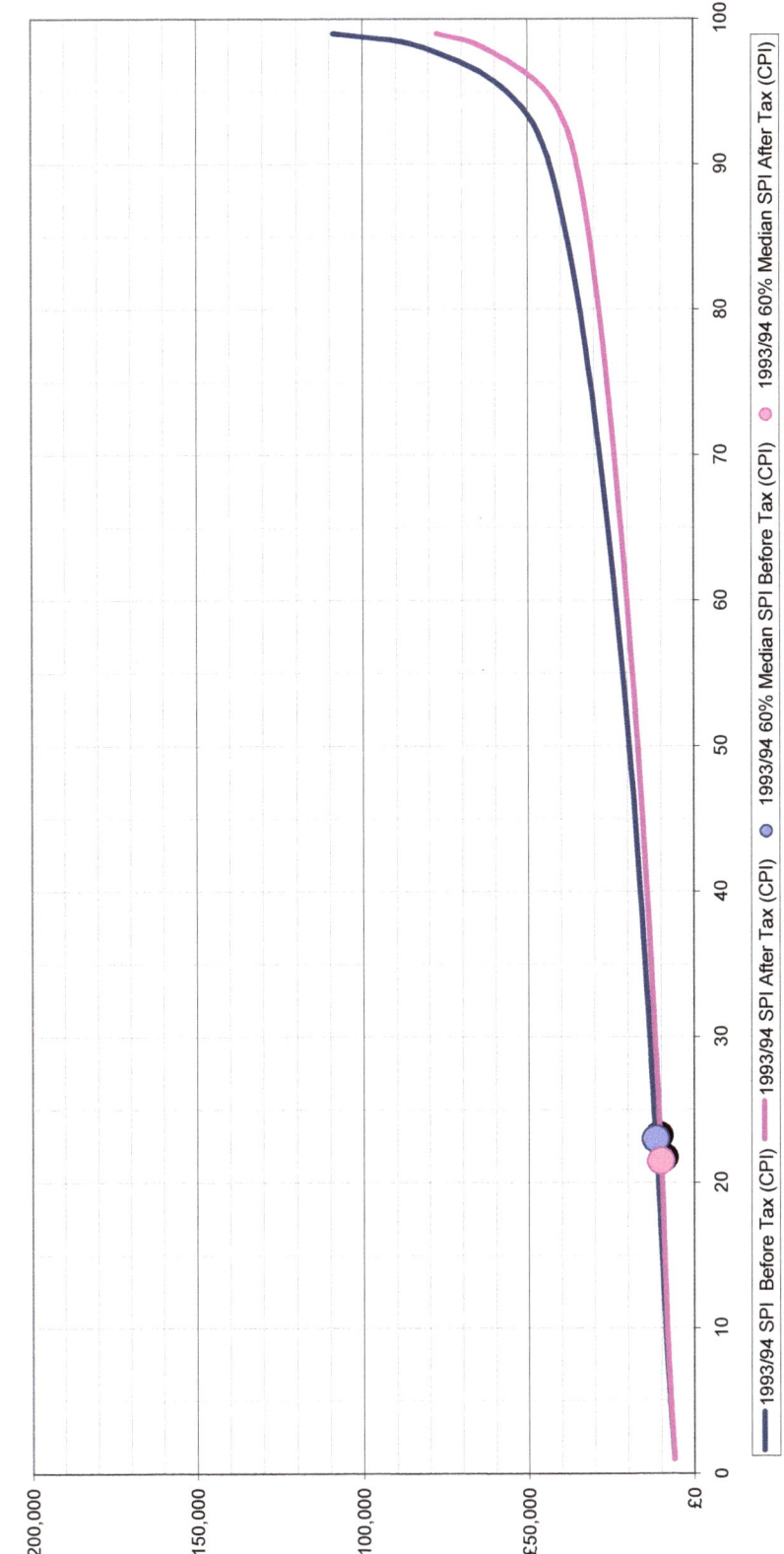

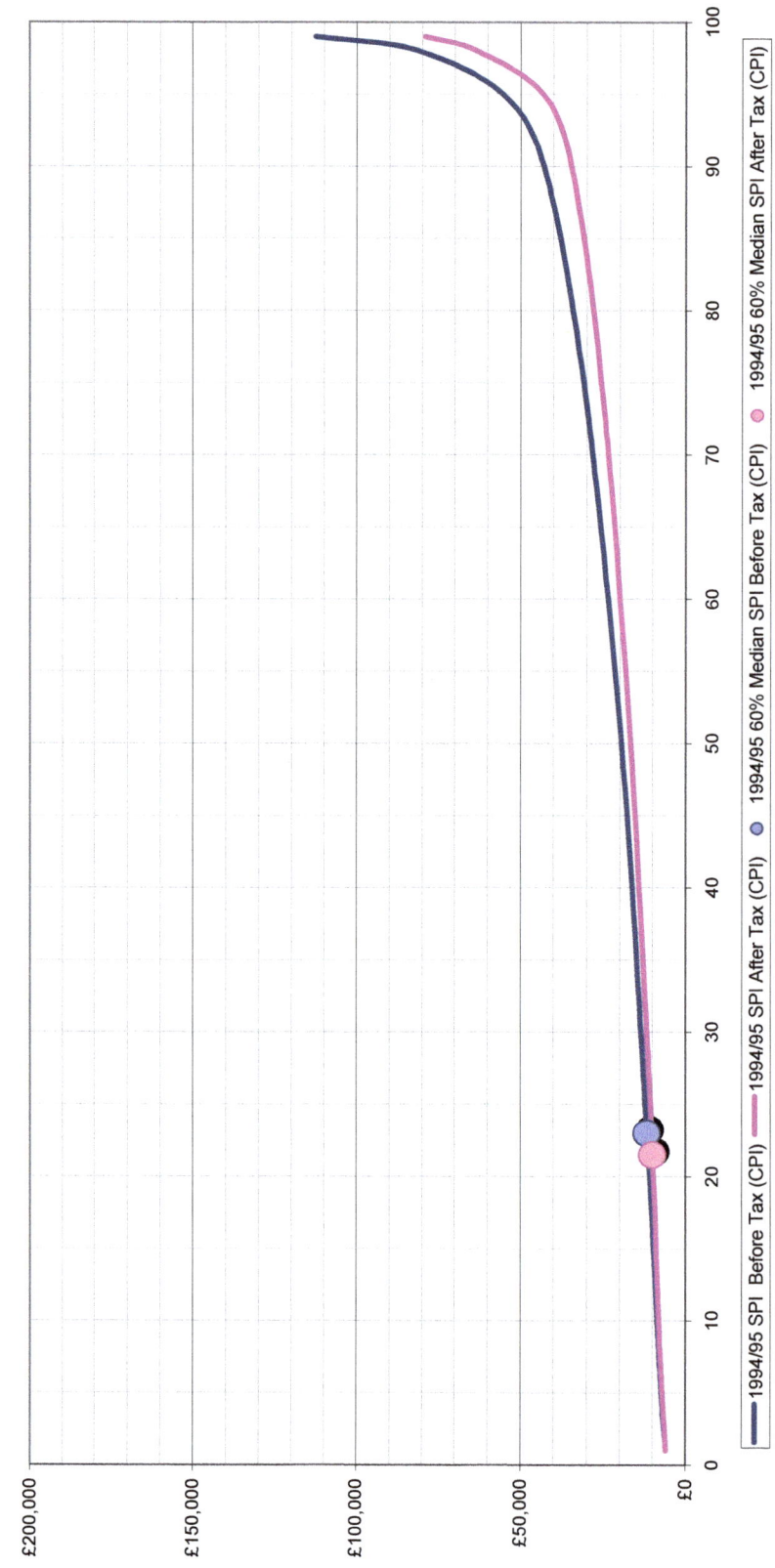

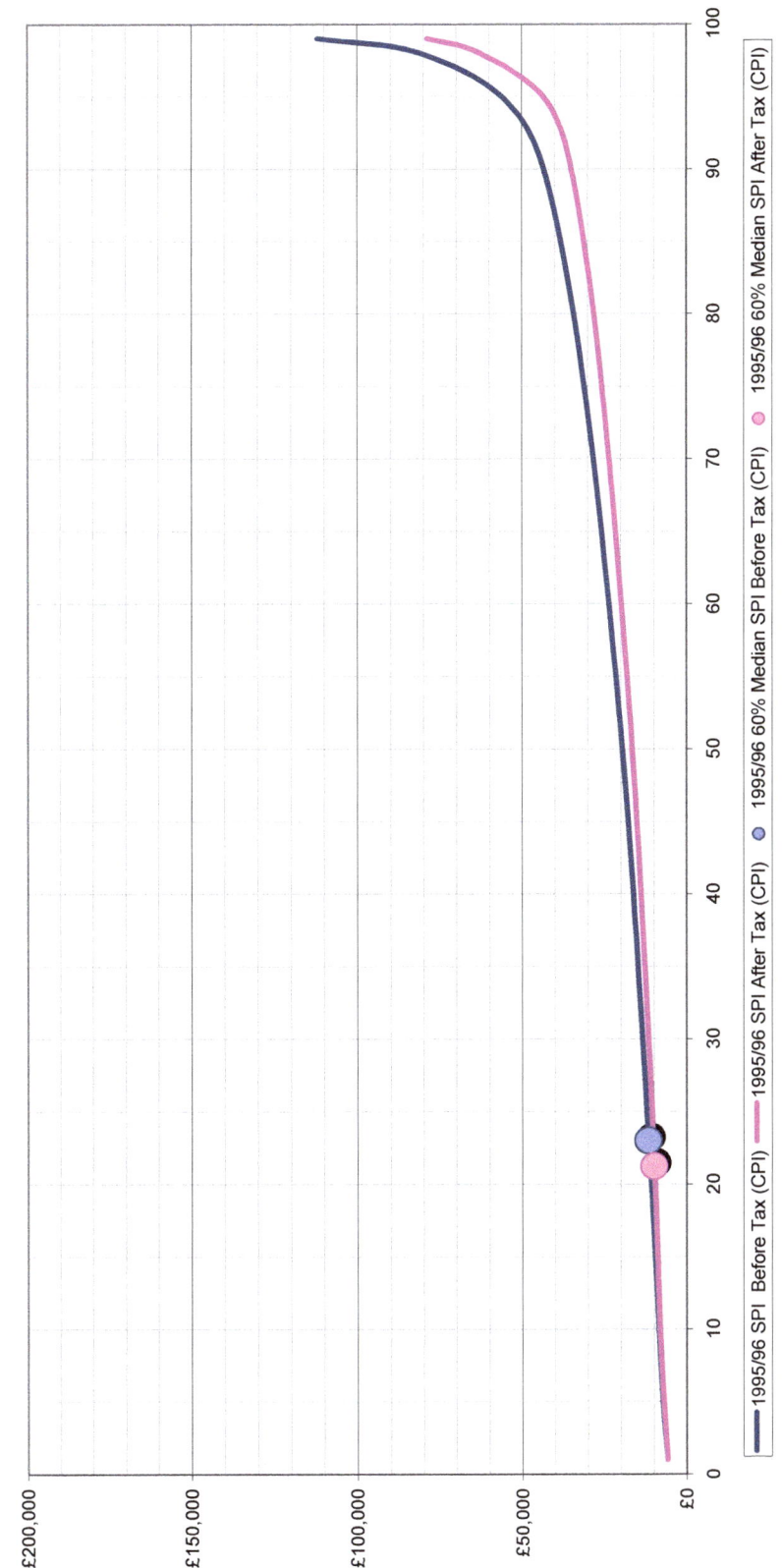

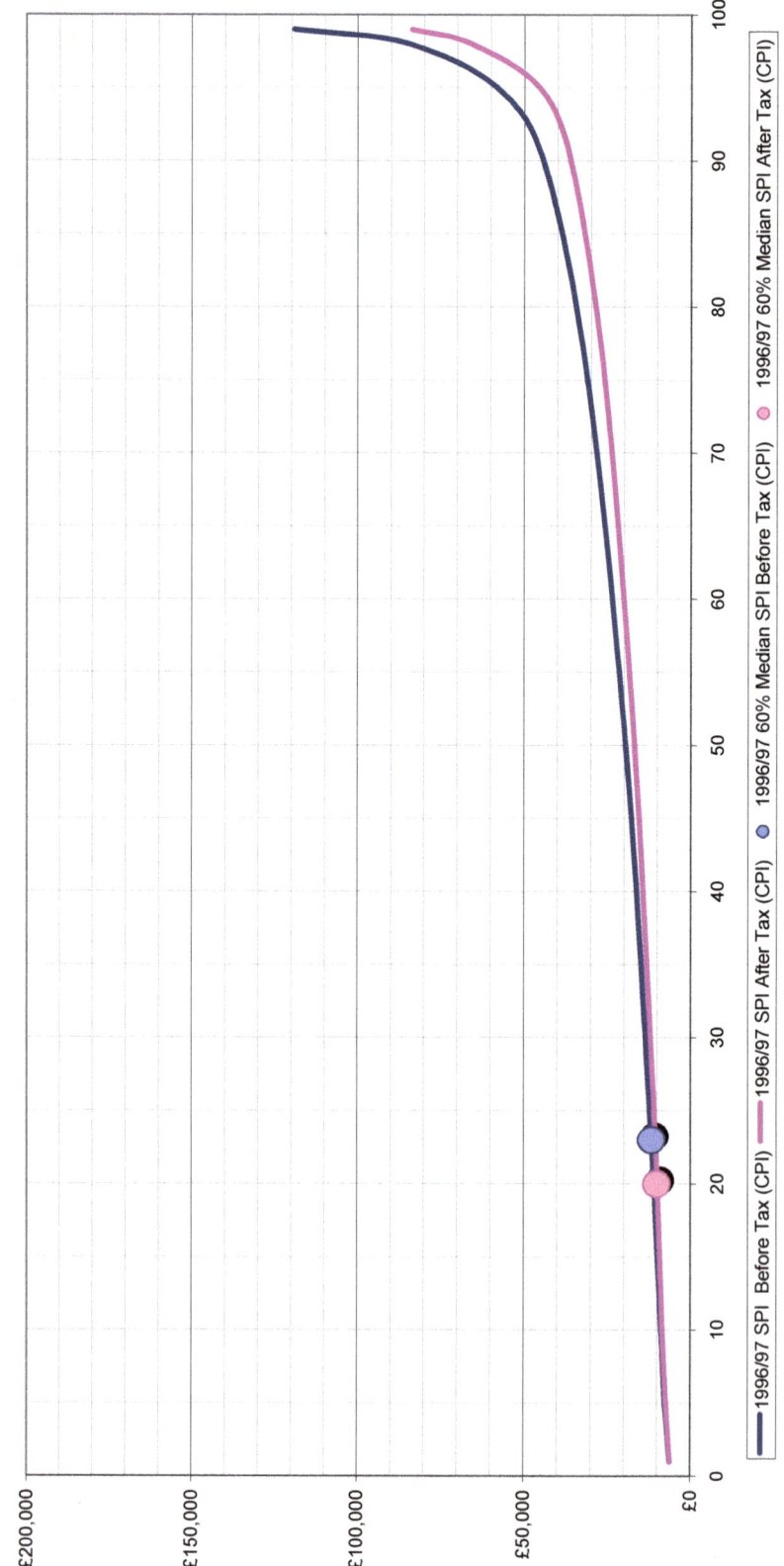

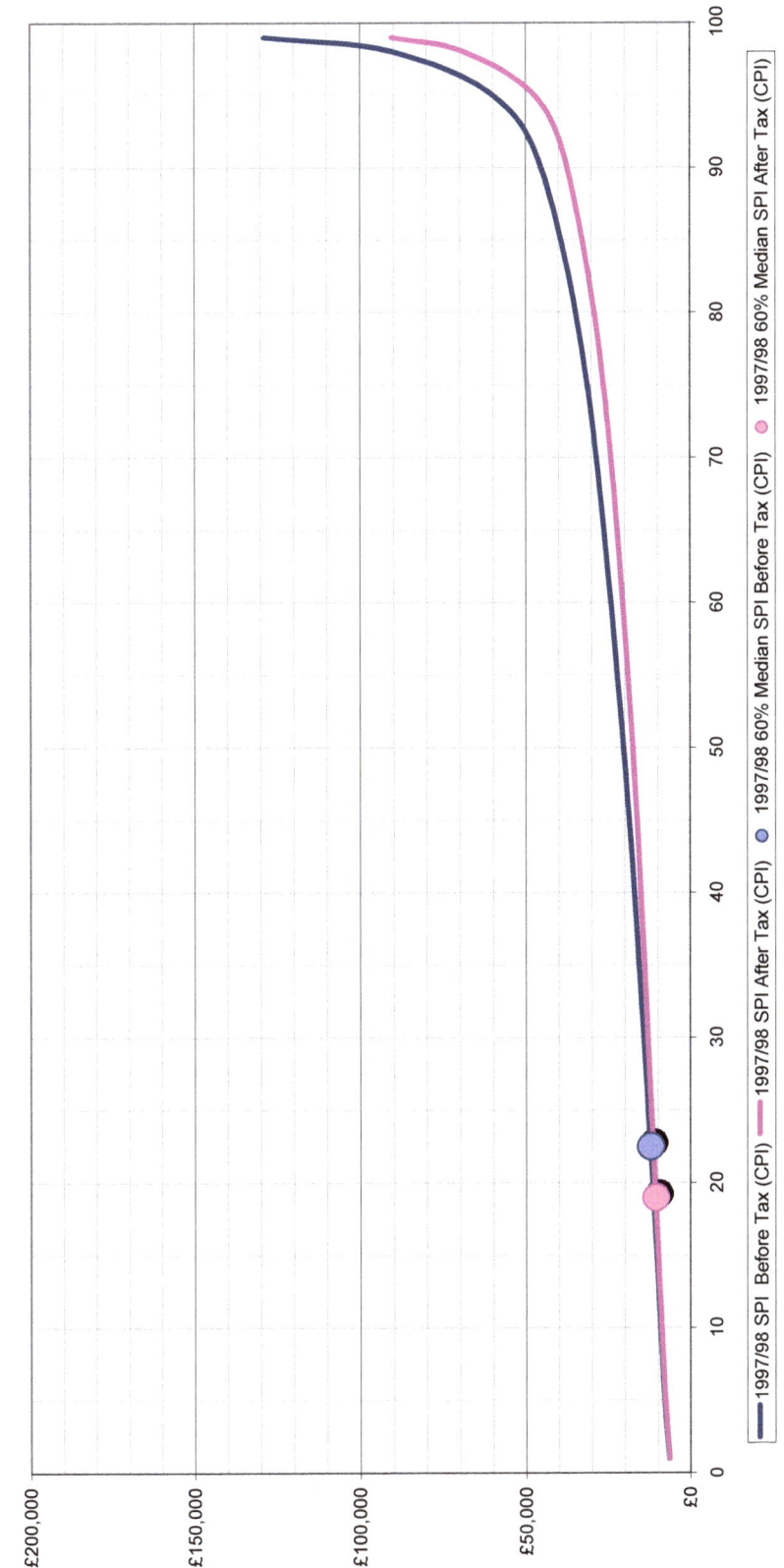

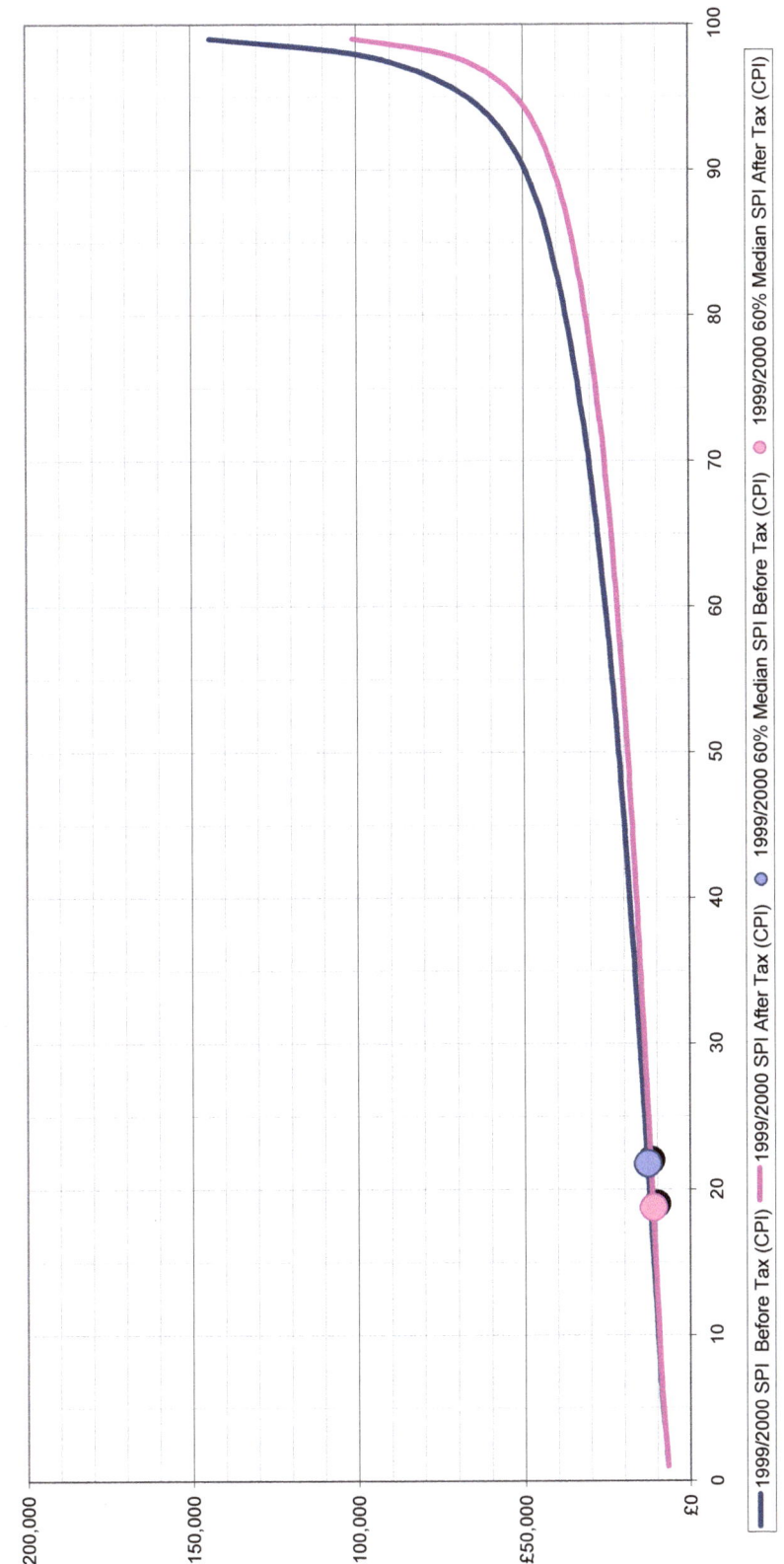

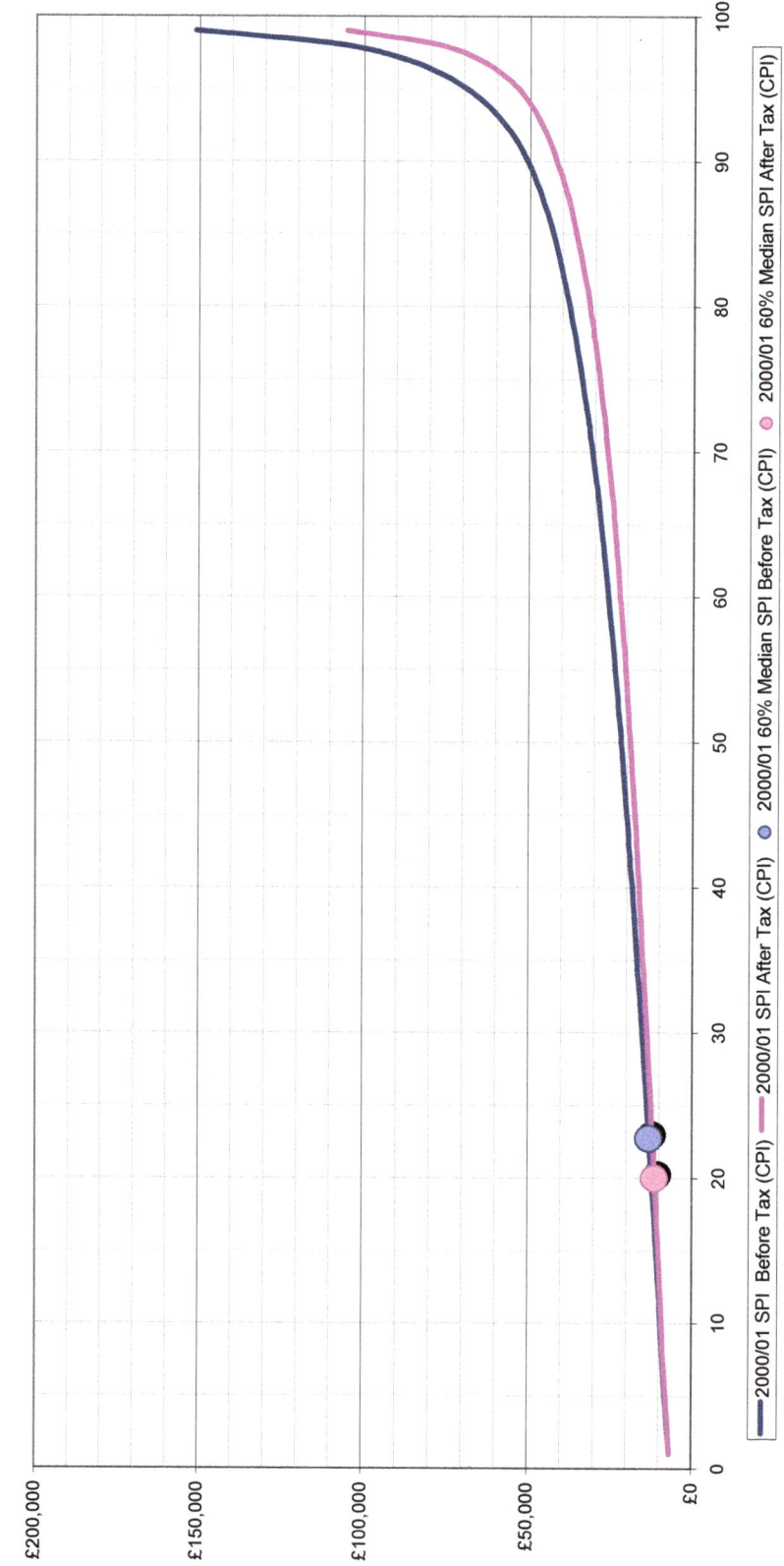

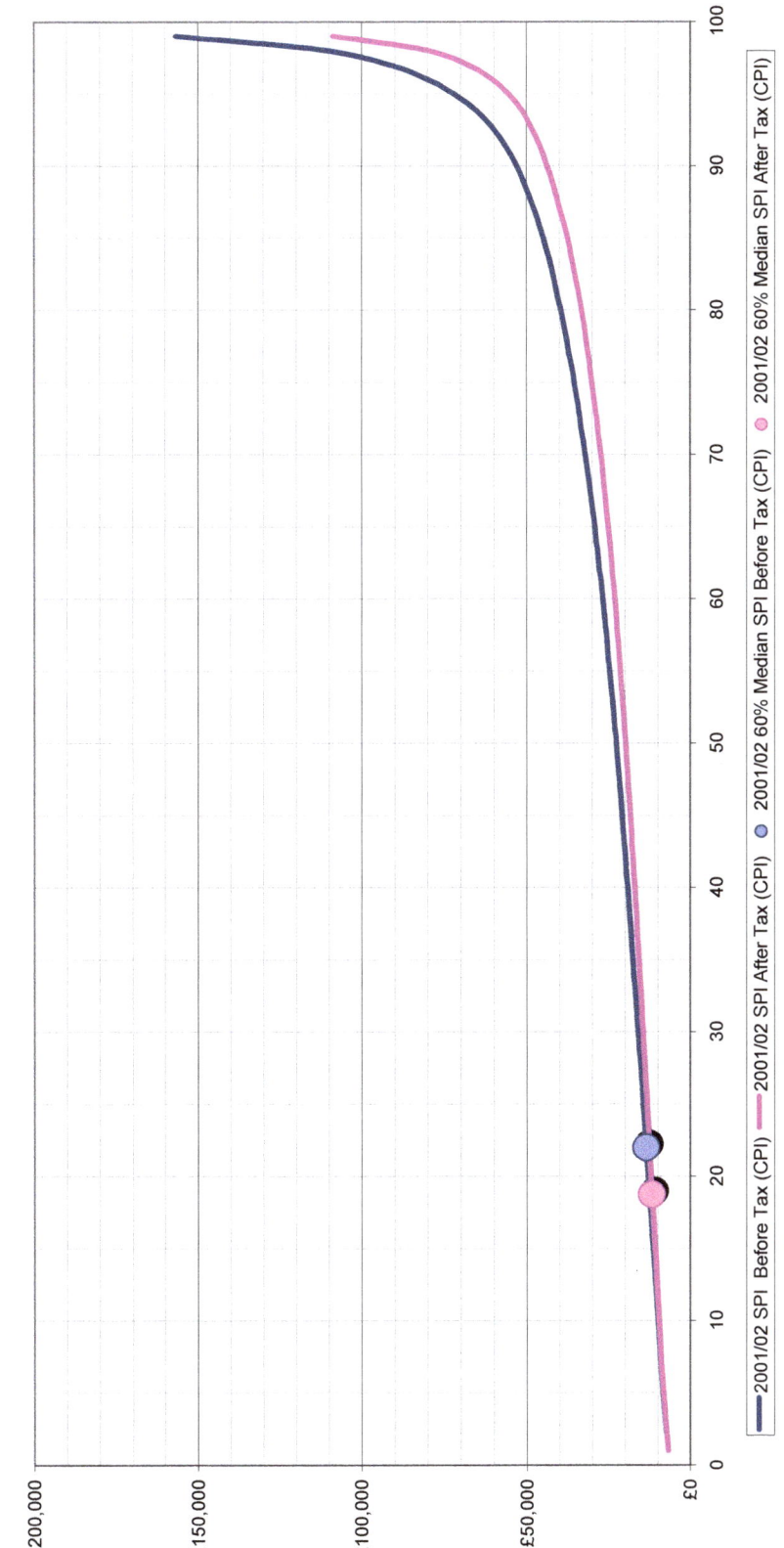

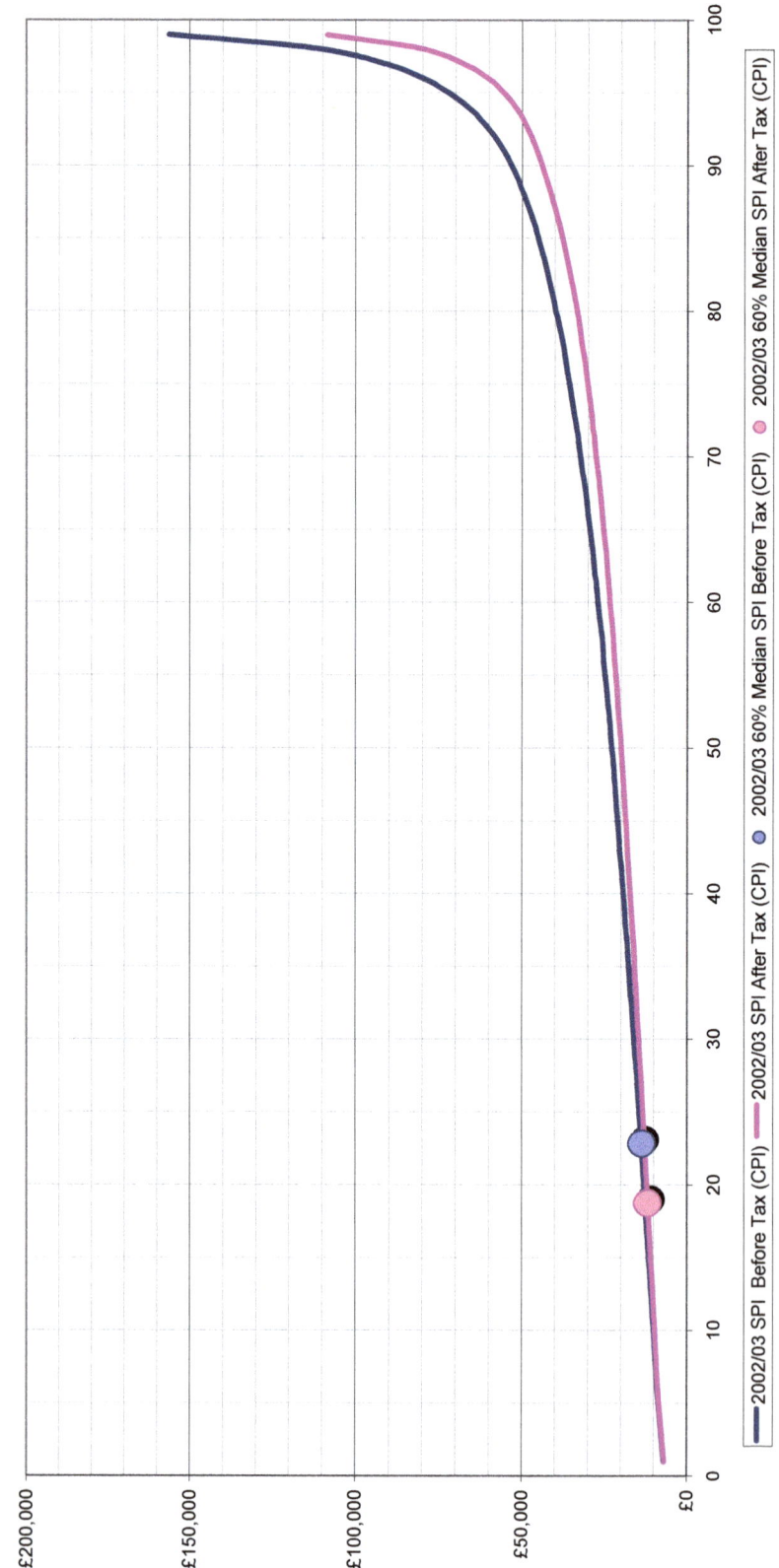

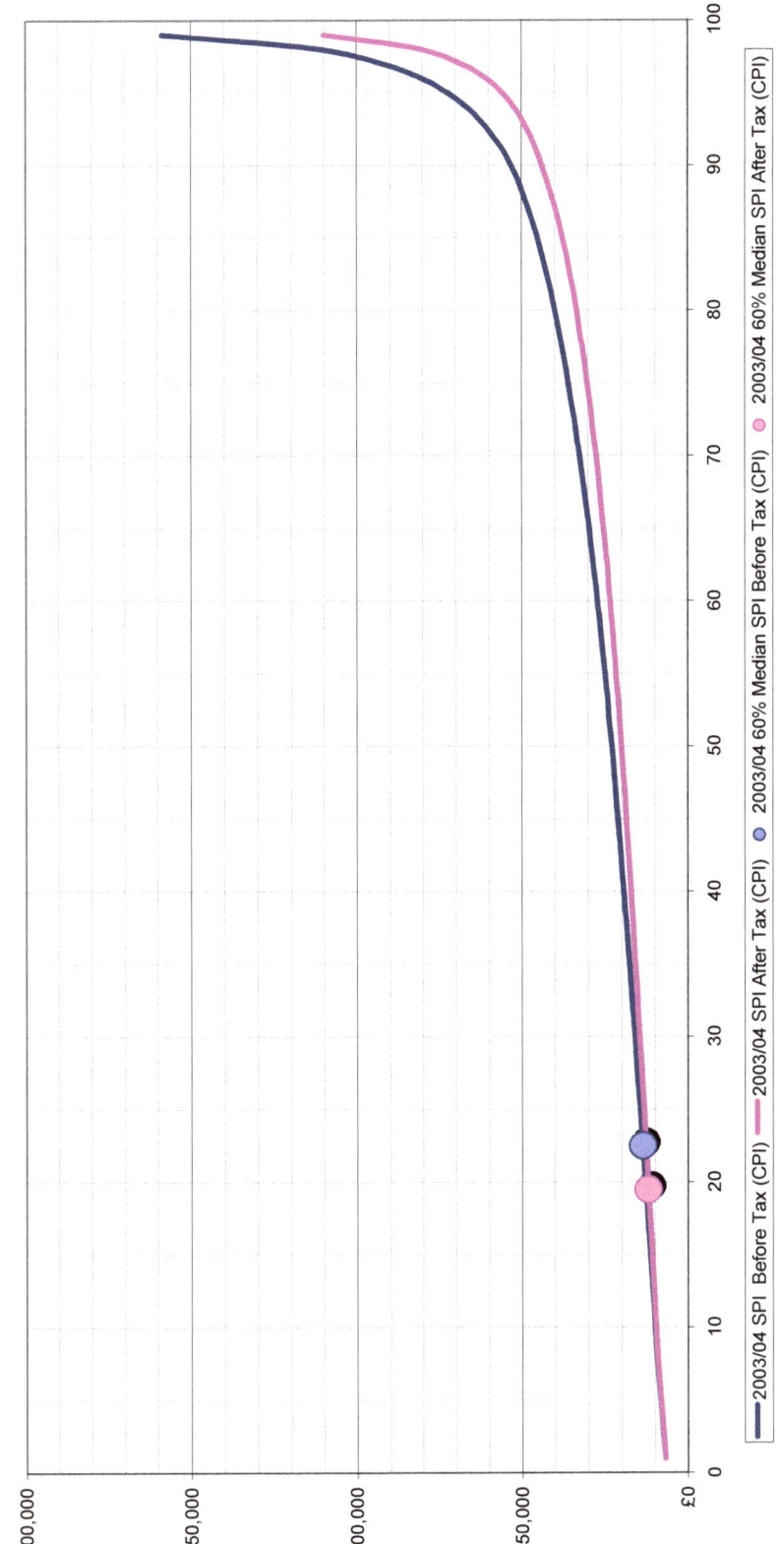

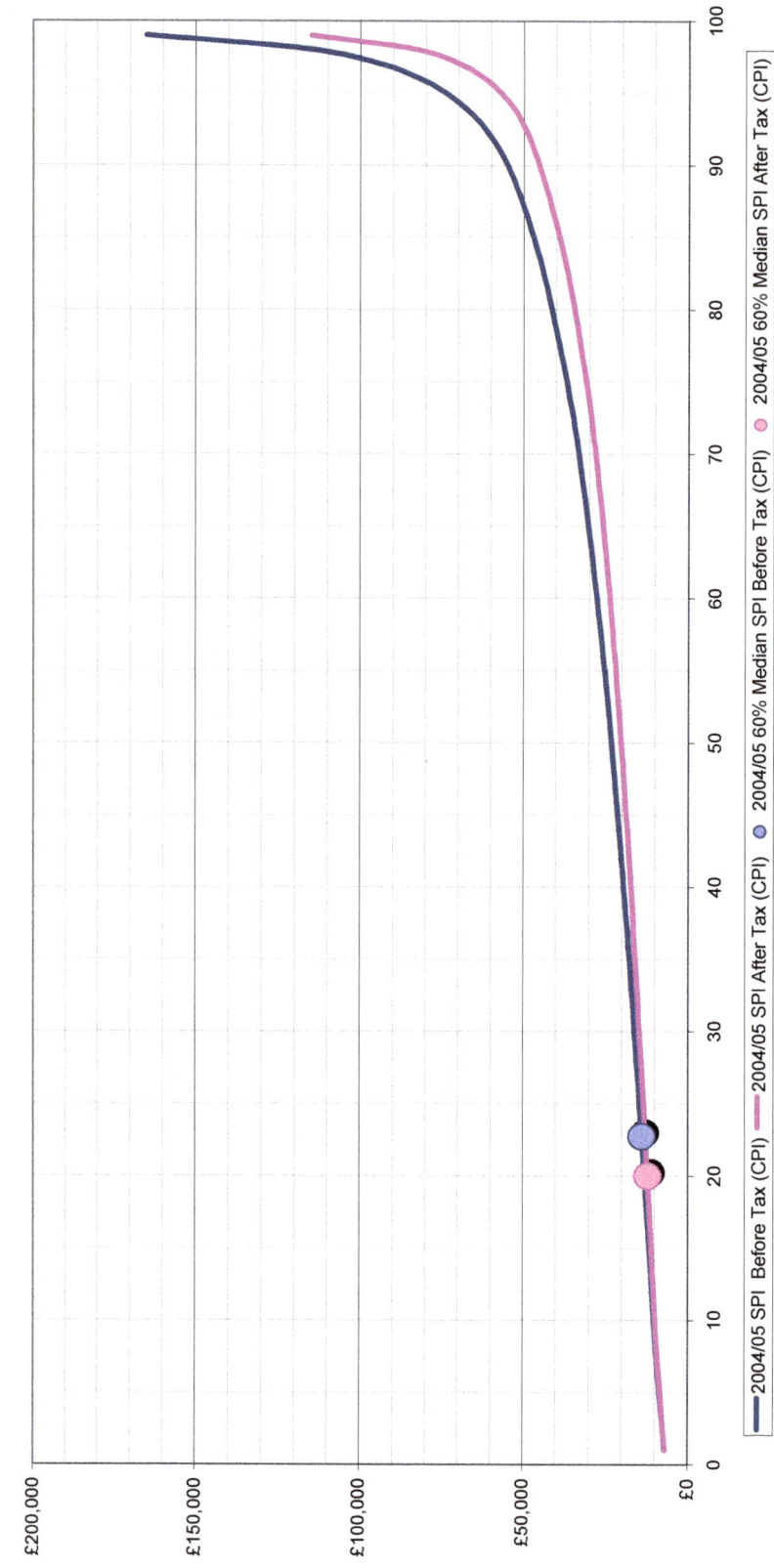

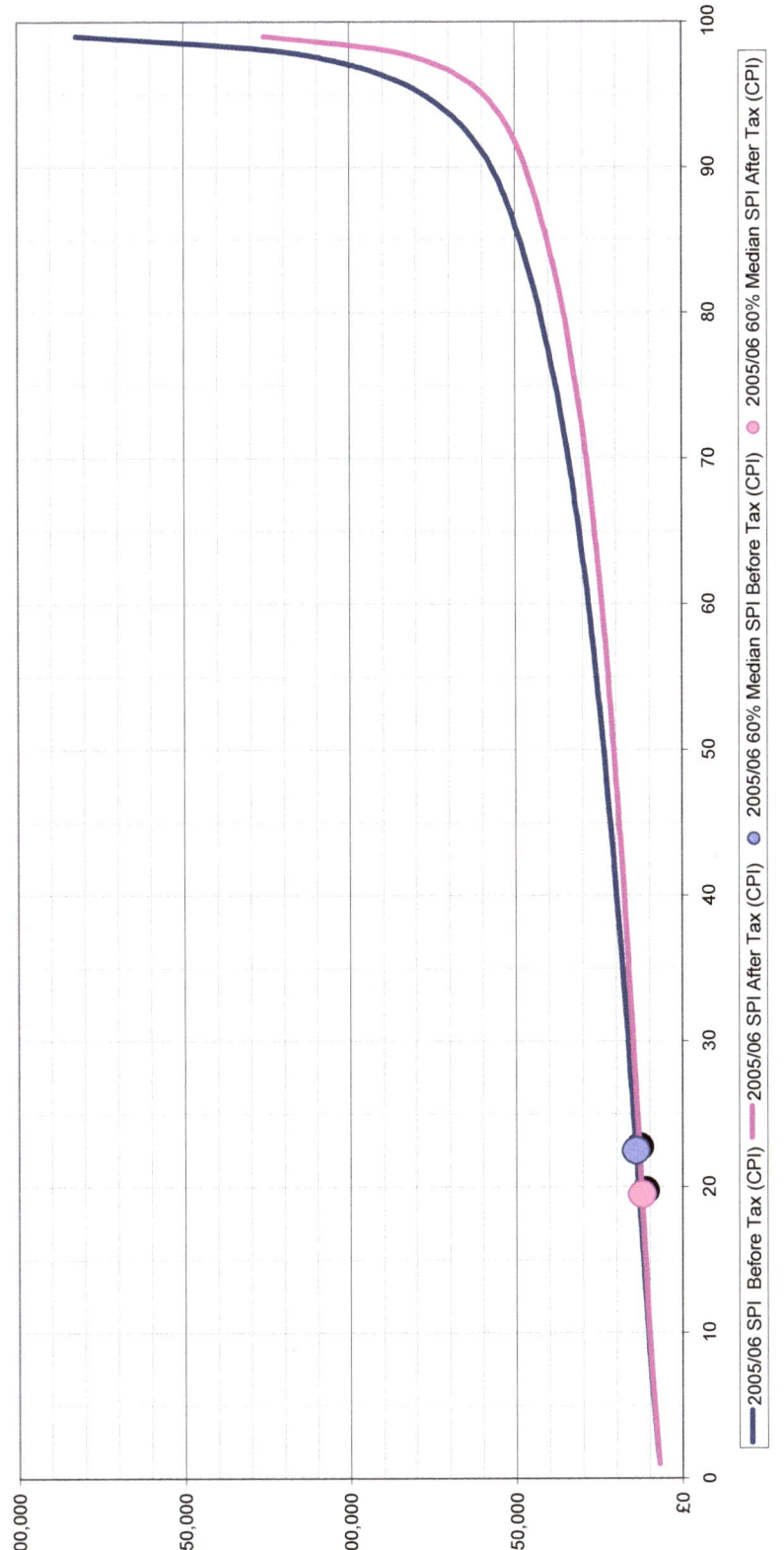

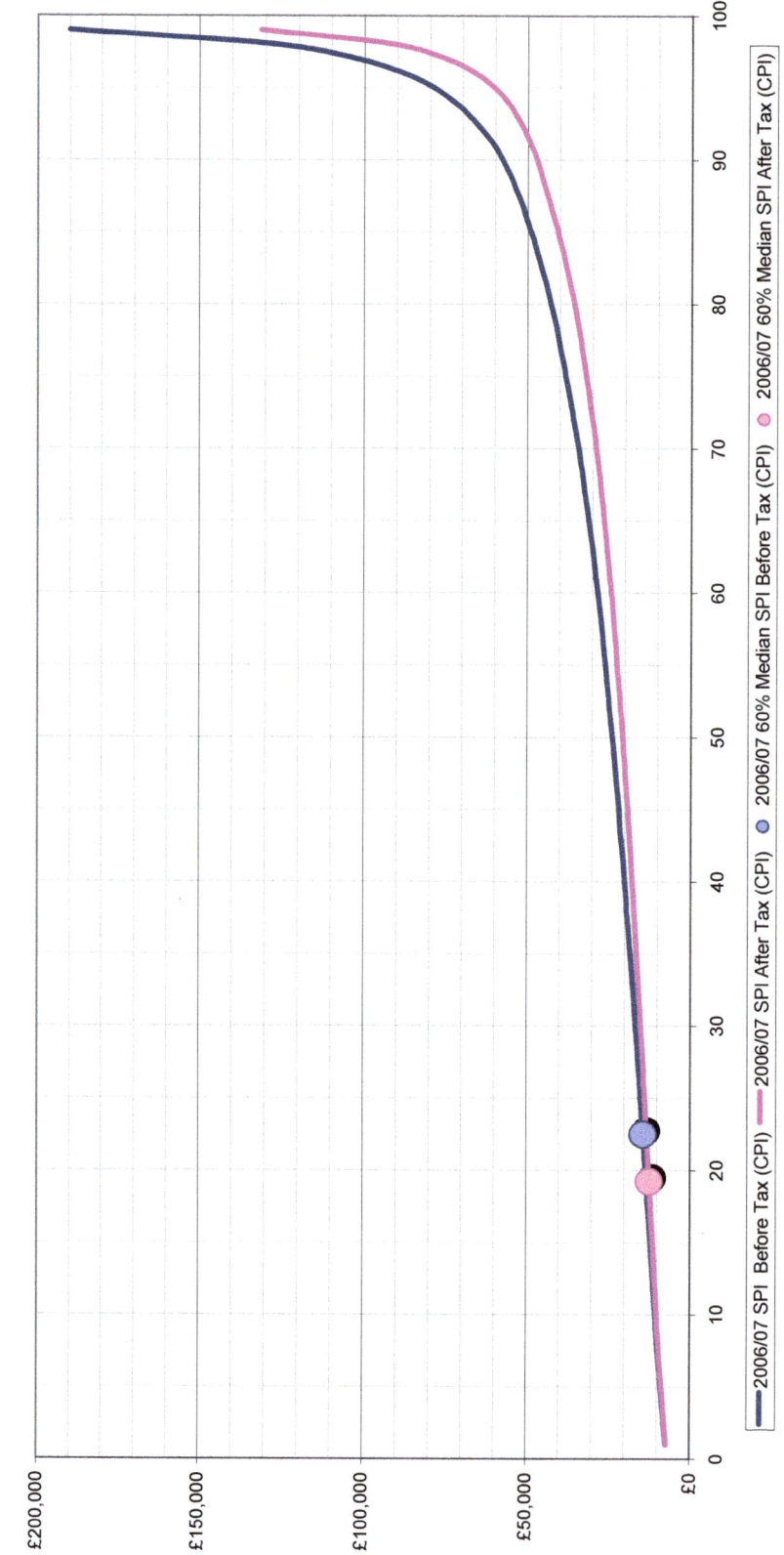

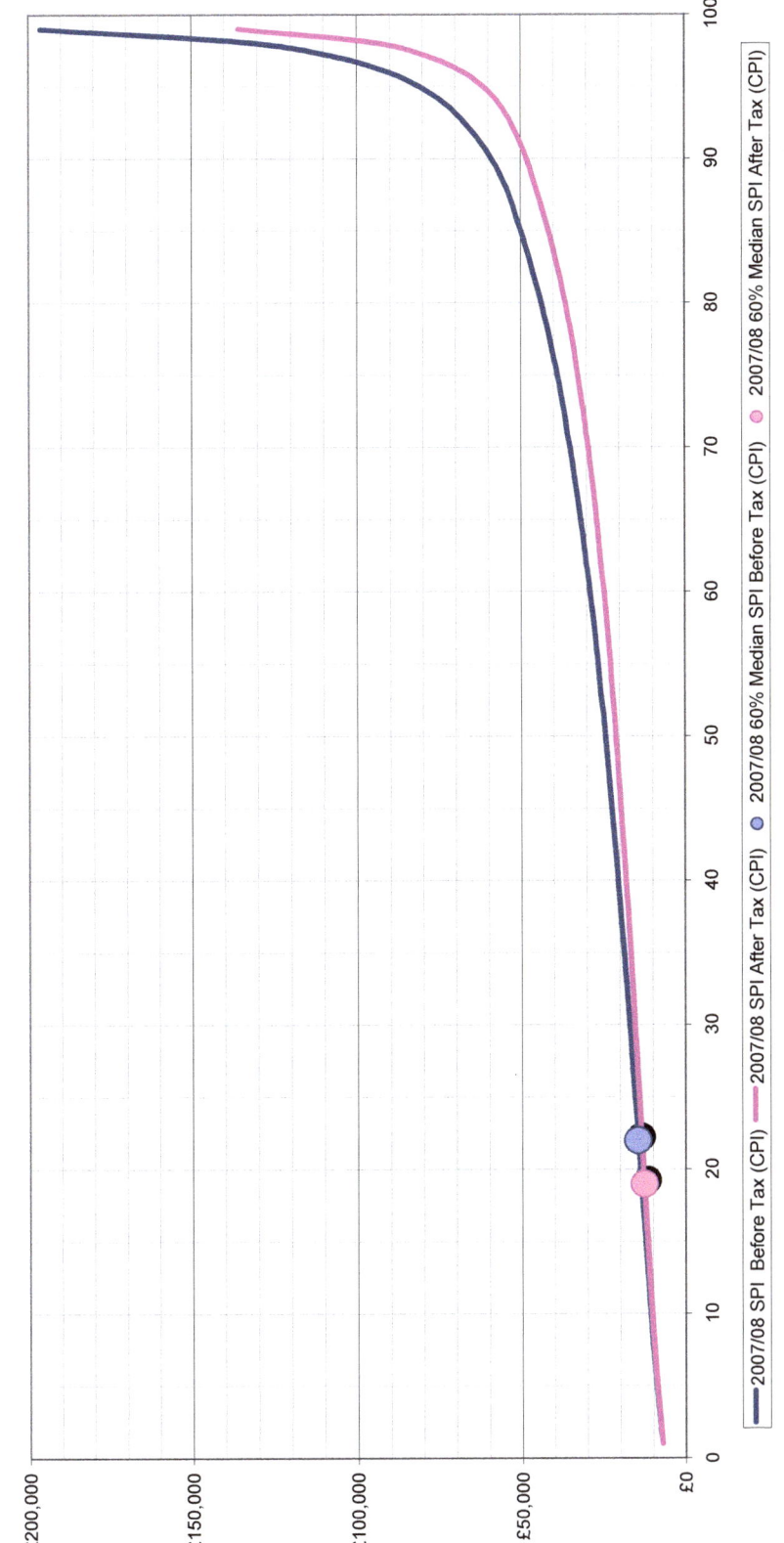

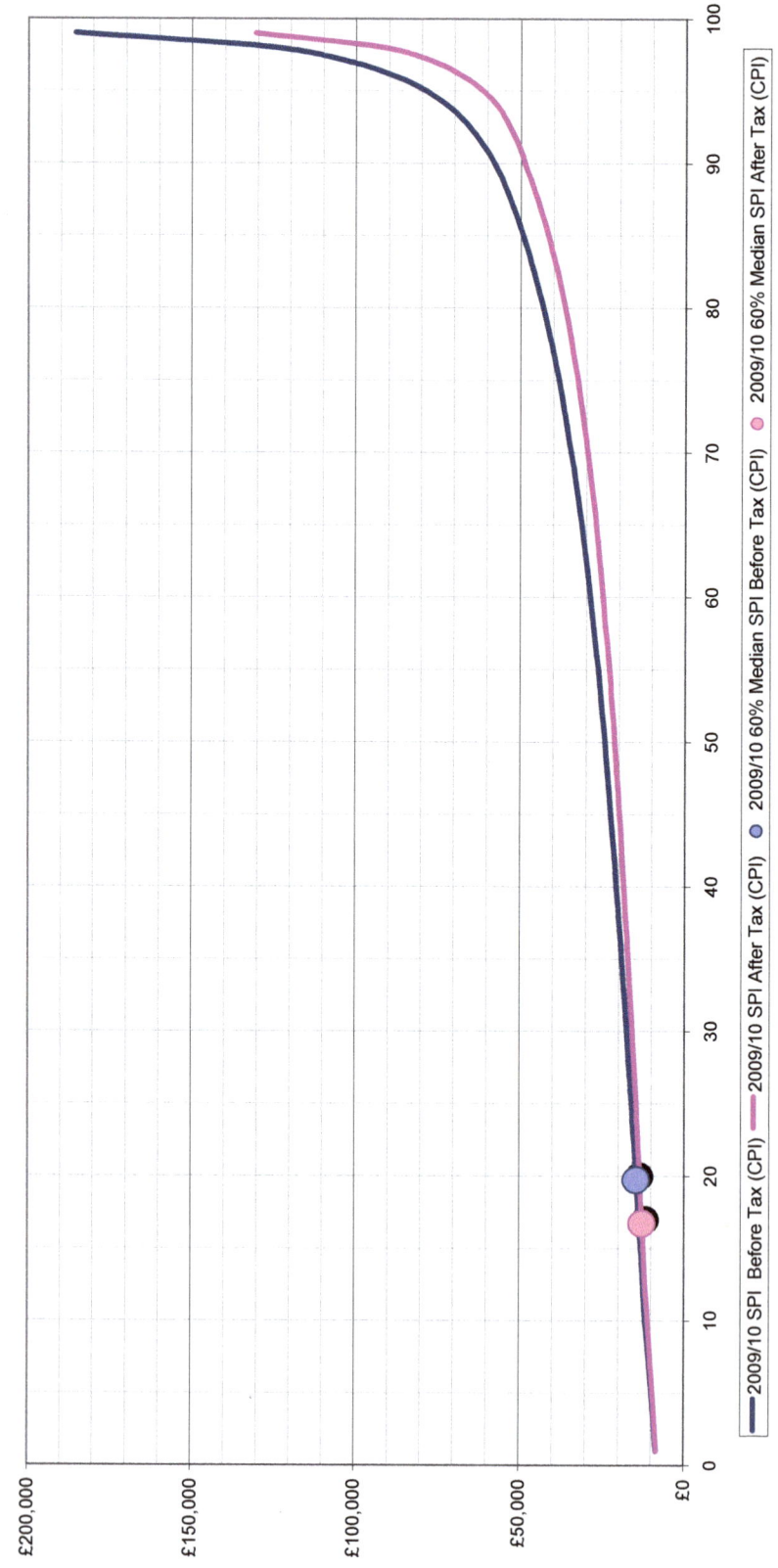

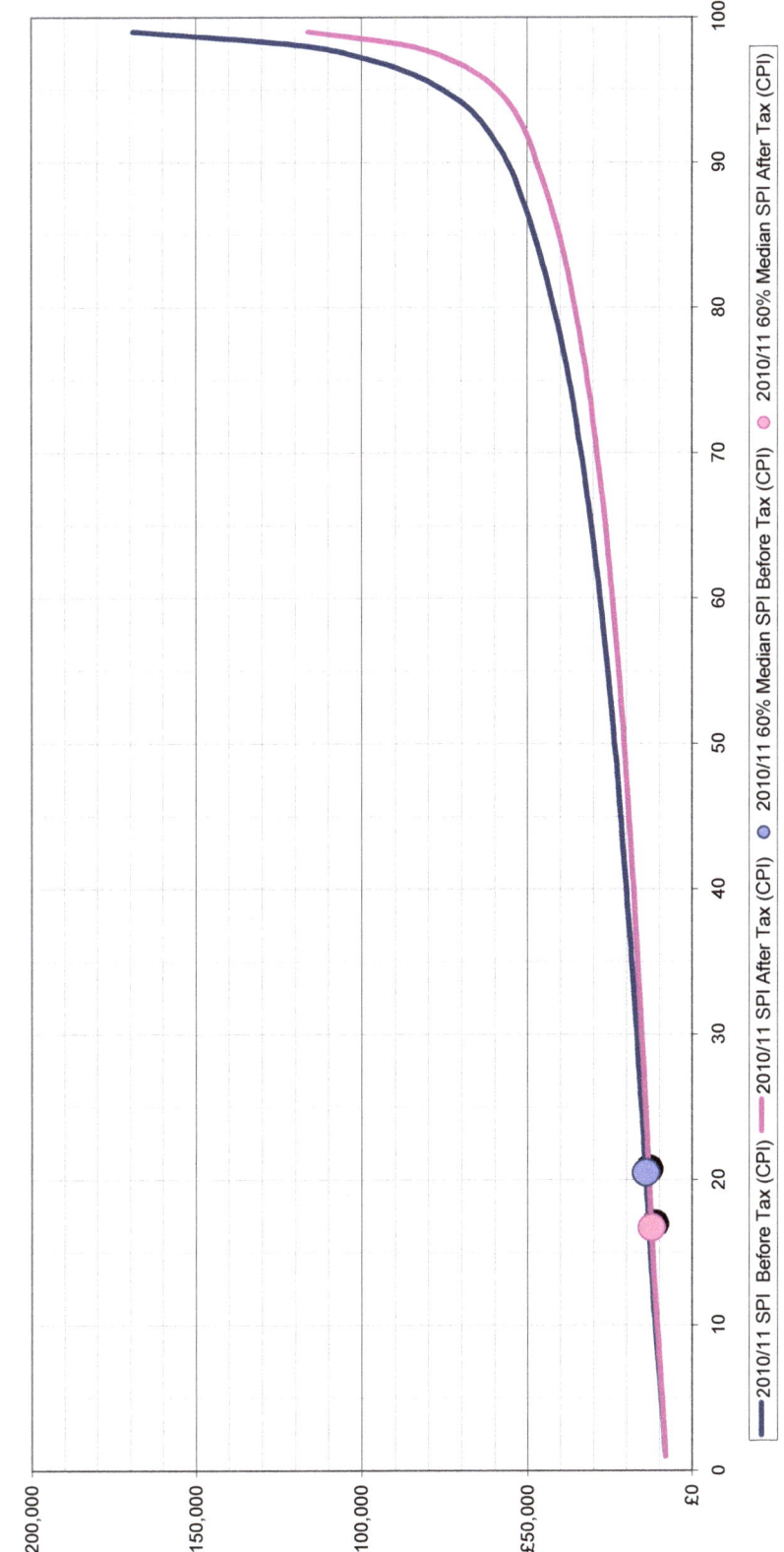

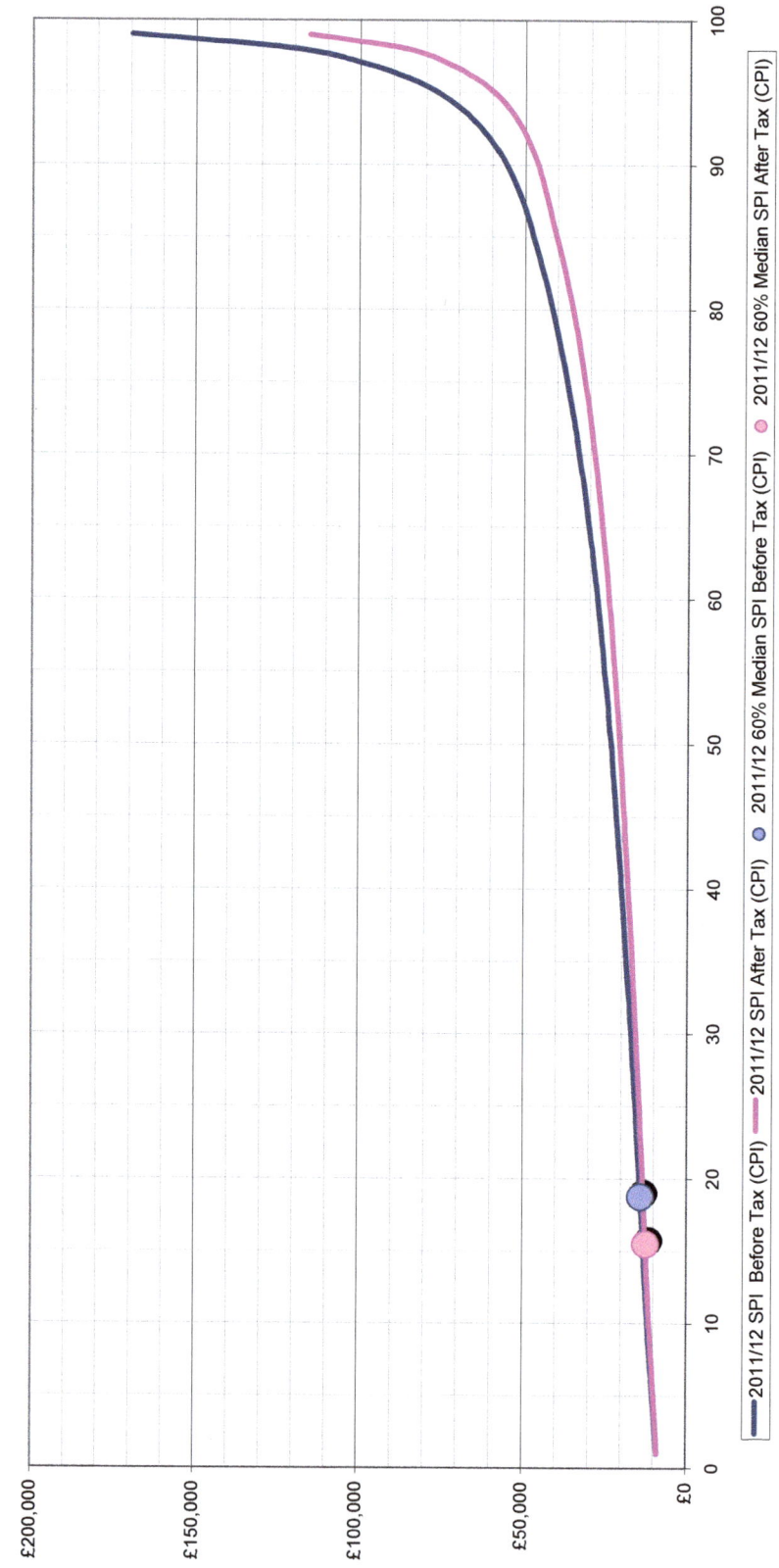

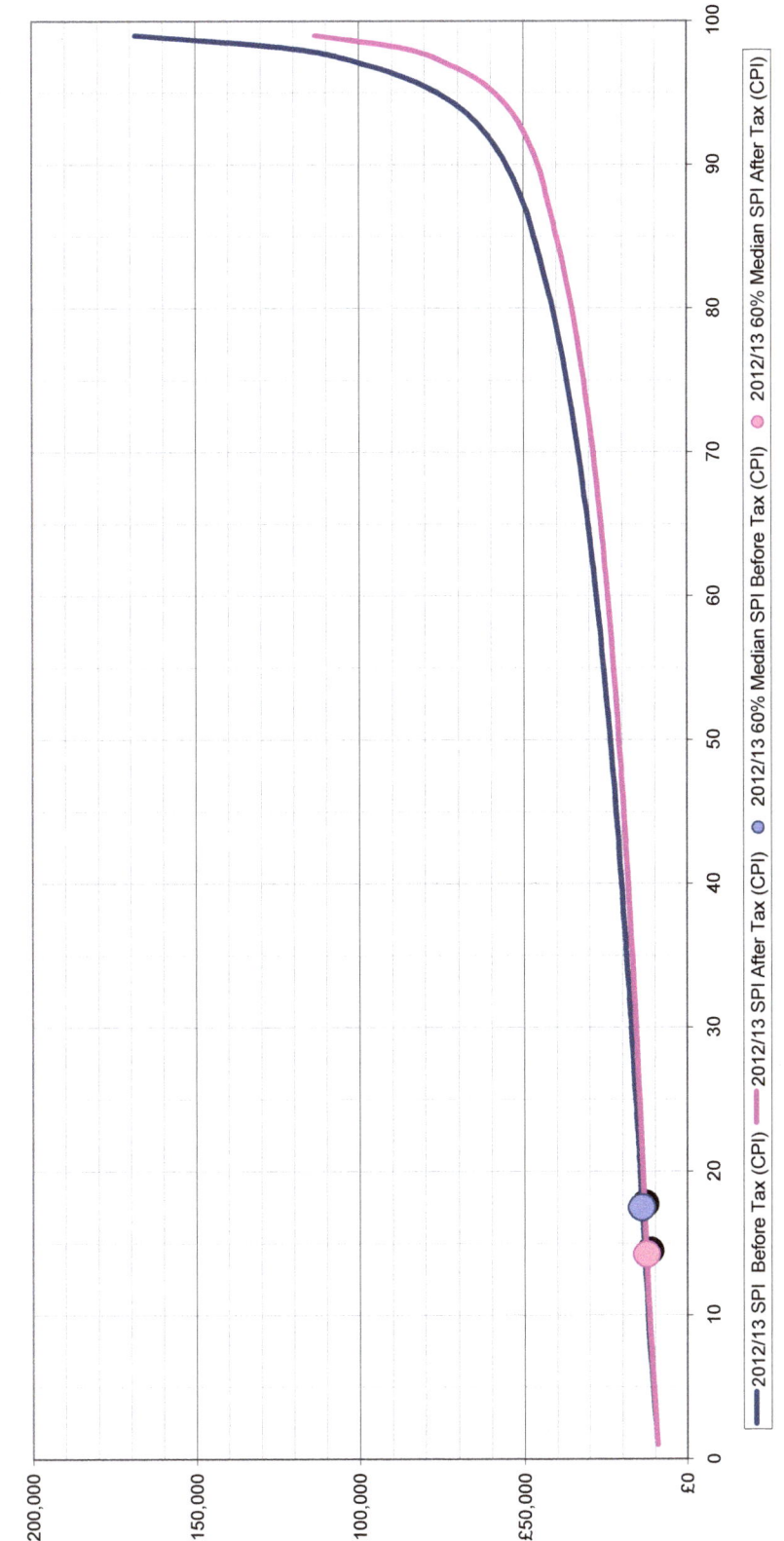

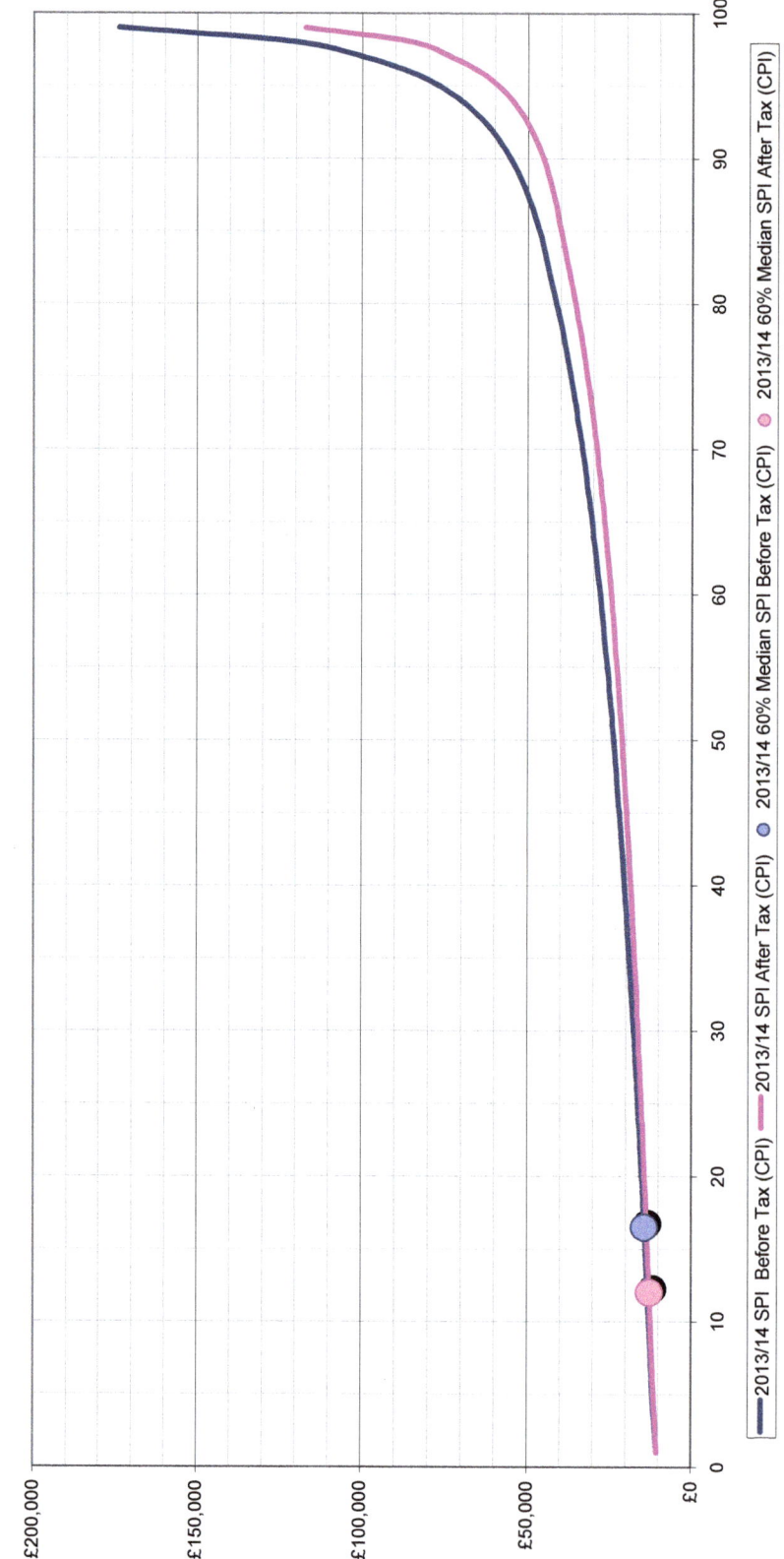

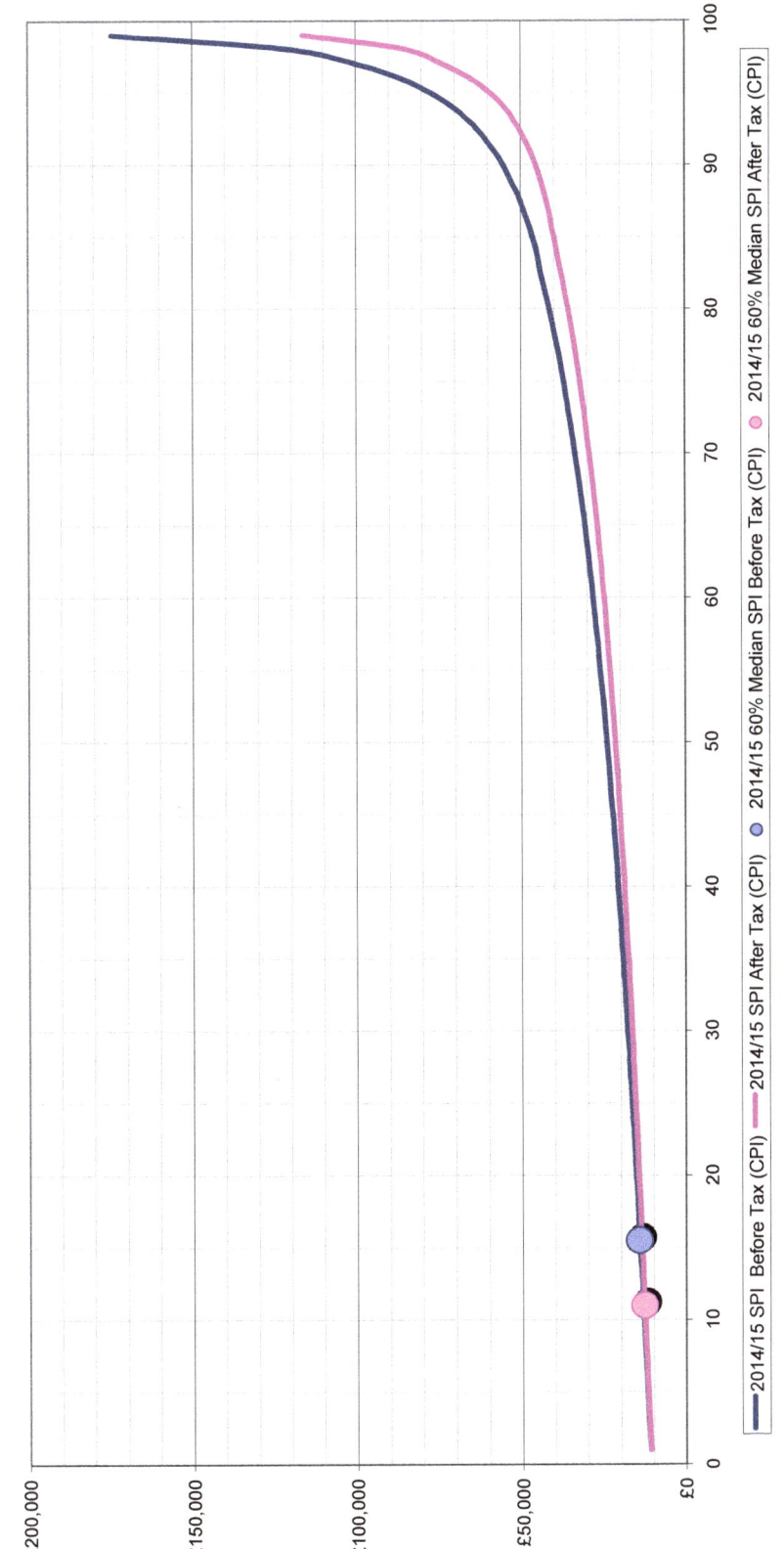

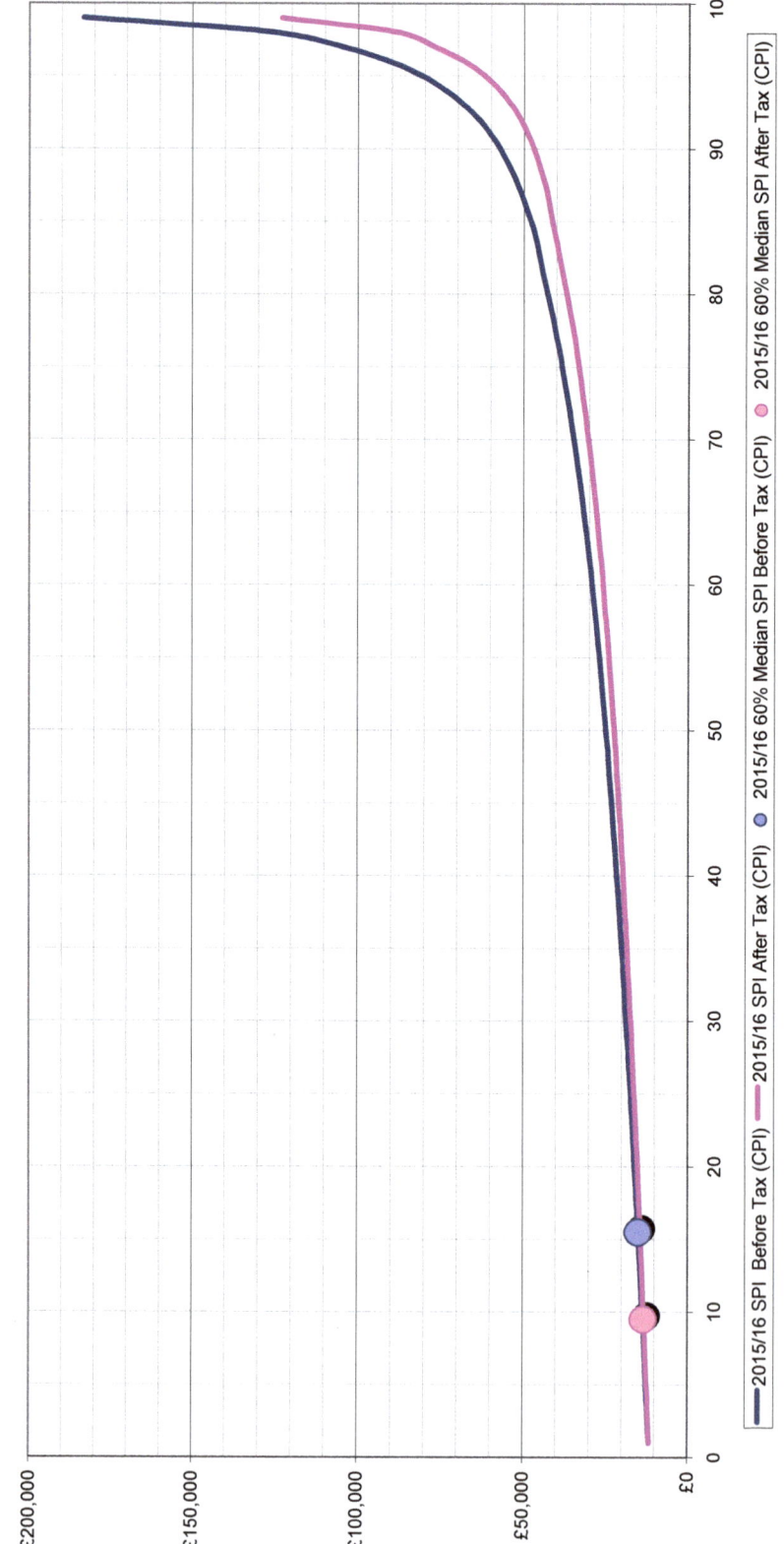

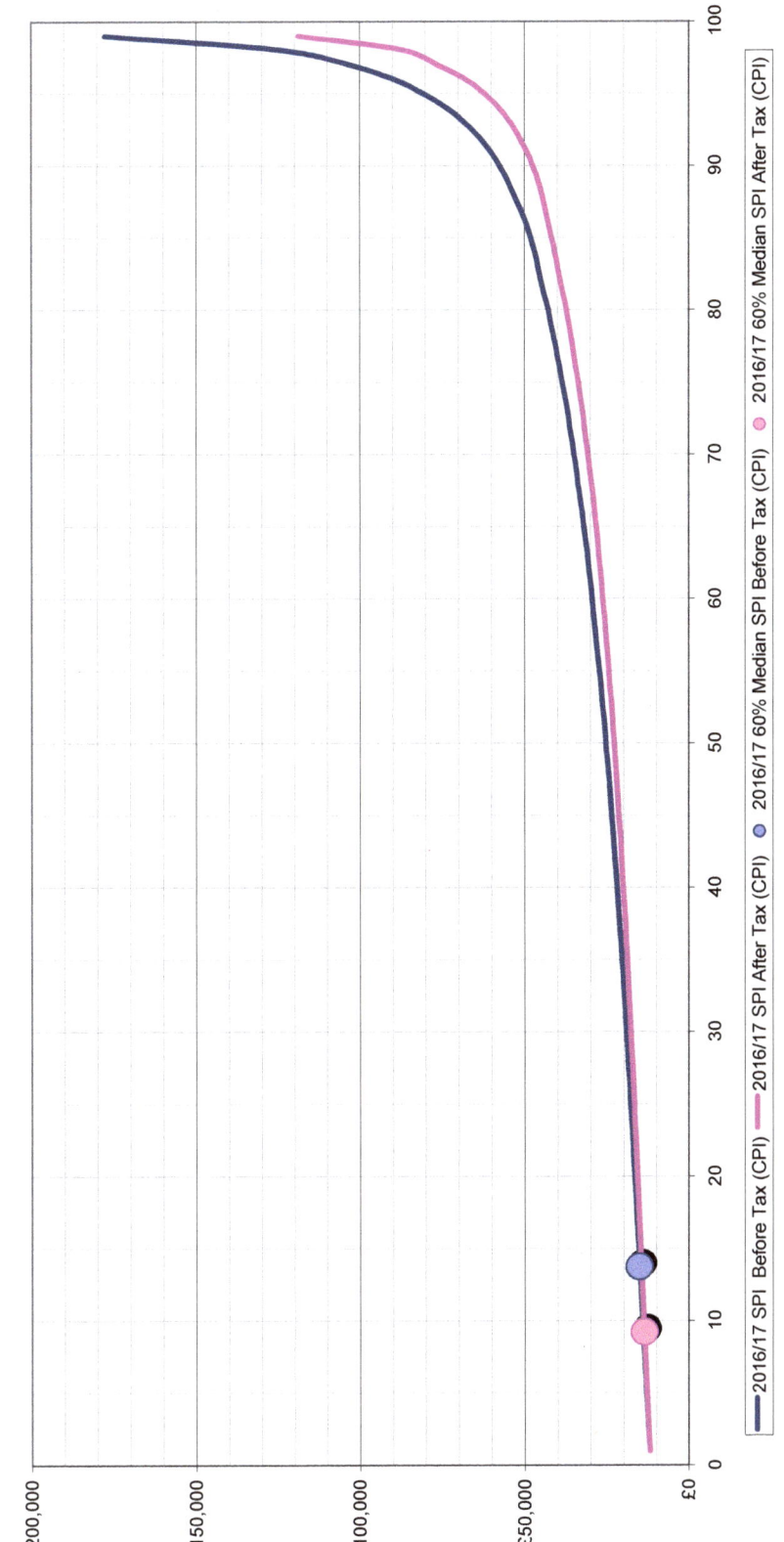

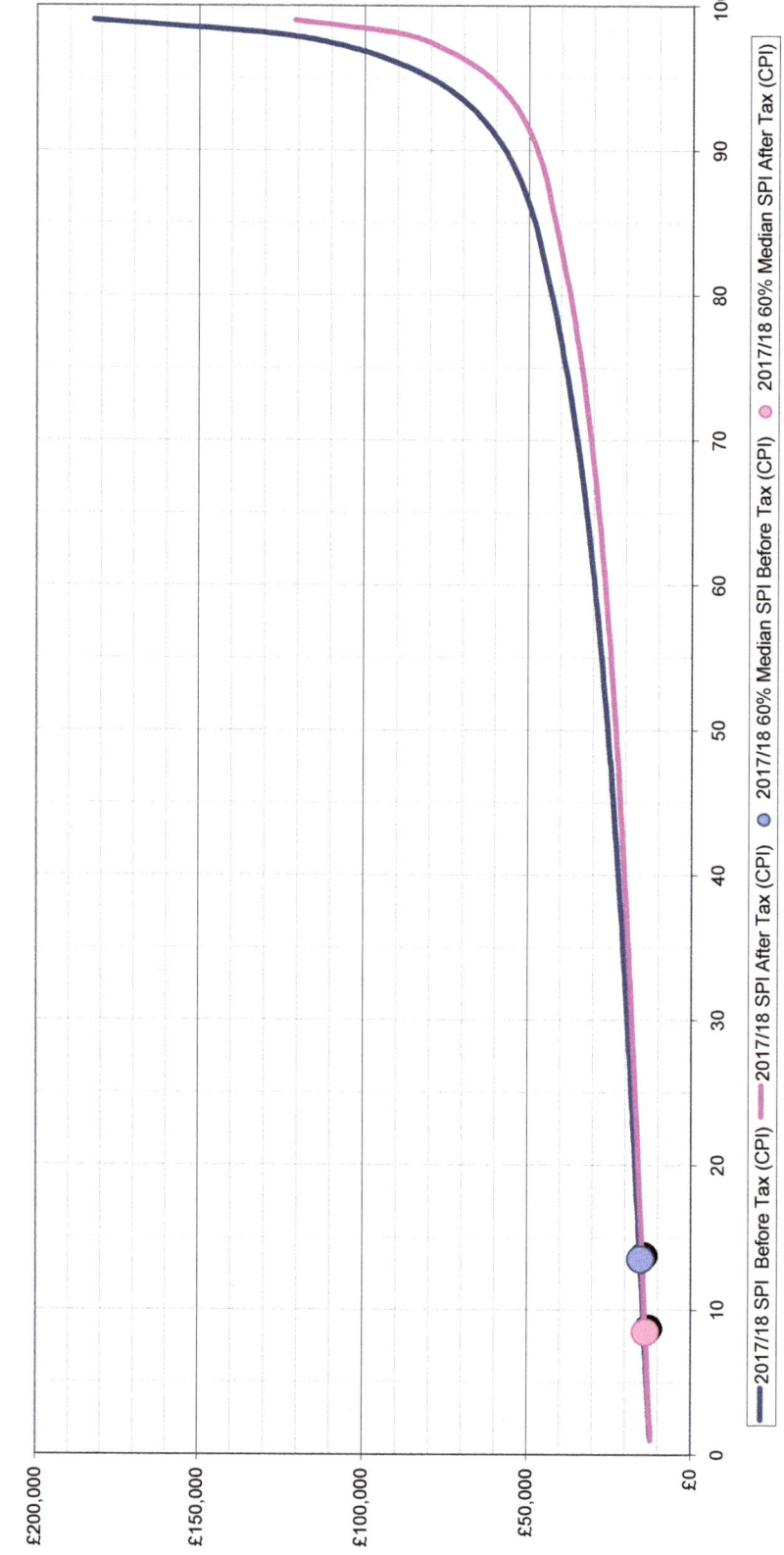

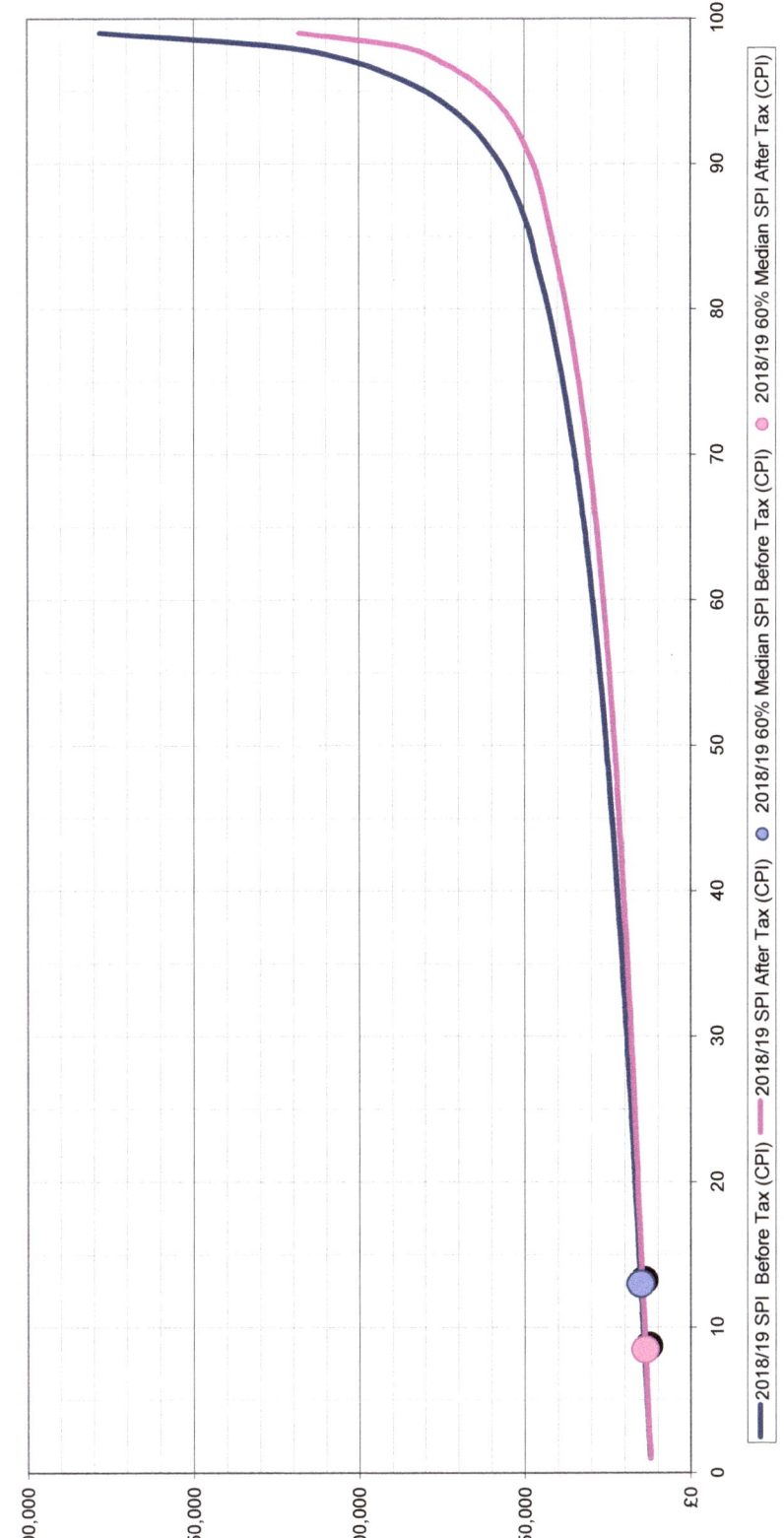

Part of a series - see also:

- UK Economic & Social Change – 1700-2019 – Three centuries of progress
- UK Economy – 1700-1913 – An economy in transition
- UK Economy – 1900-2019 – Growth of the state & world war
- UK Economy – 1990-2019 – Quarter of a century of new changes
- UK Economy – 1990-2019 – Stable income inequality
- UK Household Expenditure – 1700-2019 – Cost of Living
- UK Housing – 1700-2019 – Growth of home ownership
- UK Pauperism, Poverty and Hardship – 1700-2019 – The Retreat of Real Poverty
- UK Pollution (Air Quality), Cars – 1970-2019 – Continuous improvement
- UK Pollution (Air Quality), Energy – 1970-2019 – Continuous improvement
- UK Population & Life Expectancy – 1970-2019 – Continuous Improvement

Bibliography, Selected Reading and Internet Data

"For out of old fields, as men saith,
Cometh all this new corn from year to year;
And out of old books, in good faith,
Cometh all this new science that men learn."

Geoffrey Chaucer:
Parliament of Foules,
1381-1382

Bibliography and Selected Reading

Adelino, N, Schoar, A and Severino, F	(2013) 'Credit Supply and House Prices: Evidence from Mortgage Market Segmentation' National Bureau of Economic Research Working Paper 17832
Adler, Professor M.	(2017) 'Extreme Poverty in the Midst of Unprecedented Affluence - Summary' University of Edinburgh
Adler, Professor M.	(2017) 'Extreme Poverty in the Midst of Unprecedented Affluence' University of Edinburgh
Adler, Professor M.	(2018) 'Cruel, Inhuman or Degrading Treatment? Benefit Sanctions in the UK' Palgrave Macmillan ISBN: 978-3-319-90355-2
Ainsworth, R. B.	(1949) 'Earnings and Working Hours of Manual Wage-Earners the United Kingdom in October, 1938' Wiley DOI: 10.2307/2984178

Akhtar, Galaiya and Reynolds	(2014) 'Residential mortgages: a comparison of the Bank of England's published statistical and regulatory data collections' Bank of England
Allen, Professor R. C.	(1994) 'Real Incomes in the English Speaking World, 1879-1913 (from Labour Market Evolution)' Routledge ISBN: 978-0-415-10865-2
Allen, Professor R. C.	(2007) 'Pessimism Preserved: Real Wages in the British Industrial Revolution' University of Oxford Working Paper 314
Allen, Professor R. C.	(2009) 'Engels' pause: Technical change, capital accumulation, and inequality in the British Industrial Revolution' Science Direct DOI: 10.1016/j.eeh.2009.04.004
Allen, Professor R. C.	(2009) 'The British Industrial Revolution in Global Perspective' Cambridge University Press ISBN: 978-0-521-68785-0
Allen, Professor R. C.	(2016) 'Revising England's Social Tables Once Again' University of Oxford Discussion Paper Number: 146
Allen, Professor R. C.	(2018) 'Class structure and inequality during the industrial revolution: lessons from England's social tables, 1688–1867' Wiley DOI: 10.1111/ehr.12661
Alvaredo, F., Atkinson, A. B., Morelli, S.	(2018) 'Top wealth shares in the UK over more than a century' Science Direct DOI: 10.1016/j.jpubeco.2018.02.008
Anon.	(1823/1828) 'A New System of Practical Domestic Economy'
Arkell, T.	(2006) 'Illuminations and Distortions, Gregory King's Scheme Calculated for the Year 1688' Wiley DOI: 10.1111/j.1468-0289.2005.00330.x
Armstrong, W. A.	(1981) 'The Influence of Demographic Factors on the Position of the Agricultural Labourer in England and Wales, c1750-1914' British Agricultural History Society The Agricultural History Review, Vol. 29, No. 2 (1981), pp. 71-82
Ashworth, H.	(1842) 'Statistics of the Present Depression of Trade in Bolton' Wiley DOI: 10.2307/2337951
Atkinson, Professor A. B.	(1997) 'Distribution of Income and Wealth in Britain over the Twentieth Century (from Twentieth Century British Social Trends)' Springer ISBN: 978-0-333-72149-0
Atkinson, Professor A. B.	(2002) 'Top Incomes in the United Kingdom over the Twentieth Century' University of Oxford Discussion Paper No 43
Atkinson, Professor A. B.	(2005) 'Top Incomes in the United Kingdom over the Twentieth Century' Wiley DOI: 10.1111/j.1467-985X.2005.00351.x
Atkinson, Professor A. B.	(2007) 'The Distribution of Top Incomes in the United Kingdom 1908–2000 (from Top Incomes over the 20th Century)' Oxford University Press ISBN: 978-0-199-28688-1
Atkinson, Professor A. B.	(2013) 'Wealth and Inheritance in Britain from 1896 to the Present' London School of Economics CASE/178
Atkinson, Professor A. B.	(2016) 'Pareto and the upper tail of the income distribution in the UK: 1799 to the present' London School of Economics CASE papers (198)
Atkinson, Professor A. B. and Jenkins, S. P.	(2019) 'A different perspective on the evolution of UK income inequality' London School of Economics Working Paper 01-19

Atkinson, Professor A. B., Piketty, T. and Saez, E.	(2011) 'Top Incomes in the Long Run of History' American Economic Association DOI: 10.1257/jel.49.1.3
Ayres, Professor J. G. (Chair) and Hurley J. F. (Chair)	(2010) 'The Mortality Effects of Long-Term Exposure to Particulate Air Pollution in the United Kingdom' COMEAP ISBN: 978-0-85951-685-3
Banks, J. and Johnson, P.	(1998) 'How Reliable is the Family Expenditure Survey' Institute for Fiscal Studies ISBN: 978-1-873357-70-2
Baxter, R. D.	(1868) 'National Income. The United Kingdom' MacMillan and Co.
Baxter, R. D.	(1869) 'The Taxation of the United Kingdom' MacMillan and Co.
Belfield et al.	(2017) 'Two decades of income inequality in Britain: the role of wages, household earnings and redistribution' The Institute for Fiscal Studies Working Paper W17/01
Belfield, Chandler and Joyce	(2015) 'Housing: Trends in Prices, Costs and Tenure' Institute for Fiscal Studies ISBN: 978-1-909463-79-0
Berry, Harrison, Ryland & de Weymarn	(2007) 'Interpreting movements in broad money' Bank of England BofE Quarterly Bulletin
Block, F. and Somers, M.	(2003) 'In the shadow of Speenhamland Social Policy and the Old Poor Law' Sage Publications DOI: 10.1177/0032329203252272
Bogdanor, Professor V. B.	(2016) 'The IMF Crisis, 1976: Transcript' Gresham College, Oxford
Bolton	(2019) 'Student Loan Statistics' House of Commons Library Briefing Paper 1079
Booth, C.	(1892) 'Life and Labour of the People in London' MacMillan and Co.
Booth, C.	(1904) 'Life and Labour of the People in London' MacMillan and Co.
Bosanquet, S. R.	(1841) 'The Rights of the Poor and Christian Alms Giving Vindicated'
Boulter, Thorpe, Harrison and Allen	(2005) 'Road vehicle non-exhaust particulate matter: final report on emission modelling' TRL Limited
Bourquin and Waters	(2019) 'The effect of taxes and benefits on UK inequality' The Institute for Fiscal Studies Briefing Note No 249
Bourquin, Cribb, Waters and Xu	(2019) 'Living standards, poverty and inequality in the UK: 2019' The Institute for Fiscal Studies ISBN: 978-1-912-80527-3
Bowley, Professor Sir A. L.	(1900) 'Wages in the United Kingdom in the Nineteenth Century' Cambridge University Press
Bowley, Professor Sir A. L.	(1920) 'The Change in the distribution of National Income 1880-1913' Clarenden Press (Oxford)
Bowley, Professor Sir A. L.	(1937) 'Wages and Income in the United Kingdom Since 1860' Cambridge University Press ISBN: 978-1-316-50960-9
Boyer, Professor G. R.	(2019) 'The Winding Road to the Welfare State - Economic Insecurity & Social Welfare Policy in Britain' Princeton University Press ISBN: 978-0-691-17873-8
Boyer, Professor G. R. and Hatton, Professor T. J.	(1994) 'Regional Labour Market Integration in England and Wales, 1850-1913 (from Labour Market Evolution)' Routledge ISBN: 978-0-415-10865-2
Boyer, Professor G. R. and Hatton, Professor T. J.	(2002) 'New Estimates of British Unemployment, 1870-1913' Cambridge University Press DOI: 10.1017/S0022050702001031

Bradshaw, Professor J.	(2001) 'Methodologies to Measure Poverty: More Than One is Best!' University of York
Brewer, Goodman and Leicester	(2006) 'Household spending in Britain What can it teach us about poverty?' Joseph Rowntree Foundation ISBN: 978-1-861-34855-5
Brewer, Sibieta and Wren-Lewis	(2008) 'Racing away? Income inequality and the evolution of high incomes' The Institute for Fiscal Studies Briefing Note No 76
Broadberry, Professor S. N. et al.	(2015) 'British Economic Growth, 1270-1870' Cambridge University Press ISBN: 978-1-107-67649-7
Broadberry, Professor S. N. and Burhop, Professor C.	(2009) 'Real wages and labour productivity in Britain and Germany, 1871-1938: a unified approach to the international comparison of living standards' Max Planck Society DOI: 10.1017/S0022050710000331
Broadberry, Professor S. N. et al.	(2011) 'British Economic Growth and the Business Cycle 1700-1850' Broadberry et al. AnnualGDP10a
Broadberry, Professor S. N. et al.	(2011) 'British Economic Growth, 1270-1870: An Output Based Approach' Broadberry et al. BritishGDPLongRun16a.docx
Broadberry, Professor S. N. et al.	(2011) 'The Sectoral Distribution of the Labour Force and Labour Productivity of Britain, 1381-1951' Broadberry et al. SectoralSharesGB10b
Brundage, Professor A.	(2002) 'The English Poor Laws, 1700-1930' Palgrave Macmillan ISBN: 978-0-333-68271-8
BSA	(2014) 'Extract from BSA Yearbook 2013/14 - Interest Rates' Building Societies Association
Bunn and Rostom	(2014) 'Household debt and spending' Bank of England BofE Quarterly Bulletin
Burkhauser, Professor R. V. et al.	(2018) 'Top incomes and inequality in the UK: reconciling estimates from household survey and tax return data' Oxford University Press DOI: 10.1093/oep/gpx041
Burrell, Older, Watmough, Ripley and Hopkins	(2018/2020) 'The financial lives of consumers across the UK' Financial Conduct Authority
Carrington and Madsen	(2010) 'House Prices, Credit and Willingness to Lend' Monash University JEL: E44; E51
Chadwick, D.	(1849) 'Poor Rates Principle of Rating Letter to the Mayor of Salford'
Chadwick, D.	(1860) 'On the Rate of Wages in Manchester and Salford, and the Manufacturing Districts of Lancashire, 1839-59' Wiley DOI: 10.2307/2338478
Chalmers, G.	(1782/1804) 'An Estimate of the Comparative Strength of Great Britain'
Chapman, L. (revised)	(1977/1988) 'Roget's International Thesaurus - Fourth Edition' Harper Collins ISBN: 978-0-004-33176-1
Clark, Professor G.	(1999) 'Housing Rents, Housing Quality, and Living Standards in England and Wales, 1640-1909' University of California Davis
Clark, Professor G.	(2001) 'Farm Wages and Living Standards in the Industrial Revolution England, 1670-1850' University of California Davis
Clark, Professor G.	(2001) 'Land Rental Values and the Agrarian Economy - England and Wales 1500-1912' University of California Davis

Clark, Professor G.	(2002) 'The Agricultural Revolution and the Industrial Revolution, 1500-1912' University of California Davis
Clark, Professor G.	(2003) 'The Price History of English Agriculture, 1209-1914' University of California Davis
Clark, Professor G.	(2005) 'The Condition of the Working Class in England, 1209–2004' The University of Chicago Press DOI: 10.1086/498123
Clark, Professor G.	(2007) 'The Long March of History Farm Labourers Wages in England, 1208-1850' University of California Davis
Clark, Professor G.	(2011) 'Average Earnings and Retail Prices, UK, 1209-2010' University of California Davis
Clark, Professor G.	(2014) 'The Industrial Revolution' University of California Davis
Clark, Professor G.	(2018) 'Average Earnings and Retail Prices, UK, 1209-2017' University of California Davis
Clark, Professor G.	(2020) 'What Were British Earnings and Prices Then? A Question-and-Answer Guide' MeasuringWorth
Cobbett, W.	(1830/2001) 'Rural Rides' Penguin Classics ISBN: 978-0-140-43579-4
Colquhoun, P.	(1806) 'A Treatise on Indigence'
Colquhoun, P.	(1815) 'Treatise on the Wealth, Power and Resources of the British Empire'
Corlett, A. et al.	(2019) 'The Living Standards Audit 2019' Resolution Foundation
Corlett, A. and Judge, L.	(2017) 'HOME AFFRONT: Housing across the generations' Resolution Foundation
Coulson, R. L.	(2017) 'Clarifying Income Distribution' Policy Exchange ID report mon-2347
Crafts, Professor N. F. R.	(1985) 'British Economic Growth during the Industrial Revolution' Oxford University Press ISBN: 978-0-198-73067-5
Crafts, Professor N. F. R.	(1995) 'Recent research on the national accounts of the UK, 1700–1939' Routledge DOI: 10.1080/03585522.1995.10415893
Crafts, Professor N. F. R.	(1997) 'Some Dimensions of the Quality of Life during the British Industrial Revolution' London School of Economics ISBN: 978-0-85328-387-7
Crafts, Professor N. F. R.	(2020) 'Slow Real Wage Growth during the Industrial Revolution: Productivity Paradox or Pro-Rich Growth?' CAGE Working paper no. 474
Crafts, Professor N. F. R. and Harley, Professor C. K.	(1992) 'Output Growth and the British Industrial Revolution: A Restatement of the Crafts-Harley View' Wiley DOI: 10.2307/2597415
Crafts, Professor N. F. R. and Harley, Professor C. K.	(2002) 'Precocious British Industrialization: A General Equilibrium Perspective (from British Exceptionalism)' Cambridge University Press ISBN: 978-0-511-52383-0
Crafts, Professor N. F. R. and Mills, Professor T. C.	(2017) 'Six centuries of British economic growth: a time-series perspective' Oxford University Press DOI: 10.1093/ereh/hew020
Crafts, Professor N. F. R. and Mills, Professor T. C.	(2020) 'The Race between Population and Technology: Real Wages in the First Industrial Revolution' University of Warwick ISSN: 2059-4283

Crafts, Professor N. F. R., Gazeley and Newell (Ed.)	(2007) 'Work and Pay in Twentieth-Century Britain' Oxford University Press ISBN: 978-0-199-21266-8
Cribb, J. et al.	(2017) 'Living standards, poverty and inequality in the UK: 2017' Institute for Fiscal Studies ISBN: 978-1-911102-56-4
Darton, D. and Streilitz, J. (Ed.)	(2003) 'Tackling UK poverty and disadvantage in the twenty-first century' Joseph Rowntree Foundation ISBN: 978-1-85935-090-9
Davenant, C.	(1695) 'An Essay of the Ways and Means of Supplying the War'
Davies, Rev. D.	(1795) 'The Case of Labourers in Husbandry, Stated and Considered'
Deane, Professor P. M.	(1979) 'The First Industrial Revolution' Cambridge University Press ISBN: 978-0-521-29609-0
Deane, Professor P. M. and Cole, Professor W. A.	(1962/1969) 'British Economic Growth 1688-1959 (Second Edition)' Cambridge University Press 978-0-521-09569-7
DEFRA	(2019) 'Defra National Statistics Release: Air quality statistics in the UK 1987 to 2018' DEFRA
DEFRA	(2020) 'Air Pollution in the UK 2019' DEFRA
DEFRA	(2020) 'Air Pollution in the UK 2019: Compliance Assessment Summary' DEFRA
DEFRA	(2022) 'Air quality statistics in the UK - https://www.gov.uk/government/statistics/air-quality-statistics' DEFRA
Department of Employment	(1978) 'British Labour Statistics, Year Book 1976' Her Majesty's Stationery Office SBN 11 360695 8
Department of Employment and Productivity	(1971) 'British Labour Statistics, Historical Abstract 1886-1968' Her Majesty's Stationery Office
Devine	(2020) 'Poverty in the UK: Statistics' House of Commons Library Briefing Paper 7096
Devine	(2021) 'Income inequality in the UK' House of Commons Library Briefing Paper 7484
Devlin, S.	(2016) 'Agricultural labour in the UK' Food Research Collaboration ISBN: 978-1-903-95717-2
Dorling, D. et al.	(2007) 'Poverty, wealth and place in Britain, 1968 to 2005' Joseph Rowntree Foundation ISBN: 978-1-86134-995-8
Eden, Sir F. M. (Bart.)	(1797) 'The State of the Poor, or An History of the Labouring Classes in England (Three volumes)'
Emmerson and Leicester	(2002) 'A survey of the UK benefit system' The Institute for Fiscal Studies Briefing Note No 13
Engels, F.	(1845/1969) 'The Conditions of the Working Class in England - From Personal Observations and Authentic Sources' Panther Books Limited ISBN: 978-0-586-02880-3
English Housing Survey	(2020) 'English Housing Survey: Headline Report, 2019-20' Ministry of Housing, Communities and Local Government
Favara and Imbs	(2012) 'Credit Supply and the Price of Housing' HEC Lausanne
Feinstein, Professor C. H.	(1972) 'National Income Expenditure and Output of the United Kingdom 1855-1965' Cambridge University Press ISBN: 978-0-521-07230-1

Feinstein, Professor C. H.	(1988) 'The Rise and Fall of the Williamson Curve' Cambridge University Press DOI: 10.1017/S0022050700005969
Feinstein, Professor C. H.	(1990) 'New estimates of average earnings in the United Kingdom, 1880-1913' Wiley DOI: 10.1111/j.1468-0289.1990.tb00547.x
Feinstein, Professor C. H.	(1995) 'Changes in nominal wages, the cost of living and real wages in the United Kingdom over two centuries' Edward Elgar Publishing ISBN: 978-1-85278-971-9
Feinstein, Professor C. H.	(1996) 'Conjectures and Contrivances - Economic Growth and the Standard of Living in Britain during the Industrial Revolution' Oxford University Press Pubs. Id. 1167895
Feinstein, Professor C. H.	(1998) 'Pessimism Perpetuated Real Wages & Standard of Living in Britain during & after the Industrial Revolution' Cambridge University Press DOI: 10.1017/S0022050700021100
Ferragina, E., Tomlinson, M. and Walker, R.	(2013) 'Poverty, Participation And Choice, The Legacy Of Peter Townsend' Joseph Rowntree Foundation ISBN: 978-1-85935-976-1
Fitzpatrick, S. et al.	(2016) 'Destitution in the UK' Joseph Rowntree Foundation ISBN: 978-1-91078-356-6
Fitzpatrick, S. et al.	(2018) 'Destitution in the UK 2018' Joseph Rowntree Foundation ISBN 978-1-911581-35-2
Floud, Professor Sir R., Humphries and Johnson (Ed.)	(2014) 'The Cambridge Economic History of Modern Britain Volume I, 1700-1870' Cambridge University Press ISBN: 978-1-107-63143-4
Floud, Professor Sir R., Humphries and Johnson (Ed.)	(2014) 'The Cambridge Economic History of Modern Britain Volume II, 1870 to the Present' Cambridge University Press ISBN: 978-1-107-68673-1
Floud, Professor Sir R., Wachter and Gregory	(1990) 'Height, health and history - Nutritional status in the United Kingdom, 1750-1980' Cambridge University Press ISBN: 978-0-521-02998-8
Foreman-Peck, Professor J. (Ed.)	(1991) 'New perspectives on the late Victorian economy - Essays in quantitative economic history, 1860-1914' Cambridge University Press ISBN: 978-0-521-89085-3
Freeman, M. D.	(1999) 'Social Investigation in Rural England, 1870-1914' Mark David Freeman PhD Thesis
Freud, Baron D.	(2021) 'Clashing Agendas - Inside the Welfare Trap' Nine Elms Books Limited ISBN: 978-1-910-53352-9
Gazeley, Professor I.	(1989) 'The Cost of Living for Urban Workers in late Victorian and Edwardian Britain' Wiley DOI: 10.1111/j.1468-0289.1989.tb00494.x
Gazeley, Professor I. and Newell, Professor A.	(2007) 'Poverty in Britain in 1904' University of Sussex PRUS Working Paper no. 38
Gazeley, Professor I. and Newell, Professor A.	(2009) 'No Place to Live, Urban Overcrowding in Edwardian Britain' IZA Discussion Paper 4209
Gazeley, Professor I. and Newell, Professor A.	(2009) 'The End of Destitution' IZA Discussion Paper 4295
Gazeley, Professor I. and Newell, Professor A.	(2011) 'The end of destitution: evidence from urban British working households 1904–37' Oxford University Press DOI: 10.1093/oep/gpr032

Gazeley, Professor I. and Verdon, Professor N.	(2014) 'The first poverty line? Davies and Eden's investigation of rural poverty in late 18th century England' Science Direct DOI: 10.1016/j.eeh.2012.09.001
Gazeley, Professor I. et al.	(2017) 'The poor and the poorest, 50 years on: evidence from British Household Expenditure surveys of the 1950s and 1960s' Wiley DOI: 10.1111/rssa.12202
Gazeley, Professor I. et al.	(2017) 'What Really Happened to British Inequality in the Early 20th Century? Evidence from National Household Expenditure Surveys 1890-1961' IZA DP No. 11071
Gazeley, Professor I.	(2003) 'Poverty in Britain, 1900-1965' Palgrave Macmillan ISBN: 979-0-333-71619-1
Giles, C. and Webb, S	(1993) 'Poverty Statistics: a Guide for the Perplexed' Institute for Fiscal Studies ISBN: 978-1-873357-24-9
Gillie, A.	(1996) 'The origin of the poverty line' Wiley DOI: 10.2307/2597970
Gillie, A.	(2008) 'Identifying the Poor in the 1870s and 1880s' Wiley DOI: 10.1111/j.1468-0289.2007.00395.x
Glennerster H. et al.	(2004) 'One hundred years of poverty and policy' Joseph Rowntree Foundation ISBN: 978-1-85935-222-7
Gordon, D. and Pantazis, C	(1997) 'Breadline Britain in the 1990s' Routledge DOI: 10.4324/9780429460173
Grannum, C	(2006) 'Policy briefing: Home ownership' Shelter ISBN: 978-1-903595-63-0
Grant and Williams - Kantar Public	(2017) 'The FCA's Financial Lives Survey 2017 - Technical Report' Kantar Public
Gregory, I. N., Dorling, D. and Southall, H. R.	(2001) 'A century of inequality in England and Wales using standardized geographical units' Royal Geographical society DOI: 10.1111/1475-4762.00033
Gregory, Mclaughlin, Mullender and Sundararajah	(2016) 'New solutions to air pollution challenges in the UK' Imperial College London
Griffin, E.	(2018) 'Diets, Hunger and Living Standards During the British Industrial Revolution' Oxford University Press DOI: 10.1093/pastj/gtx061
Grigoratos and Martini	(2014) 'Non-exhaust traffic related emissions. Brake and tyre wear PM' EU Commission - JRC Report EUR 26648 EN
Harari	(2018) 'Household debt: statistics and impact on economy' House of Commons Library Briefing Paper 7584
Harley, Professor C. K.	(1982) 'British Industrialization Before 1841: Evidence of Slower Growth During the Industrial Revolution' Cambridge University Press DOI: 10.1017/S0022050700027431
Harley, Professor C. K.	(2019) 'The Industrial Revolution in General Equilibrium' University of Oxford Working Paper 170
Harley, Professor C. K. and Crafts, Professor N. F. R.	(2000) 'Simulating the Two Views of the British Industrial Revolution' Cambridge University Press ISSN: 0022-0507
Hatton, Professor T. J., Bailey, R. E.	(2000) 'Seebohm Rowntree and the post-war poverty puzzle' Wiley DOI: 10.1111/1468-0289.00169

Hatton, Professor T. J., Boyer and Bailey	(1994) 'The union wage effect in late nineteenth century Britain' Wiley DOI: 10.2307/2555032
Hatton, Professor T. J., Boyer and Bailey	(2005) 'Unemployment and the UK Labour Market Before, During and After the Golden Age' Cambridge University Press DOI: 10.1017/S1361491604001376
Hick, Dr. R.	(2013) 'On 'Consistent' Poverty' London School of Economics CASE/167
Hicks and Allen	(1999) 'A Century of Change: Trends in UK statistics since 1900' House of Commons Library ISSN: 1368-8456
Hills, Ryland (BofE) and Dimsdale (Oxford)	(2010) 'The UK recession in context — what do three centuries of data tell us?' Bank of England BofE Research and analysis
Hinde, Professor A.	(2003) 'England's Population - A History Since the Domesday Survey' Hodder Education ISBN: 978-0-340-78190-8
HM Treasury	(2019) 'Public Expenditure Statistical Analyses 2019' HM Treasury CP 143
HM Treasury	(2020) 'Public Expenditure Statistical Analyses 2020' HM Treasury CP 276
HM Treasury	(2021) 'Public Expenditure Statistical Analyses 2021' HM Treasury CP 507
Hobsbawm, Professor E. J. E. and George Rudé	(1969) 'Captain Swing' Penguin University Books ISBN: 978-0-140-60013-2
Holgate CBE, Professor S. (Working Party Chair) et al.	(2016) 'Every breath we take: The lifelong impact of air pollution. Report of a working party' Royal College of Physicians ISBN: 978-1-86016-568-9
Holmans, Dr. A.	(2005) 'Historical Statistics of Housing in Britain' University of Cambridge ISBN: 978-1-86190-218-2
Holmans, Dr. A.	(2014) 'Housing need and effective demand in England: A look at "the bigger picture"' University of Cambridge
Holmans, Dr. A.	(2014) 'new estimates of housing demand and need in england, 2011 to 2031' Town & Country Planning Tomorrow Series Paper 16
Holmes, G. S.	(1977) 'King and the Social Structure of Pre-Industrial England' Cambridge University Press DOI: 10.2307/3679187
Hood and Keiller	(2016) 'A survey of the UK benefit system' The Institute for Fiscal Studies Briefing Note No 13
Hopkins et al.	(2018) 'Financial Lives Survey 2017 - Weighted Data Tables User Guide' Financial Conduct Authority
Horrell, Professor S.	(1996) 'Home Demand and British Industrialisation' Cambridge University Press DOI: 10.1017/S0022050700016946
Horrell, S., Humphries, J. and Weisdorf, J.	(2019) 'Family standards of living over the long run, England 1280-1850' University of Warwick Working Paper 419
Howard, Beevers and Dajnak	(2015) 'UP IN THE AIR How to Solve London's Air Quality Crisis: Part 2' Capital City Foundation
Howard, R.	(2015) 'UP IN THE AIR How to Solve London's Air Quality Crisis: Part 1' Capital City Foundation

Hume, Professor R. D.	(2015) 'The Value of Money in Eighteenth-Century England: Incomes, Prices, Buying Power— and Some Problems in Cultural Economics' Henry E. Huntington Library and Art Gallery DOI: 10.1525/hlq.2014.77.4.373
Humphries, Professor J.	(2012) 'Childhood and child labour in the British industrial revolution' Wiley DOI: 10.1111/j.1468-0289.2012.00651.x
Inglis, B.	(1971) 'Poverty and the Industrial Revolution' Panther Books Limited ISBN: 978-0-586-03792-8
Jefferys, J. B. and Walters D.	(1952) 'National Income and Expenditure of the United Kingdom, 1870-1952' Wiley DOI: 10.1111/j.1475-4991.1955.tb01075.x
Jenkins, Professor S. P.	(1999) 'Trends in the UK Income Distribution' Institute for Social and Economic Research
Jenkins, Professor S. P. and Micklewright, Professor J.	(2007) 'New Directions in the Analysis of Inequality and Poverty' Institute for Social and Economic Research ISER Working Paper 2007-11
Jin, W. et al.	(2011) 'Poverty and Inequality in the UK: 2011' Institute for Fiscal Studies ISBN: 978-1-903274-84-2
Johnson, S.	(1755/1758/1818) 'A Dictionary of the English Language'
Jones, F. et al.	(2008) 'The distribution of household income 1977 to 2006/07' Office for National Statistics Economic & Labour Market Review, Vol 2, No 12, pp. 18-31
Jones, F. et al.	(2009) 'The redistribution of household income 1977 to 2006/07' Office for National Statistics Economic & Labour Market Review, Vol. 3, No 1, pp. 31-43
Joyce and Xu	(2019) 'Inequalities in the twenty-first century, Introducing the IFS Deaton Review' The Institute for Fiscal Studies ISBN: 978-1-912-80521-1
Joyce, Mitchell and Norris Keiller	(2017) 'The cost of housing for low-income renters' Institute for Fiscal Studies ISBN: 978-1-911102-66-3
Justiniano, Primiceri, and Tambalotti	(2017) 'Credit Supply and the Housing Boom' Federal Reserve Bank etc. css6-7
Keep	(2020) 'The budget deficit: a short guide' House of Commons Library Briefing Paper 06167
Kelly, M. and O'Grada, C.	(2016) 'Adam Smith, Watch Prices, and the Industrial Revolution' Oxford University Press DOI: 10.1093/qje/qjw026
Kelly, M., O'Grada, C. and Mokyr, J.	(2013) 'Precocious Albion: a New Interpretation of the British Industrial Revolution' University College Dublin WP13/11
Kennedy	(2004) 'Poverty: Measures and Targets' House of Commons Library RP04-23
Kennedy, L. and Solar, P. M.	(2012) 'Markets and Price Fluctuations in England and Ireland, 1785-1913' Taylor Francis ISBN: 978-1-315-85237-9
Keohane and Broughton	(2013) 'The Politics of Housing' National Housing Federation
Kitson, Professor M. and Michie OBE, Professor J.	(2014) 'The De-industrial Revolution - The Rise and Fall of UK Manufacturing, 1870-2010' University of Cambridge Working Paper No. 459
Knowles, J. (Ed.)	(1888) 'The Nineteenth Century. A Monthly Review. Volume XXIII' Keegan Paul

Kyd, James G. (Ed.)	(1952) 'Scottish Population Statistics - Including Webster's Analysis of Population 1755' University of Edinburgh
Laybourn-Langton, Quilter-Pinner and Ho	(2016) 'LETHAL & ILLEGAL Solving London's Air Pollution Crisis' IPPR
Lindert, Professor P. H.	(1986) 'Unequal English Wealth since 1670' The University of Chicago Press DOI: 10.1086/261427
Lindert, Professor P. H.	(1998) 'Three Centuries Of Inequality In Britain And America' University of California Davis Working Paper Series 97-09
Lindert, Professor P. H.	(2000) 'When did inequality rise in Britain and America?' Elsevier Science Inc. DOI: 10.1016/S0926-6437(99)00012-8
Lindert, Professor P. H. and Williamson, Professor J. G.	(1982) 'Revising England's Social Tables 1688-1812' Academic Press, Inc. DOI: 10.1016/0014-4983(82)90009-2
Lindert, Professor P. H. and Williamson, Professor J. G.	(1983) 'English Workers' Living Standards During the Industrial Revolution' Wiley DOI: 10.2307/2598895
Lindert, Professor P. H. and Williamson, Professor J. G.	(1983) 'Reinterpreting Britain's Social Tables' Academic Press, Inc. DOI: 10.1016/0014-4983(83)90044-X
Long et al. (Shelter commissioners)	(2018) 'A vision for social housing' Shelter
Lupton et al.	(2009) 'Growing up in social housing in Britain' Joseph Rowntree Foundation
Lyle, M. A.	(2007) 'Regional agricultural wage variations in early nineteenth-century England' British Agricultural History Society The Agricultural History Review, Vol. 55, No. 1 (2007), pp. 95-106
Lyons, Murphy, Snelling and Green	(2017) 'What More Can Be Done To Build The Homes We Need?' IPPR
Malthus, Rev. T. R.	(1798) 'An Essay on the Principle of Population' Oxford University Press ISBN: 978-0-192-84747-8
Marner, Dr. B.	(2016) 'Deriving Background Concentrations of NOx and NO2' Air Quality Consultants
Marner, Dr. B.	(2016) 'Emissions of Nitrogen Oxides from Modern Diesel Vehicles' Air Quality Consultants
Massie, J.	(1756) 'Calculations of Taxes for a Family of Each Rank, Degree or Class: for One Year'
Massie, J.	(1758) 'A Plan for the Establishment of Charity Houses'
Mathias, P.	(1957) 'The Social Structure in the Eighteenth Century: A Calculation by Joseph Massie' Wiley DOI: 10.2307/2600060
Mayhew, H.	(1851/1987) 'London Labour and the London Poor' Wordsworth Classics ISBN: 978-1-840-22619-5
Mayor of London (GLA)	(2019) 'PM2.5 in London: Roadmap to meeting World Health Organization guidelines by 2030' Greater London Authority
McCloskey, Professor D. N.	(2014) 'Measured, unmeasured, mismeasured, and unjustified pessimism: a review essay of Thomas Piketty's Capital in the twenty-first century' EJPE Erasmus Journal for Philosophy and Economics, Volume 7, Issue 2, Autumn 2014, pp. 73-115

McDonald and Whitehead	(2015) 'new estimates of housing demand and need in England, 2012 to 2037' Town & Country Planning Tomorrow Series Paper 17
McGuinness and Harari	(2019) 'Income inequality in the UK' House of Commons Library Briefing Paper 7484
McLeay, Radia and Thomas	(2014) 'Money creation in the modern economy' Bank of England BofE Quarterly Bulletin
McLeay, Radia and Thomas	(2014) 'Money in the modern economy: an introduction' Bank of England BofE Quarterly Bulletin
Mearns, Rev. A.	(1883) 'The Bitter Cry of Outcast London'
Meen, Professor G.	(2018) 'How should housing affordability be measured?' UK Collaborative Centre for Housing Evidence R2018_02_01
Miles and Monro	(2019) 'UK house prices and three decades of decline in the risk free real interest rate' Bank of England Staff Working Paper No. 837
Ministry of Labour	(1940) 'The Ministry of Labour Gazette' Her Majesty's Stationery Office Vol. 48, No. 12
Ministry of Labour	(1941) 'The Ministry of Labour Gazette' Her Majesty's Stationery Office Vol. 49, No. 1
Ministry of Labour	(1941) 'The Ministry of Labour Gazette' Her Majesty's Stationery Office Vol. 49, No. 2
Mitchell, B. R.	(1988) 'British Historical Statistics' Cambridge University Press ISBN: 978-1-107-40244-7
Mitchell, B. R. and Deane, Professor P. M.	(1962) 'Abstract of Historical Statistics' Cambridge University Press ISBN: 978-0-521-05738-8
Mokyr, Professor J. (Ed.)	(1999) 'The British Industrial Revolution - An Economic Perspective' Westview Press ISBN: 978-8-813-33389-2
Monks, Professor P. et al.	(2019) 'Non-Exhaust Emissions from Road Traffic' Air Quality Expert Group PB14581
Mulheirn, I.	(2019) 'Tackling the UK housing crisis: is supply the answer?' UK Collaborative Centre for Housing Evidence
Neild, W.	(1842) 'Comparative Statement of the Income and Expenditure of Certain Families of the Working Class in Manchester and Dukinfield, in the Years 1836 and 1841' Wiley DOI: 10.2307/2337693
Nesteling, H. P. H.	(1993) 'English population statistics for the first half of the Nineteenth Century : a new answer to old questions' Societe de Demographie Historique DOI: 10.3406/adh.1993.1840
Niemietz, Dr. K.	(2011) 'A New Understanding of Poverty - Poverty Measurement and Policy Implications' The Institute of Economic Affairs ISBN: 978-0-255-36638-0
Niemietz, Dr. K.	(2012) 'Redefining the Poverty Debate - Why a War on Markets is No Substitute for a War on Poverty' The Institute of Economic Affairs ISBN: 978-0-255-36652-6
O'Donoghue (ONS), Goulding (ONS) & Allen (HofC Lib.)	(2004) 'Consumer Price Inflation since 1750' Office for National Statistics Economic Trend 604

Officer, Professor L. H.	(2007) 'What Were the U.K. Earnings Rate and Consumer Price Index Then? A Data Study' University of Illinois at Chicago
Officer, Professor L. H.	(2007) 'What Were the UK Earnings and Prices Then? A Question-and-Answer Guide' MeasuringWorth
Onions, C. T. (Ed.), Little, Fowler and Coulson	(1932/1983) 'The Shorter Oxford English Dictionary on Historical Principles (2 volumes)' Guild Publishing CN 5647
ONS	(2014) 'UK Wages Over the Past Four Decades' Office for National Statistics
ONS	(2021) 'A guide to sources of data on income and earnings' Office for National Statistics
ONS	(2021) 'Average household income, UK: financial year 2020' Office for National Statistics
Orr, J. et al.	(2021) 'Regional differences in short stature in England between 2006 and 2019: A cross-sectional analysis from the National Child Measurement Programme' PLOS Medicine DOI: 10.1371/journal.pmed.1003760
Ortiz-Ospina, Esteban and Hannah Ritchie	(2018) 'What's happening to life expectancy in Britain?' Our World in Data
Palma, N.	(2016) 'Book review of Broadberry, Campbell, Klein, Overton, and van Leeuwen, British Economic Growth, 1270-1870' Maddison-Project Working Paper WP-5
Patriquin, Professor L.	(2007) 'Agrarian Capitalism and Poor Relief in England, 1500–1860' Palgrave Macmillan ISBN: 978-0-230-59138-7
Perkin, Professor H.	(1969/2002) 'The Origins of Modern English Society' Routledge ISBN: 978-0-415-29880-2
Perkin, Professor H.	(1989/2002) 'The Rise of the Professional Society - England Since 1880' Routledge ISBN: 978-0-415-30178-5
Perkin, Professor H.	(1996) 'The Third Revolution - Professional Elites in the Modern World' Routledge ISBN: 978-0-415-14338-1
Phaup, H.	(2015) 'Historical sources of mortgage interest rate statistics' Bank of England
Piddington, Nicol, Garrett and Custard	(2020) 'The Housing Stock of The United Kingdom' BRE Trust PEN02 20
Pinker, Professor S. A.	(2018) 'Enlightenment Now' Allen Lane ISBN: 978-0-241-00431-9
Platt, L.	(2003) 'Putting Childhood Poverty on the Agenda: The Relationship Between Research and Policy in Britain 1800-1950' Young Lives
Polanyi, K.	(1944/2001) 'The Great Transformation: The Political and Economic Origins of Our Time' Beacon Press ISBN: 978-0-8070-5643-x
Pope and Waters	(2016) 'A survey of the UK tax system' The Institute for Fiscal Studies Briefing Note No 09
Raleigh, Veena (Senior Fellow, King's Fund)	(2021) 'What is happening to life expectancy in England' The Kings Fund
Rashid, T. et al.	(2021) 'Life expectancy and risk of death in 6791 communities in England from 2002 to 2019' The Lancet DOI: 10.1016/S2468-2667(21)00205-X

Ravallion, Professor M.	(2013) 'The Idea of Anti-Poverty Policy' National Bureau of Economic Research Working Paper 19210
Ravallion, Professor M.	(2016) 'The Economics of Poverty - History, Measurement and Policy' Oxford University Press ISBN: 978-0-190-21276-6
Ravallion, Professor M.	(2020) 'On the Origins of the Idea of Ending Poverty' National Bureau of Economic Research Working Paper 27808
Razzell, P. E.	(2016) 'Mortality, Marriage and Population Growth in England, 1550-1850' Caliban Books ISBN: 978-0-904573-19-0
Razzell, P. E.	(2018) 'Population Growth and the Increase of Socio-Economic Inequality in England, 1550-1850' Razzell, P.
Registrar General	(1904) 'Census of England and Wales, 1901, General Report with Appendices' Her Majesty's Stationery Office
Ridley, Dr. Viscount M. W.	(2011) 'The Rational Optimist' 4th Estate (Harper Collins) ISBN: 978-0-007-26712-5
Roantree and Shaw	(2017) 'What a difference a day makes: inequality and the tax and benefit system from a long-run perspective' Springer DOI: 10.1007/s10888-017-9362-x
Roser, Max	(2020) 'The Spanish flu (1918-20): The global impact of the largest influenza pandemic in history' Our World in Data
Rosling, Dr., H., Rosling and Ronnlund	(2018) 'Factfulness' Sceptre (Hodder & Stoughton) ISBN: 978-1-473-63746-7
Rowntree, B. Seebohm	(1901) 'Poverty: A Study of Town Life' MacMillan and Co. ISBN 978-1-86134-202-0
Samaras, Professor Z. et al.	(2013) 'Transport related Air Pollution and Health impacts – Integrated Methodologies for Assessing Particulate Matter' TRANSPHORM
Scott, Professor P. M. and Walker, Professor J. T.	(2014) 'Demonstrating Distinction at 'the Lowest Edge of the Black-coated Class': The Family Expenditures of Edwardian Railway Clerks' Henley Business School Discussion Paper Number: IBH-2014-04
Scott, Professor P. M. and Walker, Professor J. T.	(2020) 'The Comfortable, the Rich, and the Super-Rich. What Really Happened to Top British Incomes during the First Half of the Twentieth Century?' Cambridge University Press DOI: 10.1017/S0022050719000767
Scott, Professor P. M., Walker, J. T. and Miskell, P. M.	(2014) 'British Working-class Household Composition, Labour Supply and Commercial Leisure Participation during the 1930s' Henley Business School Discussion Paper Number: IBH-2014-03
Sen, Professor A. K.	(1982) 'Poor, Relatively Speaking' The Economic and Social Research Institute ISBN: 978-0-7070-0055-6
Shaw-Taylor, Dr. L.	(2009) 'The Occupational Structure of England 1750-1871 Some Preliminary Results' University of Cambridge
Shaw-Taylor, Dr. L. and Wrigley, E. A.	(2006) 'The Occupational Structure of England c.1750-1871: A Preliminary Report' University of Cambridge
Shaw-Taylor, Dr. L. et al.	(2010) 'The Occupational structure of England and Wales c.1817-1881' University of Cambridge
Shaw-Taylor, Dr. L. et al.	(2010) 'The Occupational structure of England c.1710 to c.1871 Work in progress' University of Cambridge

Smee, W. R.	(1846) 'THE INCOME TAX: Its Extension at the Present Rate Proposed to all Classes'
Snell, Professor K. D. M.	(1985) 'Annals of the Labouring Poor - Social Change in Agrarian England, 1660-1900' Cambridge University Press ISBN: 978-0-521-33558-4
Solomou, Professor S. and Ryland Thomas	(2019) 'Feinstein Fulfilled: Updated Estimates of UK GDP 1841-1920' ESCOE (NIESR) and ONS ISSN: 2631-3588
Spiegelhalter OBE, Professor Sir D. J.	(2017) 'Does air pollution kill 40,000 people each year in the UK?' Winton Centre
Spiegelhalter OBE, Professor Sir D. J.	(2019) 'The Art of Statistics - Learning from Data' Pelican (Penguin Books) ISBN: 978-0-241-25876-7
Starling, B. and Bradbury, D.	(2020) 'The Official History of Britain - Our story in numbers as told by the Office for National Statistics' Harper Collins ISBN: 978-0-008-41219-7
Stroud, P. (Chair)	(2019) 'Equivalisation In Poverty Measures: Can We Do Better?' Social Metrics Commission ISBN: 978-1-911125-52-5
The Intergenerational Commission	(2018) 'A New Generational Contract' Resolution Foundation ISBN: 978-1-999-72011-7
The Trussell Trust	(2019) 'The State of Hunger' The Trussell Trust
Thomas	(2015) 'Analysis of Long-run Historical Data at the Bank of England' Bank of England BofE Archival Worksop
Thompson et al.	(2012) 'Olympic Britain: Social and economic change since the 1908 and 1948 London Games' House of Commons Library
Thompson, E. P.	(1963) 'The Making of the English Working Class' Vintage Books ISBN: 978-0-394-70322-0
Timmers and Achten	(2016) 'Non-exhaust PM emissions from electric vehicles - 134 (2016) 10e17' Atmospheric Environment DOI: 10.1016/j.atmosenv.2016.03.017
Townsend, Professor P.	(1954) 'Measuring Poverty' Wiley DOI: 10.2307/587651
Townsend, Professor P.	(1966) 'Poverty, socialism and Labour in power' Fabian Society Fabian Tract 371
Townsend, Professor P.	(1979) 'Poverty in the United Kingdom' Penguin Books ISBN: 978-0-140-22139-8
Townsend, Professor P.	(2010) 'The meaning of poverty' Wiley DOI: 10.1111/j.1468-4446.2009.01241.x
Turner, C. and NHBC	(2015) 'Homes through the decades' NHBC Foundation ISBN: 978-0-9930691-3-0
Twigger, R.	(1999) 'Inflation: the Value of the Pound 1750-1998' House of Commons Library Research Paper 99/20
UK Statistics Authority	(2019) 'Statistics on air quality and emissions of air pollutants' UK Statistics Authority Assessment Report 344
Vamplew, W.	(1980) 'A Grain of Truth The Nineteenth-Century Corn Averages' British Agricultural History Society The Agricultural History Review, Vol. 28, No. 1 (1980), pp. 1-17 (17 pages)

van de Ven, Dr. J.	(2011) 'Expenditure and Disposable Income Trends of UK Households: Evidence from Micro-Data' National Institute of Economic and Social Research DOI: 10.1177/002795011121800105
Vanderlint, J.	(1734) 'Money Answers all Things'
Voth, H.-J.	(2003) 'Living Standards During the Industrial Revolution: An Economist's Guide' American Economic Association DOI: 10.1257/000282803321947083
Watts, Fitzpatrick, Bramley and Watkins	(2014) 'Welfare Sanctions and Conditionality in the UK' Joseph Rowntree Foundation ISBN: 978-1-909-58646-8
Welshman, J.	(2006/2013) 'Underclass: A History of the Excluded Since 1880' Bloomsbury ISBN: 978-1-4725-0498-2
WHO	(2006) 'WHO Air quality guidelines for particulate matter, Ozone, Nitrogen Dioxide and Sulphur Dioxide' World Health Organisation
Williamson, Professor J. G.	(1984) 'Why Was British Growth So Slow During the Industrial Revolution' Cambridge University Press DOI: 10.1017/S0022050700032320
Williamson, Professor J. G.	(1985) 'Did British Capitalism Breed Inequality?' Routledge ISBN: 978-1-138-86489-4
Wilson	(2019) 'Under-occupying social housing: Housing Benefit entitlement' House of Commons Library Briefing Paper 06272
Wilson and Barton	(2018) 'Tackling the under-supply of housing in England' House of Commons Library Briefing Paper 07671
Wilson and Barton	(2020) 'Overcrowded housing (England)' House of Commons Library Briefing Paper 1013
Wilson Fox, A.	(1903) 'Agricultural Wages in England and Wales during the Last Fifty Years' Wiley DOI: 10.2307/2339234
Wilson, W	(2019) 'Stimulating housing supply - Government initiatives (England)' House of Commons Library Briefing Paper 06416
Wolff, J. et al.	(2015) 'A Philosophical Review of Poverty' Joseph Rowntree Foundation ISBN: 978-1-90958-659-8
Wrigley, Professor Sir E. A. and Dr. R. S. Schofield	(1982/1989) 'The Population History of England, 1541-1871, A reconstruction' Cambridge University Press ISBN: 978-0-521-35688-6
Wrigley, Professor Sir E. A. and Dr. R. S. Schofield	(1997) 'English Population History from Family Reconstitution, 1580-1837' Cambridge University Press ISBN: 978-0-521-59015-0
Zmolek, M. A.	(2019) 'The Dark World of Reverend Malthus' University of Nebraska Omaha ISSN: 2476-0269

Internet Data

Bank of England - "Millennium Database"	https://www.bankofengland.co.uk/statistics/research-datasets
BRE Trust - UK Housing Stock Report	https://files.bregroup.com/bretrust/The-Housing-Stock-of-the-United-Kingdom_Report_BRE-Trust.pdf
Building Societies Association - Mortgage interest rates	https://www.bsa.org.uk/BSA/files/f8/f86888ee-716c-4f95-9c63-1dfa26d86742.xlsx
Building Societies Association - Mortgages and housing	https://www.bsa.org.uk/statistics/mortgages-housing
Chartered Institute of Housing	https://www.ukhousingreview.org.uk/ukhr21/compendium.html
Christopher Chantrill - UK Public Revenue	https://ukpublicrevenue.co.uk/
Christopher Chantrill - UK Public Spending	https://ukpublicspending.co.uk/
Clark, Professor G. - Downloads	http://faculty.econ.ucdavis.edu/faculty/gclark/data.html
DEFRA - Air Pollution in the UK	https://uk-air.defra.gov.uk/library/annualreport/
DEFRA - Air Quality and Emissions Statistics	https://www.gov.uk/government/collections/air-quality-and-emissions-statistics
DEFRA - UK Air Information Resource - Data	https://uk-air.defra.gov.uk/data/
Department for Transport - Coronavirus transport use	https://www.gov.uk/government/statistics/transport-use-during-the-coronavirus-covid-19-pandemic
Department for Transport - Vehicle statistics	https://www.gov.uk/government/collections/vehicles-statistics
Department for Work and Pensions - Statistics	https://www.gov.uk/government/collections/dwp-statistical-summaries
Drax Electric Insights	https://electricinsights.co.uk/#/homepage?&_k=o6odgj
Economic Statistics Centre of Excellence	https://www.escoe.ac.uk
Economic Statistics Centre of Excellence - Documents	https://www.escoe.ac.uk/research/historical-data/etarticles/
Economic Statistics Centre of Excellence - Historical data	https://www.escoe.ac.uk/research/historical-data/
Halifax - House price data	https://www.halifax.co.uk/media-centre/house-price-index.html
HM Treasury - Country and regional analysis	https://www.gov.uk/government/collections/country-and-regional-analysis

HM Treasury - Public expenditure statistical analysis	https://www.gov.uk/government/collections/public-expenditure-statistical-analyses-pesa
HMRC - Survey of personal incomes	https://www.gov.uk/government/collections/personal-incomes-statistics
Human Mortality Database	https://www.mortality.org/
Institute for Fiscal Studies - Living standards, poverty and inequality in the UK	https://ifs.org.uk/tools_and_resources/incomes_in_uk
Lindert, Professor P. H. - Downloads	https://gpih.ucdavis.edu/files/
London Air Quality (Imperial College London) - Data	https://www.londonair.org.uk/london/asp/datadownload.asp
London Average Air Quality Levels (Kings College London)	https://data.london.gov.uk/dataset/london-average-air-quality-levels
London Congestion Zone - Camera captures	https://data.london.gov.uk/dataset/vehicles-entering-c-charge-zone-month
Measuring Worth	https://www.measuringworth.com/
Ministry of Housing, Communities and Local Government - English housing survey	https://www.gov.uk/government/collections/english-housing-survey
Ministry of Housing, Communities and Local Government - House building	https://www.gov.uk/government/statistical-data-sets/live-tables-on-house-building
Ministry of Housing, Communities and Local Government - Housing	https://www.gov.uk/government/statistical-data-sets/live-tables-on-dwelling-stock-including-vacants
National Atmospheric Emissions Inventory - Data	https://naei.beis.gov.uk/data/
National Infrastructure Commission - Historic Energy Dataset	https://nic.org.uk/data/all-data/historic-energy/
Nationwide - Housing historic data	https://www.nationwidehousepriceindex.co.uk/resources/
NHS - National child measurement programme	https://digital.nhs.uk/data-and-information/publications/statistical/national-child-measurement-programme
NHS - Workforce statistics	https://digital.nhs.uk/data-and-information/publications/statistical/nhs-workforce-statistics
NOMIS - Official census and labour market statistics	https://www.nomisweb.co.uk/
OECD - Housing prices	https://data.oecd.org/price/housing-prices.htm

Office for Budget Responsibility	https://obr.uk/
Office for Budget Responsibility - Data banks	https://obr.uk/data/
Office for Budget Responsibility - Welfare spending by age (Chart 3.2)	https://obr.uk/docs/dlm_uploads/Welfare-Trends-Report.pdf
Office for Budget Responsibility - Welfare spending by age (Removed)	https://obr.uk/forecasts-in-depth/brief-guides-and-explainers/an-obr-guide-to-welfare-spending/
Ofgem - Electricity prices	https://www.ofgem.gov.uk/data-portal/breakdown-electricity-bill
Ofgem - Energy bills explained	https://www.ofgem.gov.uk/publications-and-updates/infographic-bills-prices-and-profits
Ofgem - Gas prices	https://www.ofgem.gov.uk/data-portal/breakdown-gas-bill
ONS - Average equivalised household disposable income	https://www.ons.gov.uk/peoplepopulationandcommunity/personalandhouseholdfinances/expenditure/datasets/detailedhouseholdexpenditurebyequiv aliseddisposableincomedecilegroupoecdmodifiedscaleuktable31e
ONS - Deaths by single year of age	https://www.ons.gov.uk/peoplepopulationandcommunity/birthsdeathsandmarriages/deaths/datasets/deathregistrationssummarytablesenglandandwalesdeathsbysingleyearofagetables
ONS - Deaths registered weekly in England and Wales, provisional	https://www.ons.gov.uk/peoplepopulationandcommunity/birthsdeathsandmarriages/deaths/datasets/weeklyprovisionalfiguresondeathsregisteredinenglandandwales
ONS - Environmental accounts	https://www.ons.gov.uk/economy/environmentalaccounts
ONS - GDP	https://www.ons.gov.uk/economy/grossdomesticproductgdp
ONS - Gross disposable household income	https://www.ons.gov.uk/economy/regionalaccounts/grossdisposablehouseholdincome
ONS - Health inequalities	https://www.ons.gov.uk/peoplepopulationandcommunity/healthandsocialcare/healthinequalities
ONS - House building	https://www.ons.gov.uk/peoplepopulationandcommunity/housing/datasets/ukhousebuildingpermanentdwellingsstartedandcompleted
ONS - Housing	https://www.ons.gov.uk/peoplepopulationandcommunity/housing/datasets/dwellingstockbytenureuk
ONS - Income and wealth	https://www.ons.gov.uk/peoplepopulationandcommunity/personalandhouseholdfinances/incomeandwealth
ONS - Inflation and price indices	https://www.ons.gov.uk/economy/inflationandpriceindices
ONS - Labour force survey, earnings and working hours	https://www.ons.gov.uk/employmentandlabourmarket/peopleinwork/earningsandworkinghours

ONS - Life expectancy	https://www.ons.gov.uk/peoplepopulationandcommunity/healthandsocialcare/healthandlifeexpectancies/datasets/lifeexpectancyestimatesallagesuk
ONS - National balance sheet	https://www.ons.gov.uk/economy/nationalaccounts/uksectoraccounts/datasets/thenationalbalancesheetestimates/current
ONS - National life tables	https://www.ons.gov.uk/peoplepopulationandcommunity/birthsdeathsandmarriages/lifeexpectancies/datasets/nationallifetablesunitedkingdomreferencetables
ONS - Percentage of households with durable goods	https://www.ons.gov.uk/file?uri=/peoplepopulationandcommunity/personalandhouseholdfinances/expenditure/datasets/percentageofhouseholdswithdurablegoodsuktablea45/1970tofinancialyearending2018/a45201718rerun.xls
ONS - Population and migration	https://www.ons.gov.uk/peoplepopulationandcommunity/populationandmigration
ONS - Population estimates	https://www.ons.gov.uk/peoplepopulationandcommunity/populationandmigration/populationestimates
ONS - Population, Our population - Where are we?	https://www.ons.gov.uk/peoplepopulationandcommunity/populationandmigration/populationestimates/articles/ourpopulationwherearewehowdidwegetherewherearewegoing/2020-03-27
ONS - Retail Prices Index: average price of selected food items: 1914 to 2004	https://www.ons.gov.uk/file?uri=/economy/inflationandpriceindices/methodologies/consumerpricesindexcpiandretailpricesindexrpibasketofgoodsandservices/rpiaverageprices19142004tcm77168515tcm77420253.xls
ONS - UK Families and households	https://www.ons.gov.uk/peoplepopulationandcommunity/birthsdeathsandmarriages/families/datasets/familiesandhouseholdsfamiliesandhouseholds
ONS - Vital statistics, births, deaths and marriages	https://www.ons.gov.uk/peoplepopulationandcommunity/populationandmigration/populationestimates/datasets/vitalstatisticspopulationandhealthreferencetables
ONS - Workbook 4 - Expenditure by Household Characteristics	https://www.ons.gov.uk/file?uri=/peoplepopulationandcommunity/personalandhouseholdfinances/expenditure/datasets/familyspendingworkbook4expenditurebyhouseholdcharacteristic/2020/familyspendingworkbook4expenditurebyhouseholdcharacteristics.xlsx
Our World in Data	https://ourworldindata.org/
Our World in Data - CO2 and GHG emissions	https://github.com/owid/co2-data
Our World in Data - Coronavirus pandemic (Covid-19)	https://ourworldindata.org/coronavirus
Our World in Data - Excess mortality during the Coronavirus pandemic (COVID-19)	https://ourworldindata.org/excess-mortality-covid
Our World in Data - Excess mortality P-scores	https://ourworldindata.org/grapher/excess-mortality-p-scores-average-baseline
Our World in Data - Life expectancy	https://ourworldindata.org/life-expectancy

Oxford Dictionary - Lexico	https://www.lexico.com/en
Peter Lindert - Data-garden	https://psychology.ucdavis.edu/people/fzlinder/peter-linderts-webpage/data-garden
Rashid et al (Imperial College) - Life expectancy and risk of death in 6791 communities in England	https://globalenvhealth.org/download/24423/
Renewable Energy Foundation	https://www.ref.org.uk
UK Data Service	https://beta.ukdataservice.ac.uk/
UK Government – Air Quality Standards Regulation 2010	https://www.legislation.gov.uk/uksi/2010/1001/made
UK Government - Coronavirus dashboard	https://coronavirus.data.gov.uk/
UK Government - Stat-Xplore	https://stat-xplore.dwp.gov.uk/webapi/jsf/login.xhtml
UK Government BEIS - Annual January prices of road fuels and petroleum products	https://www.gov.uk/government/statistical-data-sets/oil-and-petroleum-products-annual-statistics
UK Government BEIS - Crude oil and petroleum: production, imports and exports	https://www.gov.uk/government/statistical-data-sets/crude-oil-and-petroleum-production-imports-and-exports
UK Government BEIS - Digest of UK Energy Statistics (DUKES)	https://www.gov.uk/government/collections/digest-of-uk-energy-statistics-dukes
UK Government BEIS - Energy Consumption in the UK	https://www.gov.uk/government/statistics/energy-consumption-in-the-uk
UK Government BEIS - Historical coal data: coal production, availability and consumption	https://www.gov.uk/government/statistical-data-sets/historical-coal-data-coal-production-availability-and-consumption
UK Government BEIS - Historical electricity data	https://www.gov.uk/government/statistical-data-sets/historical-electricity-data
UK Government BEIS - Historical gas data: gas production and consumption and fuel input	https://www.gov.uk/government/statistical-data-sets/historical-gas-data-gas-production-and-consumption-and-fuel-input
Vision of Britain - Census	https://www.visionofbritain.org.uk/census/
Wages through history - A. Wilson Fox agricultural wages	https://historyofwages.blogspot.com/2011/02/agricultural-labourers-wages-1850-1914.html
World Bank - Life expectancy	https://data.worldbank.org/indicator/SP.DYN.LE00.IN

Worldometers - Covid-19   https://www.worldometers.info/coronavirus/
Coronavirus Pandemic

www.ingramcontent.com/pod-product-compliance
Lightning Source LLC
Chambersburg PA
CBHW061150170426
43209CB00035B/1955/J